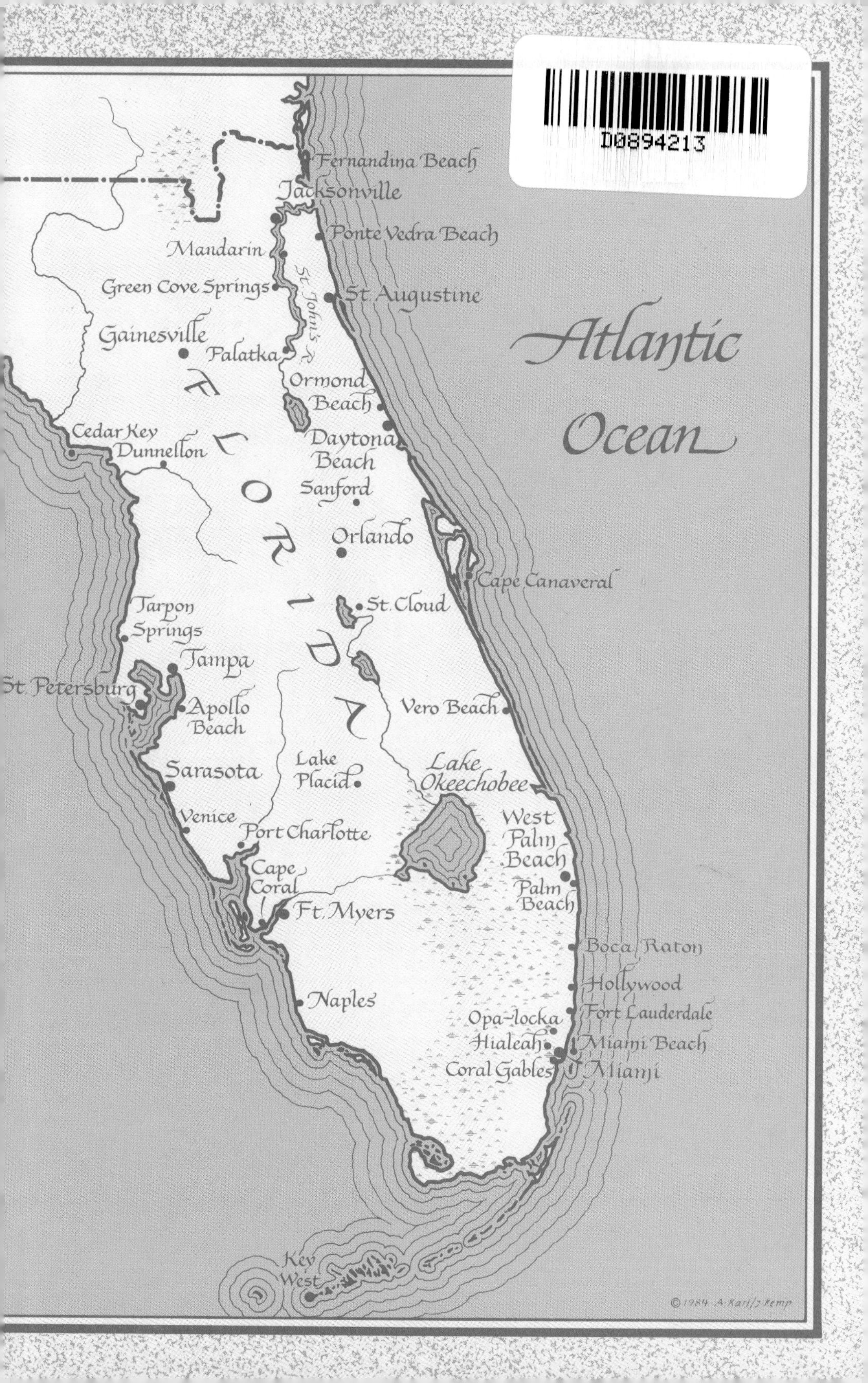

Atlantic Ocean
FLORIDA
Fernandina Beach
Jacksonville
Ponte Vedra Beach
Mandarin
Green Cove Springs
St. Johns R.
St. Augustine
Gainesville
Palatka
Ormond Beach
Cedar Key
Dunnellon
Daytona Beach
Sanford
Orlando
Cape Canaveral
St. Cloud
Tarpon Springs
Tampa
St. Petersburg
Apollo Beach
Vero Beach
Lake Placid
Sarasota
Lake Okeechobee
Venice
Port Charlotte
West Palm Beach
Cape Coral
Palm Beach
Ft. Myers
Boca Raton
Hollywood
Naples
Opa-locka
Fort Lauderdale
Hialeah
Miami Beach
Coral Gables
Miami
Key West
©1984 A. Karl/J. Kemp

FIFTY FEET IN PARADISE

• • • • • •

FIFTY FEET IN PARADISE

• • • • •

THE BOOMING OF FLORIDA

DAVID NOLAN

HARCOURT BRACE JOVANOVICH, PUBLISHERS
SAN DIEGO NEW YORK LONDON

The author and publisher are grateful for permission to quote from the following material: The lines in the epigraph are quoted from the song, "Farther Along," by permission of Stamps-Baxter Music of the Zondervan Corporation. [TBS]

Except as indicated, all photographs in the text are from the Florida Photographic Collection, Florida State Archives.

Library of Congress Cataloging in Publication Data
Nolan, David.
Fifty feet in paradise.
Bibliography: p.
Includes index.
1. Florida—Economic conditions. 2. Capitalists and financiers—Florida—History. 3. Florida—History.
I. Title.
HC107.F6N64 1984 330.9759 84-529
ISBN 0-15-130748-2

Designed by Dalia Hartman
Endpapers map by Anita Karl and James Kemp

Printed in the United States of America
FIRST EDITION
A B C D E

For Sudie and
Hamilton Nolan,
young Floridians

Farther along
we'll know all about it,
Farther along
we'll understand why;
Cheer up, my brother,
live in the sunshine,
We'll understand it
all by and by.

—OLD SOUTHERN
CHURCH HYMN

CONTENTS

FIFTY FEET IN PARADISE

THE BOOMING OF PARADISE

•

Florida is not just any place.

It is one of the largest and fastest-growing parts of the country, one of the world's most popular destinations.

It is many things to many people. Drawing jet-setters and migrant laborers, it is home to the idle rich, the grindingly poor, and quite a few of the in-betweens.

Florida is a state of the Union. It is also a state of mind.

Every snowstorm in Chicago or Buffalo makes more people dream about the Sunshine State. They flee south for vacations and plan for retirement. People do things in Florida they would never think of trying in the staid elsewhere. Architecture bristles with fantasy. Tourists dress in eye-blinding fashions. Prim and proper people shed almost all their clothes in the most public places.

It is a mecca, a magnet for dreamers.

Take the dreams, the influx of newcomers, and money, money, money. Mix them together and you have a boom.

Ask an old-time Floridian about The Boom and his mind will go back to the 1920s. He'll snort derisively about peddlers of swampland and the suckers who bought it, about people chasing after easy money until they lost it all.

During those heady, roaring years, speculators dealt in Florida property just as they did in stocks—with the same ultimate results. The collapse of the boom predated and presaged the stock-market crash by three years and should have served as a word to the wise—but it didn't.

Afterward, people preferred to forget it. They didn't want to be reminded of their follies. But the physical evidence remained, to leap out at the eye in multitudes of stuccoed buildings with red tile roofs on streets with grandiose Spanish, Tahitian, or Venetian names.

The 1920s boom was one of those episodic madnesses in history so concentrated and so colorful as to erase the memory of similar but less startling events. This is unfortunate because it consigns the madness merely to the past, whereas nothing is more certain than that it shall happen again.

Far from being an isolated incident, it is in fact the basic pattern of Florida's growth. (Listen closely and you will hear a chorus in the background, like a Vachel Lindsay poem, with a boom, Boom, BOOM!)

The Sunshine State has never been a place for slow-paced growth or the quiet processes of augmentation. It has, rather, followed cycle after cycle of hopes, hypes, dizziness, collapse, forgetfulness, and rebirth.

Each stage has its distinctive personality: the pioneer, the visionary, the promoter, the speculator, the fast-buck artist, the victim, the rediscoverer. Taken together, they are the recurrent cast of characters parading across the Florida scene, from buckskin times to bikini days.

The booms have focused on many different things. There have been cotton crazes and mulberry manias and orange fevers. Each generation has had its own sure way of squeezing easy money out of Florida.

At the base of all of them has been the land. In the beginning, settlers bought it in 640-acre sections or 160-acre quarters. In the age of the robber barons it was gobbled up in million-acre parcels. By the Roaring Twenties it had become so precious that speculators pinned their hopes on footage. A building lot of fifty feet in paradise was the irresistible commodity of 1925. There were not enough of them high and dry to go around, so swamps and lowlands became negotiable—particularly with those who bought sight-unseen.

They wound up sharing the sentiments of the rueful mid-westerner who surveyed his purchase and remarked that he had never bought land by the gallon before.

Still they came and bought, and the sounds emanating from Florida were two:

BOOM!

POP!!

For the booms were invariably punctuated by the revenge of God, man, and Mammon: hurricane, frost, yellow fever, insect plague, war, and financial panic.

"When you're hot, you're hot. When you're not, you're not" would be a fitting motto to adopt for the state seal.

It used to take a long time to forget the busts. They were memorable. One boom per generation was about par for the course—it took that long for the wariness to recede. But things have speeded up: now three or four can be crammed into the same period of time.

This has led to cynicism on the part of long-time observers.

One bit of conventional wisdom holds, "If a man comes to Florida poor, he stays poor. If he comes rich and stays long enough, he gets poor."

But that is phrasing it too dismally. Some of the poor have become rich and some of the rich have grown richer. They too figure in the kaleidoscopically changing pattern of dreamers and doers, millionaires and malefactors, salesmen and scamps.

They have given Florida a history as colorful as its foliage, peopled by characters as exotic as its wildlife. A veritable zoo of human types—bulls and bears, foxes and peacocks, skunks and snakes—fill its pages.

It is a cash-encrusted tale all the way back to the Spanish conquistadores. Once Florida went on the dollar standard, it really got in high gear.

RED, WHITE, AND BLUEBLOODS

•

History, in its shorthand, has labeled the administration of President James Monroe, from 1817 to 1825, as the Era of Good Feeling. The felicitous description covers a multitude of warts and hard times. Just two years into this era, the booming economy, which had been fueled by war spending, expansive credit, land speculation, and rising cotton prices, collapsed ignominiously in the Panic of 1819—America's first great depression.

Factories closed their doors. Unemployment and pauperism grew. Soup lines were set up in major cities. Banks could not honor their notes. Land values dropped abruptly by half or more. A national mood of buoyant expansion was replaced by one of gloom and doom. Good Feeling indeed!

It was a young country then, which had only in recent decades hacked its way inland from the Eastern Seaboard and crossed the first of many mountain chains to the west. People knew that you pushed out into the frontier when the old lands no longer provided a living.

America did not lack a frontier. In fact, in that same year of panic it was significantly enlarged. Secretary of State John Quincy Adams and Spanish Minister Luis de Onis signed a treaty in 1819 which would transfer Florida to the United States, after three centuries as an outpost of the Spanish empire.

It would take two years for both countries to ratify the treaty, and several months beyond that to accomplish the actual change of power. But the course was clear and the interim served merely to whet ravenous appetites. A new territory meant new government jobs, and the job seekers lined up. Endorsements were sought from senators and representatives, and the White House was soon flooded with requests.

Among those seeking posts were the scions of the nation's founding fathers. Increasingly impoverished by the hard times they shared with those of less distinguished ancestry, they looked to the government their forebears had founded to bail them out of economic distress. They did not hesitate to flaunt their red, white, and blueblood as a qualification for public office. Niches were found for many of them in the territorial government of Florida.

But not at the top. The post of governor, though sought by many, was reserved almost by divine right for Andrew Jackson, the nation's greatest military hero since George Washington.

One of the budget-cutting measures adopted to deal with the hard times was a reduction in the size of the military establishment. The new streamlined army had room for only one major general, and Jackson lacked the seniority to fill the post. Unwilling to accept a demotion in rank, he was therefore out of a job.

But where was the government official bold enough to dispense with the services of Old Hickory? Who would risk running afoul, not only of Jackson, whose wrath was considerable and legendary, but also of his supporters and idolizers, who were legion? Political imperatives required that another job of sufficient dignity be found for the nation's hero.

The Florida post was an answer to the politicians' prayers. Twice in his stormy career Jackson had invaded Florida. Acting on his own authority, he had battled Indians and Spaniards, executed British subjects, and provoked international incidents.

No American's name was so closely linked with Florida in the days prior to its acquisition.

The only hitch was Old Hickory himself. "I can never descend to become a governor of a Territory, after the offices I have filled," he vowed to his friends.

But President Monroe approached him with honeyed words. "It must be agreeable to you," he wrote, "from many considerations which will occur, to take possession of the Floridas, & cause the Spanish authorities & troops to be removed to Cuba."

The thought of returning triumphant was indeed agreeable. It would put the national seal of approval on his past, controversial invasions, and shame those rascally politicians who had dared to criticize him.

There was another consideration as well. In the course of his military campaigns, from the War of 1812 on, Jackson had built up a corps of young protégés who served him bravely and well, giving the utter loyalty he demanded. What would they do now that he was leaving the army? As governor of Florida he could at least help them get established on the civil side of public employment. His adjutant general, Robert Butler (who was married to Mrs. Jackson's niece); his aide-de-camp, Richard Keith Call; and his personal physician, Dr. James Bronaugh, were among those anxious to cast their lot with Florida. As governor he would be in a position to launch their careers, in repayment for past services.

So Old Hickory consented to take the office. Then he learned that the politicians in Washington had already filled the choicest positions, which he was counting on for his aides. Furious as only he could get, he ranted and raved and liberally hurled his favorite curse of "By the Eternal!"

He wrote to Dr. Bronaugh, "Had I anticipated this I should have adhered to my first determination not to have accepted the Government." He vowed "never to be associated with such men as some of those who are appointed."

He proceeded to Florida in a foul mood, which was aggravated by his chronic diarrhea, and presided over the changing of flags in July 1821. It was nothing new to Jackson: "Thrice have I seen the Spanish coulours lowered and the American coulours waving over this place," he noted wearily. But this time it was for keeps.

His stay in Florida was brief, lasting only a few months. He proclaimed the new government, established its basic laws, and provoked yet another international incident by clapping the former Spanish governor in jail for noncooperation. Then he took off for his beloved Hermitage, a brief way station on his road to Washington and the White House.

His loyal followers, however, stayed behind and left their mark on Florida. Robert Butler became surveyor general. Dr. Bronaugh was president of the legislative council, and Richard Keith Call served as congressional delegate and governor. Old Hickory looked out for his own, one way or another, no matter what the Washington politicians did.

• • •

Andrew Jackson was the most visible veteran of old battles with Spain, but he was not the only one who showed up to claim the spoils.

A precocious warrior named William Steuben Smith had thrown down his gauntlet to Spanish might long before Jackson ever thought to. Now he pressed his claim for public gratitude through government employment, and he had a certain inside track in doing so.

When President Monroe informed Jackson that Smith had been appointed naval officer at Pensacola, his description of the young man's qualifications rested entirely on family relations. He was "the son of Col. Wm. Smith, who was aid de camp to Genl. Washington in the revolutionary war, & afterwards Secry. of legation at London, where he married the daughter of Mr. Adams, former President. He is the nephew of the present Secry.

of State, & his wife is the sister of Mrs. Adams." He was also, said the president, "literally poor."

This had not always been true. Smith's childhood had been spent partly in the relative luxury of the vice-presidential mansion in New York, and then at the White House in Washington, under the watchful eye of his ever-doting grandmother Abigail. Then he went off to Columbia College for an education.

While there, he became involved with Francisco de Miranda, one of those soldiers of fortune who had aided the American Revolution and then sought other areas to liberate. The target for 1806 was the Spanish colony of Venezuela, and the nineteen-year-old Smith dropped out of school to join the crusade.

Today Miranda is hailed as the precursor of Latin American independence, but old John Adams had a somewhat less exalted opinion, calling him "a vagrant, a vagabond, a Quixotic adventurer."

Smith's participation appalled Adams. "I gave up my grandson as lost forever," he wrote. "I can truly say that information that the ship had gone to the bottom would at the same moment have been an alleviation of my grief."

In due course, word came back that the expedition had failed and young Smith was in prison, awaiting execution. When it was suggested that Adams should seek a pardon, he replied vehemently: "No! My blood should flow upon a Spanish scaffold, before I would meanly ask or accept a distinction in favor of my grandson. No! He should share the fate of his colleagues, comrades, and fellow-prisoners."

But family connections never hurt, and although some of the adventurers paid with their lives, Smith eventually made his way safely back. He was installed at the Adams home in Massachusetts, where a close eye could be kept on him while he finished his schooling at Harvard. He thought about being a lawyer, but then decided against it. He tried his hand at farming, unsuccessfully. What was a man to do?

Grandmother Abigail knew. When her son John Quincy Adams traveled to Russia as American minister in 1809, Smith went along as his secretary. The young man enjoyed the social life, hobnobbing with counts and princes and dukes. But he was forced, after a dalliance, to marry the younger sister of Mrs. John Quincy Adams. And he got into financial difficulties from gambling, causing his uncle to despair that "he has been unfortunately deficient in that without which no good qualities can avail—prudence." Smith was shipped back home.

Over the next few years, he faced a succession of heartbreaking losses. His sickly firstborn child, who had barely survived the grueling journey across the Atlantic, died just after arrival. Then his father went to the grave, leaving his worldly affairs in "inextricable confusion." Finally came the loss of Grandmother Abigail, who had so loved and watched over him and pressed his claims on less willing members of the family.

A government clerkship helped him keep body and soul together, but this would soon be snatched away to serve the nepotism of another family equally needy and well connected in those hard times.

It was a good omen that the Adams-Onis Treaty contained a clause by which Spain renounced claims for "all injuries caused by the expedition of Miranda, that was fitted out and equipped at New York." Taking this as a sign that there might be a future for him in Florida, Smith leaped at it. His appointment as naval officer for the port of Pensacola was announced in May 1821, and a month later the brig *Enterprise* was ordered to convey the Smiths and other appointees to their new posts. They did not arrive until August 12, nearly a month after the change of flags.

President Monroe asked Andrew Jackson to provide housing for the Smiths in one of the public buildings at Pensacola. But Old Hickory replied that "the public buildings are in such a state of dilapidation, that it will not be in my power to accommodate Mr. Smith." He also testily added his "regret" that Smith and the other unwelcome Washington appointees "were not here to aid me in the labours of organizing the Government." Fortunately, he had been able to fill their posts on an interim basis with his protégés.

Housing was not the only thing that the new naval officer for the port of Pensacola found lacking on his arrival: boats were in short supply as well. In his first communication with Washington, Smith put in his request for a revenue cutter. If that wasn't possible, he would settle for a rowboat, noting that "hitherto the Inspectors have been able to hire one for the occasion as requisite, but the practice if continued will be found bad economy."

His tenure in Pensacola was short, and this was not to his regret. After the social life of the courts of Europe, the sleepy, shabby, dirty Florida port lacked something in style and glamour. Fortunately, the hard times were easing up. The political fortunes of John Quincy Adams were on the rise, and Washington beckoned to Smith even as Pensacola threatened.

He left in time to avoid the fate of many new American residents: death by the "vile black vomit" of yellow fever. An epidemic hit the city in 1822, causing government officials to flee as far and as fast as they could. Those who stayed, like Dr. Bronaugh, paid with their lives. From the safety of the Hermitage, Andrew Jackson mourned the passing of his old physician and ventured his own considered medical opinion that the outbreak had been caused by rotten fish.

• • •

At the height of hard times it would have been foolish to present a claim for office based on the pre-eminent contributions of one's father to a then-faltering economic system. But by 1822 the situation had improved, and the whole raft of New York congressmen who recommended Alexander Hamilton, Jr., for a job in Florida felt little embarrassment in so doing. President Monroe was happy to oblige with an appointment as U.S. attorney for East Florida, based in the ancient city of St. Augustine.

Young Hamilton had studied at Columbia, where he was a contemporary of Steuben Smith, though he avoided the senior excursion to Venezuela. After graduating, he traveled in Europe, to imbibe military tactics first-hand by watching the campaigns of the Duke of Wellington against Napoleon. Then he returned to the United States in time to fight the British in the War of 1812.

With the postwar reduction in ranks, Hamilton left the army and sought to make his living as a lawyer. Business was not brisk, and after the acquisition of Florida he was ready to follow in his father's footsteps as a public official.

Hamilton took pride in his name, his ability, and his integrity. A $200-a-year post in a backwater like St. Augustine was hardly the pinnacle of his ambition, but just a starting place. By applying his talents there for a short time, he could earn the recognition and attendant promotion that would give him an office worthy of his heritage.

Even as a steppingstone the Ancient City left much to be desired, from Hamilton's point of view. It was dirty, ruinous, and crumbling. Many ambitious public improvements had been talked up, but only one had actually been completed: a new cemetery for the victims of the previous year's yellow-fever epidemic.

It was a divided society.

The natives adhered to a pace of life that was slow and easy, oriented toward the bare necessities. They fished and gathered oysters and picked oranges and made do. They were Catholic, Spanish-speaking, and mainly of Minorcan descent. Their ancestors had come in the 1760s to carve a plantation out of the Florida wilderness. Finding the countryside inhospitable, their working conditions unendurable, they took refuge in St. Augustine. Even at that early date the Ancient City had two centuries of history behind it as the first permanent European settlement on the North American continent.

The newcomers, on the other hand, could scarcely be restrained in their quest for instant riches, by fair means or foul. They were mostly Protestant, English-speaking, and American. Impelled south by a variety of causes, some were honorable men while others were sheer rascals. These latter turned the Ancient City into "a refuge for bankrupts in fame and fortune" and a "mart for placehunters," according to one disgusted observer.

Almost inevitably, Hamilton came into conflict with both groups. The *mañana* spirit was anathema to him as a young man on the make. But, as a self-appointed rock of integrity, he did not see the fast-and-loose machinations of the newcomers as any more admirable.

It was the natives he offended first. He decreed that the property of the Catholic Church had actually been owned by the Spanish crown and with the change of power had therefore become the property of the United States government. Officials in Washington were far more sensitive then he to the hornets' nest that was being stirred up. They pointedly suggested that he focus his efforts on other problems, but to no avail. It finally took two acts of Congress to undo Hamilton's ruling and restore peace between the Catholic residents and their new Protestant government.

Having made this initial splash, Hamilton headed north to lobby with President Monroe for a better job. The post of naval agent at New York attracted his attention first, but he finally opted for an appointment as land commissioner back in St. Augustine in the spring of 1823.

The land commissioners (there were three each for East and West Florida) had to rule on the validity of titles to property originating in grants from Spanish kings over the centuries. What was not declared private property would become part of the public lands of the United States, to be sold as one means of recouping the costs of acquiring Florida. Speculators were anxious to acquire these lands as soon as clear title could be guaranteed. A potential boom awaited the handing down of Land Commission verdicts, and the whole situation was fraught with opportunities for chicanery.

Before buckling down to this work, Hamilton engaged in a couple of diversions that threatened to cut short his career.

John Rodman, another transplanted New Yorker, was collector of customs at St. Augustine. Besides carrying out his official duties, Rodman was given to flooding Washington with letters bitterly critical of other political appointees. Those to which he signed his name were augmented by a steady stream of anonymous ones. For years he functioned as a one-man complaint bureau.

As the target of one of these missives, Hamilton responded in a way that had become traditional in his family: he demanded "personal satisfaction" in the form of a duel. Prospects of the Burr-Hamilton tragedy at Weehawken's being re-enacted on the mudflats of the Matanzas River were averted when Rodman—whose favorite weapon was the pen, not the sword—issued an apology.

Then, seeing a chance to advance his career, Hamilton threw his hat in the ring for Congress. The incumbent territorial delegate in the House of Representatives, Joseph Hernandez, was a leader of the Minorcan community who had held political office under both the Spanish and the American regimes.

The question of church property came back to haunt Hamilton. He repented his involvement in the matter, but left the unfortunate impression that if the Catholics did not send him to Congress, he would use his position on the Land Commission to do them further damage.

Smoldering resentment burst into open flame. A petition weighted with signatures went to Washington asking the president to "depose Col. Alexander Hamilton" because he "does not possess those good qualities that ought to adorn a Public Officer."

Hamilton was livid. He branded his accusers "damned liars,"

"damned rascals" and "ignorant Minorcans." He filed suits for libel and conspiracy against his opponent, and wrote to President Monroe that "this is a most despicable community."

The election results reflected the ethnic makeup of the area—249 votes for Hamilton and 252 for Hernandez—but neither of them won. Their division of the East Florida vote handed the victory to Old Hickory's protégé Richard Keith Call, who received every one of West Florida's 496 votes.

After this stormy interlude, Hamilton settled down to work on the vexing question of land titles. But on the Land Commission he soon found himself odd man out. It was a difficult situation. One of the other commissioners was an old friend of Aaron Burr—hardly a good omen for their ability to work together. The third was in the advanced stages of terminal illness, and when not languishing on his deathbed seemed mainly interested in getting a good job for his brother-in-law.

In January 1824 Hamilton announced he was withdrawing from his post. He sent to Washington a list of seventeen points justifying his action and condemning his fellow commissioners. Then, having second thoughts, he tried to rescind his resignation—but to no avail. His career as stormy petrel in "despicable" St. Augustine was over.

He was esteemed in Washington as a man of integrity. But in that city of politicians his proven inability to work with others marked him a failure as a public official. No one rushed to offer him another job on the government payroll. He returned to New York, made his fortune in real estate—for which his Florida experience was certainly not bad training—and survived until 1875, dying at the ripe old age of eighty-nine (those Hamiltons who didn't die in duels were blessed with extremely long life spans).

As the bearer of one of the country's distinguished names, he took part in political debates over the years, but always from the outside. Having burned his fingers as office seeker and government employee in Florida, he proclaimed ever afterward that "in the cause of the public, I am a volunteer."

• • •

For such a recent addition to the country, Florida was amazingly intertwined with the lives of those in the news in 1824.

It was an election year. The bitterly fought presidential race pitted John Quincy Adams, who had negotiated Florida's acquisition, against Andrew Jackson, who had been its first governor.

The divisiveness of the campaign not only brought the Era of Good Feeling to a decisive end, but threatened to tear the country apart as well.

It was a good thing for national harmony that, in this time of flaring tempers, most Americans still found one thing around which they could unite to celebrate: the triumphant return to their shores of Marie Joseph Paul Yves Roch Gilbert du Motier.

To generations of Americans who have idolized him, he is best known as the Marquis de Lafayette—though he himself renounced the noble title of marquis during the French Revolution and preferred to be called simply General Lafayette.

But during the year he spent traveling the country and receiving the pent-up accolades of a people, you could merely have referred to "the Nation's Guest" or "the greatest man in the world" and been easily understood without mention of his actual name in either the long or the short form. Florida frontiersmen, Boston merchants, Virginia planters, Ohio riverboatmen, Carolina slaves, and Georgia Indians, whatever vast gulfs separated them—and these were many and growing—could raise their voices in common cheers for "Lafayette and Liberty."

The "canine appetite for popularity" that Thomas Jefferson had noted in Lafayette must have been fully satiated during that year-long orgy of celebration. There was not a city, not a crossroads, not an isolated farmhouse along the route, that didn't offer its hospitality to the Nation's Guest. Schoolchildren sang his praises. Poets penned rhymes in his honor. Young belles clamored to dance with him. Manufacturers produced souvenir trinkets to commemorate his visit, and legions of merchants and peddlers sold them to an enthusiastic public.

Lafayette! The name was magic. He had been the comrade-in-arms of George Washington. He had bled at Brandywine, shivered at Valley Forge, and triumphed at Yorktown. His contributions—financial and diplomatic as well as military—had helped to forge a nation.

With good reason did Americans feel they were in Lafayette's debt. Nor were they stingy or begrudging when it came to repayment. This visit was not arranged just to rewelcome the hero, but also to provide some security for his old age. The topsy-turvy world of war and revolution, responsibility for a large extended family and corps of retainers, and an almost complete financial ineptitude had eaten away at the Lafayette fortune and left the aging general in debt.

Congress relieved that burden with an outright gift of $200,000, and to provide for his future they made him a land baron. A township—36 square miles—was to be given him from the most fertile public lands in the country.

Representative John McKee of Alabama, a veteran land speculator knowledgeable in trends and values, was chosen to make the selection for Lafayette. The township he picked formed the northeast quadrant of the old Indian village of Tallahassee—surely due to boom, since it had just been designated the new capital of Florida. Lafayette hoped that this land, judiciously managed, could produce a sum equal to the monetary gift he had received, thus providing him an old age unhampered by the nagging worry of debt.

It is ironic that he never visited the territory where he had suddenly become one of the largest landowners—this despite his invitation from the legislative council not only to visit but to make his home there. However, if he had any questions about the value of Florida real estate, he had unparalleled opportunities to question the experts first-hand. He met them everywhere he went. Colonel Alexander Hamilton, Jr., greeted him in New York. Richard Keith Call, who had bested Hamilton in the congressional race, met Lafayette in Washington and sang the praises of Florida in his ear. A White House dinner given by President Adams for the visiting general included among its guests the inevitable family retainer, William Steuben Smith. He was happier in Washington than at Pensacola, and busied himself with escorting the presidential children to the racetrack rather than begging for rowboats. Old Hickory welcomed Lafayette at the Hermitage, and his successor as governor, William Pope Duval, greeted the Nation's Guest at Cincinnati. Greeted his landlord, as a matter of fact, since Duval had unwittingly built his home on Lafayette's property.

Those were Floridians past and present. Then there were the Floridians-to-be.

Though tart-tongued Representative John Randolph of Roanoke had asserted that no one would immigrate to Florida, "Not from Hell itself," a whole passel of his Virginia cousins and constituents were preparing to do just that. The once-rich soils of their plantations had been exhausted after generations of slave cultivation and could no longer provide a living for the masters. Scions of the Old Dominion's most distinguished families were preparing to decamp for the fertile fields of Florida, taking their slaves and society with them.

Still, there was time for one last party, and what better occasion than Lafayette's visit? At Fredericksburg the Nation's Guest was introduced to the public on the arm of George Washington's charmingly attractive grandniece, Catherine Willis Grey. Only twenty-one, she had already been married and widowed. But thoughts of mourning were far from her mind as she accompanied the visiting hero to his waiting audience.

Lafayette, a noted connoisseur of women, would not be the last Frenchman to cast an appreciative eye upon her. She would soon settle near the general's land in Tallahassee and be courted by one of his countrymen.

At nearby Charlottesville, Lafayette was hosted by his old friend Thomas Jefferson. The Sage of Monticello, now past eighty, was devoting his final years to establishing the University of Virginia. The Frenchman was honored with the first banquet held in the school's rotunda. Many rounds of toasts were offered, one by the Sage's grandson, Francis Wayles Eppes, who had come of age just in time to share the economic woes of the former president's last years. After Jefferson's death, Eppes would pack up family, goods, and slaves for the long trek to Florida.

Farther south, in Savannah, Lafayette met a different sort of Floridian: a planter with a marked French accent. Planting was but a recent vocation, and Florida a recent residence, for twenty-four-year-old Charles Louis Napoleon Achille Murat.

As eldest son of the legendary Marshal Joachim Murat and his wife, Caroline, sister of Napoleon Bonaparte, Achille had spent his early life at Elysée Palace—more recently the residence of the president of France.

In the redistribution of crowns that took place on the heels of Napoleonic conquest, Joachim Murat wound up a king, and Achille, at the tender age of seven, was proclaimed crown prince of Naples. The defeat of Napoleon resulted in a firing squad for Joachim. At the age of fourteen, the crown prince became king of nowhere. In no land did armies obey him, courtiers flatter him, or tax collectors fill his coffers.

On reaching his majority, Prince Murat followed other dispossessed family members across the sea to the small principality established by his uncle Joseph Bonaparte, erstwhile king of Spain, near Bordentown, New Jersey.

With that as his halfway house and launching pad, he looked around for ways to make his fortune in America—at least until the wheel of fortune should turn again and provide him a throne. After assessing the prospects, he decided to follow the crowd to Florida.

Now, after months of hacking a plantation out of the scrub land south of St. Augustine, Murat was ready for a little more civilized company and made his way to Savannah to pay his respects to the Nation's Guest. Lafayette was delighted to meet a fellow Frenchman, even the nephew of his old nemesis Napoleon. It warmed his heart to hear the former crown prince declare himself an enemy of despotism and proclaim his pride in having become an American citizen. But the general was sad to see an acculturation so complete that it included a fervent endorsement of slavery. This was the one great blot Lafayette saw on the American escutcheon. "I would never have drawn my sword in the cause of America," he said, "if I could have conceived that thereby I was founding a land of slavery." As a Florida land baron, Lafayette would try to develop his holdings in a manner consistent with his liberal sentiments.

AMERICAN SILK AND OTHER DREAMS

•

Those in the first wave of immigrants, who sought merely the income of a government job and the prospects of advancement through government ranks—not necessarily in Florida—were soon replaced by settlers who took a more long-range view of wringing their fortunes out of the new territory.

They did not lack for advice on how to go about it. Men whose expertise lay in pushing pens rather than plows promptly provided the booksellers of the nation with volumes on the history, climate, and economic potential of Florida.

These primitive ancestors of modern Chamber of Commerce brochures (no sunny beaches, no bathing beauties) all agreed that it was primarily from the soil that the wealth of immigrants would grow. Some research, in the form of direct observation, was done by the authors, but most of the peninsula remained—to them as to everyone else—*terra incognita.* They fleshed out their recommendations by relying heavily on arguments drawn from analogy.

Florida, like the Mediterranean countries, had a warm climate. Therefore, they reasoned, the crops that grew in one area would thrive in the other. Planters were accordingly advised to go in heavily for olives—which proved an immediate and conspicuous failure.

A similar analogy made to South America resulted in assertions that the coffee bean would become a cash crop. A group of Philadelphia investors formed the East Florida Coffee Land Association in 1821 to exploit this possibility. Only the happy failure to get an appropriate land grant from Congress saved them from throwing their money away needlessly.

More realistic was the exhortation to raise citrus. Florida was littered with old orange groves that had served the Spanish, British, and Indians over the centuries. Many were overgrown and had reverted to a wild state, but at least there was visible physical evidence that citrus would grow and thrive in Florida's soil and climate. Immigrant energy reclaimed the old groves and laid out new ones; within a few years St. Augustine, the heart of the citrus region, resembled a large orange grove from one end to the other.

By 1828, when the city was harvesting an annual crop of two million oranges, it seemed time for a little protectionism. Florida's congressional delegate, Joseph White, introduced a bill that would levy "on foreign oranges, in addition to the present duty, the sum of 25 cents per hundred, imported into the United States, between the months of October and April of every year." This first attempt to legislate for the benefit of the Florida citrus industry failed in the Senate that time around, but, like so many other early notions, it would live to fight another day.

The planters who settled in Middle Florida—many of them Virginians, such as Francis Eppes—brought their own past experience with them and opted for the familiar crops of cotton and tobacco. They tried planting Cuban tobacco seed, with disappointing results; but they did meet with some success in producing tobacco for cigar wrappers. It was a good sideline, although here, as elsewhere in the South, cotton was king. Its production increased twentyfold in a decade as more and more fields were grubbed and hacked out of the virgin forest. An extra bonanza came when it was discovered that the highly prized (and higher-priced) Sea Island cotton would not just grow but thrive in this inland region—contrary to the conventional wisdom that it would deteriorate if planted away from the sea. Before the Civil War, more Sea Island cotton was being produced in Florida than in its traditional home of South Carolina.

Middle Florida had been a wilderness thinly populated by Indians. The selection of Tallahassee as the capital there was based on geographic location rather than any pre-existing development: Tallahassee was midway between the two older towns of Pensacola on the west and St. Augustine to the east. As its lands were cleared, settled and planted, however, Middle Florida boomed. In short order it came to dominate the rest of the territory, both politically and economically.

• • •

Florida settlers were not unique in trying things that wouldn't work, or in going overboard with things that would have worked if applied to a more limited extent.

The whole country was swept, in the early decades of the nineteenth century, by wave after wave of agricultural enthusiasms. Every new breed or crop introduced to the nation was touted as the ultimate solution to rural hard times, and people went for them one after another: Merino sheep, Berkshire hogs, Rohan potatoes, Chinese tree corn, Brahma and Shanghai hens and so on.

Of all these fads, none was more widespread or dramatic than that of the *Morus multicaulis* or Chinese mulberry tree, which swept the land in the 1830s. It was as a steppingstone to the production of silk that the tree owed its great popularity.

Silk, the strong fine thread and fabric from China, long the favorite of royalty, had at times in history been worth its weight in gold. Its value had made it the object of international intrigue, smuggling and spying, which broke the Chinese monopoly so that European countries also became major producers.

There had been several attempts to establish sericulture in the American colonies, with an impressive series of backers. King James of Bible fame had tried unsuccessfully to convince his Virginia colonists to produce silk rather than tobacco. Equally ill-fated were the attempts of James Oglethorpe to promote it in Georgia. Benjamin Franklin had urged Pennsylvanians to raise silkworms, but the outbreak of the Revolution made the production of foodstuffs more important, and once more sericulture died aborning. Then, after the war, interest in the exotic fineries brought back from China by American traders once more raised the silk question in the public mind.

It was only natural, given this background, that the early Florida publicists recommended sericulture as a road to wealth on the frontier. Lafayette, who came from a silk-producing country, was sure that his Florida property would be ideal for this purpose.

Idle thoughts along these lines were translated into reality in 1826 when Gideon Smith of Baltimore brought the first Chinese mulberry tree to the United States. Mulberry leaves were the favorite food of silkworms and the raw material for their valuable excrescence. The *Morus multicaulis*, more than other varieties, was blessed with enormous leaves and was very fast-growing. It could be propagated from cuttings and within a few months would start producing the broad leaves that the silkworms found so delectable.

Agricultural journals sang its praises, assuring "the farmer in moderate circumstances" that "a single acre in mulberries will clothe and educate his children; and that five will enable him to live sumptuously and lay by enough in ten years to leave his family independent."

Congress got into the act by printing a manual on sericulture. Florida's delegate, Joseph White, distributed it, along with silkworm eggs, to his constituents. State legislatures also took it up. Several of them passed measures offering bounties for any silk produced within their borders—after which the legislators rushed home to plant mulberries and make their fortunes.

Enthusiasm shook society from top to bottom as the experiment became an all-embracing mania. It was confidently and seriously predicted that "Every available acre from New England to the Gulf will be covered with the mulberry." Cuttings that had brought a penny apiece in 1830 were fetching two or even five dollars each by the end of the decade. Farmers tore other crops out of the ground to make room for mulberries, and mortgaged their farms for cash to engage in speculation. Some scamps made their money peddling fish roe as silkworm eggs.

No place was as favored by the boom as Florida, whose lengthy growing season made it the natural hothouse for the nation. Dealers in mulberry futures scoured the rural areas on horseback, contracting for whole crops not yet in the ground.

The mere service of Mammon was not a sufficient rationale for churchgoing people, so consciences were salved by those who preached the social benefits accruing from sericulture. One Florida publicist even heralded it as a cure for juvenile delinquency, noting that it provided "an employment to the children of the poor white settler who otherwise might be idle, useless, and contractive of indolent and bad habits."

As words like these soothed the mind, pocketbooks were being morally fattened by the sale of millions of mulberry cuttings, which replaced more prosaic crops on the boats going north.

It was just the kind of shot in the arm that a frontier area needed to get its economy going: mulberries did for Florida what gold would later do for California.

• • •

Getting the crops out was essential. Be they mulberry cuttings or oranges or cotton or tobacco, they were relatively worthless until they got past the borders of Florida and out into the great market place beyond.

Roads, not very good anywhere, were mostly nonexistent in the new territory. Waterways served as the main arteries of commerce. Sandwiched as it was between the Atlantic Ocean and the Gulf of Mexico, blessed with several natural harbors and navigable rivers flowing to both coasts, Florida was relatively favored when it came to waterways. But nothing, of course, was perfect, and this was an era of great belief in man-made improvements.

It was the age of canals. The brilliant success of New York's Erie Canal prompted a host of other proposals. In any town or city you had merely to scratch the surface, raise the question in a tavern, and out would come the plans. Everyone had them, complete with elaborate rationales and inside knowledge of how greatly land values would increase along the route.

Floridians had their favorite scheme as well. They pointed out that a thousand miles could be cut from a hazardous sea route if the Atlantic and the Gulf were linked by a canal through North Florida. The Florida reef had been, over the centuries, the graveyard of countless Spanish treasure ships, but hazards were man-made as well: the inlets and islands along the coast were the refuge and launching point for pirates.

Toting up the damage done in just one year by shipwrecks and pirate raids, canal proponents claimed that the insurance money paid out as a result would be enough to turn their dream into reality. Just dig a ditch linking this river with that lake and on to the next. Presto! The Atlantic and the Gulf would be connected, and sailors' wives and children need fear no more, nor become widows and orphans.

It was a good argument.

So were those of people in New York, Pennsylvania, Ohio, Maryland, and elsewhere. A political fact of life in the competition for government funds was that there were more people in those states than there were in the territory of Florida—and they could vote too.

So it was a political masterstroke that the Floridians were able to get the august Daniel Webster of Massachusetts to introduce their legislation for them. This immediately raised it from a parochial question of local self-interest to an important national need. The Congress went ahead and authorized a survey to study the feasibility of a cross-Florida canal.

Less happy were the results. The survey report in 1829 dismissed the idea as "impracticable" because there was not a suitable deep-water port on the Gulf side, nor was there a sufficient water supply atop Florida's central ridge to keep any kind of ship afloat in the canal. Despite this unfavorable initial verdict, the proposal would prove to be durable long beyond the lifetime of any of its original advocates.

Without government assistance the project was too large to undertake, but any number of smaller canal ventures were authorized by the legislature in the 1820s and 1830s. They were organized as private enterprises, with Florida investors rushing in where even Uncle Sam feared to tread.

In 1830 Peter Cooper perfected his first steam locomotive, the Tom Thumb. From then on, canal projects began to sprout railroad components. First came the mule-powered Tallahassee–St. Marks Railway, constructed in 1836. Its primitiveness was put to shame the following year when the St. Joseph–Lake Wimico Railroad commenced operation with its newfangled steam engine.

Florida's possibilities could not be exploited as long as most of the territory was inaccessible. Any proposal to improve transportation was accordingly listened to with eager ears.

• • •

It was hard work—even with slave labor—to clear fields and plant crops, not to mention promoting canals and other projects. And all work and no play was definitely not the style of the plantation aristocrats. As they transplanted their social system south to the old Indian fields and virgin timberlands of the former Spanish colony, they brought its pleasures as well as its pains, and called the whole thing civilization.

For entertainment they chose balls. For sport they chose horse racing. For pageantry they chose medieval jousting tournaments straight from the pages of Sir Walter Scott's novels. For drinks they chose mint juleps. For settling affairs of honor they chose the dueling fields.

Granted, the amenities were at first a little rude. But the bloodlines were fine: a host of First Families of Virginia and a touch of royalty. It was a point of pride that these people could endure a little hardship on the road back to affluence. Prince Murat, for instance, made his home in a log cabin, sleeping on a mattress of Spanish moss set on the floor, with a pine log for a pillow. It was a far cry from the Elysée Palace. Of course, he was never noted for his fastidiousness, unlike his father, one of the vainest characters and fanciest dressers to strut across Europe. King Murat had favored brilliant uniforms concocted of gold thread, peacock feathers, and the like. He so treasured his good looks that the last words he uttered to the firing squad about to execute him were "Save my face. Aim for my heart."

Prince Murat, by contrast, boasted that his boots, once put on, never came off until they fell apart. Only when his manservant caught him unawares could he be tricked into a change of clothes. And he disdained the use of water, either for washing or drinking purposes. Even on the frontier, this marked him as something of an eccentric. Among his neighbors he became noted for his oddments as much as for his royal blood. "He swears very much," wrote one of them, and "continually experiments on the eatability of the whole animal tribe." Rattlesnake, chameleon, stewed alligator, owl pie, and cows' ears met with his approval, though he could find no acceptable gastronomic use for the buzzard. There were virtually no limits to his quest. He once told a friend, in his broken English, that "I just as soon eat Indian as pork—if he well fried."

Some changes occurred in this style of life in the summer

of 1826 when Murat married Catherine Willis Grey, whom he had begun courting by making the romantic gesture of drinking champagne from her slipper at a picnic. The wedding of Napoleon's nephew to George Washington's grandniece was a social columnist's delight, despite the relative impecuniousness of both parties.

Achille retained his personal slovenly habits as far as possible, but his surroundings began to take on a bit more grace, thanks to his wife. Out came the gold spoons and linen with the Napoleonic crest, and the primitive log cabin was succeeded by a plantation house a bit more impressive. To foot the bills, Murat took on a variety of odd jobs.

In addition to being a planter, he hung out his shingle for the practice of law, and became a county judge and a country postmaster as well. He wrote an insightful, if not profitable, book on frontier life. He headed a canal company and speculated in Texas lands.

But, most of all, he kept his eyes glued to European politics, hoping for a Bonapartist restoration. When the status quo began to quake in 1830, he hastened to Belgium and organized a foreign legion that so upset the reigning crowned heads of Europe that they had him declared *persona non grata* and expelled from the continent. He wound up back in Florida, in considerable debt for the costs of his adventure, and looking for new avenues to riches. In the meantime, he sought solace in drink.

That other famous Frenchman General Lafayette kept one eye on politics with the other on his Florida property. He had turned down an early offer from Richard Keith Call to buy his Tallahassee township, believing he could get a better price if he held on to it. This brought down on him the unfamiliar sound of American criticism. First he was accused of retarding the development of Florida's capital by keeping such a strategic section of it off the market. Then, when he offered parts of it for sale, his prices were condemned as outrageous. For one who had so recently been lavishly praised and celebrated, these words were doubly harsh to the ear.

Lafayette toyed with the idea of retaining the township as part of the family estate to be passed on to his heirs. But the 1830 revolution in France, though it met with his enthusiastic support, had further impoverished him and required that he sell his American assets. No buyer could take on the whole tract, so it went piecemeal. It brought only about half of what the general had hoped, and took two decades to realize this reduced figure—by which time Lafayette had long been in his grave. But in light of his history of ineptitude in financial affairs, it was not a bad bargain. It had cost him nothing in the first place, and a good chunk of money came out of it. That was more than could be said for many of his ventures.

It also gave him a chance to try to show his adopted country the benefits of free versus slave labor. Many years before, he had experimented on a plantation in Cayenne by allowing the slaves to earn their freedom. Although that effort had been short-circuited by the French Revolution and Lafayette's resulting downfall, the antislavery cause was still dear to his heart, and he cherished the hope that his American friends could be won over by the example of a model colony on his Florida lands.

The vine, the olive, and the mulberry were to be the crops. Imported French peasants were to be the laborers. His friends Count de la Porte and General Morris de Veir were to be in charge. And an end to slavery was to be the final result.

It would have been a comedy of errors had not the cause been so noble and the personal tragedies of death, disease, and dashed hopes so real. Everything went wrong, from incorrect land titles to poor crop selection to lack of medical care to chicanery on the part of one of the leaders. The model colony was a monumental failure and convinced no one. Though Lafayette witnessed the debacle, his convictions never wavered: the last letter he wrote from his deathbed (in 1834) hailed the abolition of slavery in the British colonies.

In 1850 the general's grandsons visited Tallahassee, to oversee the disposition of the remaining lands. They were lionized by the residents and invited to address the legislature. Senators praised them and their ancestor effusively, heard their words politely, then moved on to the next item on the agenda, which was strengthening the slave laws.

Lafayette must have turned in his grave.

• • •

No sooner had the American flag been raised in 1821 than one of the newcomers, under the pen name "Americanus," published an open letter to the Spanish inhabitants of St. Augustine predicting that in the future the Ancient City would be "the retreat of the opulent, the gay, and the fashionable, a destiny which bountiful Nature seems to have intended."

"Americanus" was perspicacious, if a bit ahead of his time.

The same sun that nourished crops also nourished people. The summers could be unpleasant—unhealthy even, as the recurrent yellow-fever epidemics showed. But the winters, in those days of inefficient heating systems, were ever so much more pleasant than those in the north. It was natural that those who needed, and could afford, a break from the wind and chills and snow and ice should turn their thoughts to this new American territory. Of course, given the rigors of travel and the primitive accommodations, only the most desperate came in those early years. So, more immediately realistic than the predictions of "Americanus" were the hopes of the boosters that local coffers could be filled "if the physicians could be induced to recommend a winter at St. Augustine to their patients," rather than the prevailing "fashion of sending invalids from the north on an expensive journey to the south of France and Italy."

The winter boats that came into port began bringing with them a variety of invalids, and headstones in the city's cemeteries attest that some of these remained in St. Augustine permanently. While they survived, they were a profitable source of income for boardinghouse keepers and pioneer hoteliers. Most noticeable among them were those suffering from consumption and other bronchial ailments, whose hacking, racking coughs echoing through the narrow streets would for many years to come convince the healthy "opulent, gay and fashionable" that St. Augustine was no fit stopping place for them.

It was not a matter of peddling false hope to those with nowhere else to turn: lung conditions did improve in the salubrious climate, and some recovered from their ills, going on to lead long and productive lives.

Farewell; and fair befall thee, gentle town!
The prayer of those who thank thee for their life,
The benison of those thy fragrant airs,
And simple hospitality hath blest,
Be to thee ever as the rich perfume
Of a good name, and pleasant memory!

Those lines were penned by one of the grateful recoverees, a young, troubled, tubercular New England minister named Ralph Waldo Emerson. He was going through a religious crisis (which may have sparked his physical ailment) when he sojourned in the Ancient City in 1827.

He spent much of his time on the sand at the ocean's edge, hitting an orange around with a stick. He could thus be considered a pioneer of two favorite tourist pastimes: beachgoing and golfing. But he would have been horrified at the suggestion. He engaged in those activities simply because he declined to participate in the wickedness of billiards with the rest of the crowd.

The high point of his visit—apart from gaining relief from his ailment—came at the very end. A shipmate on the excruciatingly long voyage north was Achille Murat—not only the first prince, but also the first atheist Emerson had ever met.

Murat at that time was aggressive and engaging about his distaste for religion. Once, when preparing for a duel, he turned to his second and said, "I may be dead the next minute, but I declare to you that I am an entire disbeliever in any future state of existence." Fortunately, he lost only the top half of his little finger in the engagement and so did not have to face eternal judgment with blasphemy on his lips. In later years his disbelief mellowed considerably.

Emerson, in the midst of his religious crisis, took the meeting with Murat as a kind of temptation and test of faith. He was relieved to find that his beliefs came through unscathed. For the prince's role in resolving his nagging doubts on this score, Emerson was eternally grateful, paying perhaps unwarranted tribute to Murat's "sublime virtue" and "noble soul."

Among those who were not ill, mere sightseeing was not a sufficient lure: visitors usually came with some particular mission in mind. One such man with a purpose was naturalist John J. Audubon, who traveled through Florida in 1831. His impression, however, was considerably less favorable than Emerson's. The Ancient City he described as "the poorest hole in creation," and his departure was a "Happy event." Yet his trip was not without value, for he painted some of the birds that made him famous.

From feeble beginnings like these, and with many setbacks yet to come, would grow Florida's dominant modern industry of catering to tourists.

• • •

Immigrants to Florida have always brought with them ideas for how things could be improved. Not surprisingly, these have often been inspired by the way things were done back home.

The original American settlers were full of good ideas. Financing these schemes was the only problem. There were two ways to get money in the amounts needed for development. One was to tap the government purse, and Floridians did this as well as could be expected, given the serious competition they faced from the rest of the country. The other way was to establish banks—preferably ones that would raise their money elsewhere through the sale of bonds, and invest it in Florida.

Andrew Jackson, having advanced from governor to president, was busily engaged in smiting the Bank of the United States from his seat in the White House. Anti-bank sentiment dribbled all the way back to Tallahassee, where his successor, Governor Duval, regularly vetoed all bank proposals that came across his desk.

At length the governor relented, under pressure from his friends and neighbors, and in 1834 permitted the Union Bank of Tallahassee to be chartered. Other financial institutions were established in its wake. The faith of the territory was pledged to back bank bonds that would be peddled as far away as Europe.

The establishment of banks represented the completion of a system whose component parts included cotton and tobacco plantations, slaves, orange and mulberry groves, canal projects, and the increasingly delightful social life that went with a prospering economy.

Planters quickly became adept at the art of borrowing money to make money. Land and slaves could be mortgaged to the bank for two-thirds of their value. The money thus obtained would be used to buy more land and slaves. The market for cotton was so good that a couple of crops would pay off the debts incurred, and the whole cycle could be repeated on a newer, higher level. People adjusted their sights upward to keep pace with the wealth that was rolling in.

The importance of getting the highest appraisal on mortgaged property—so as to borrow more money to invest—gave rise to a variety of ways of "working the bank." Some of these were legitimate, and some merely possible to get away with.

Lands that the planters had bought at public sale for $1.25 to $2.00 an acre were valued by the bank at $5.00 an acre. Later, as the real-estate boom heated up, appraisals were increased to $15.00 an acre. Thus an initial investment of $1,000 could enable one to borrow up to $8,000—a credit arrangement that would be attractive in any day and age.

Less aboveboard were methods sometimes used to kite the

valuation of slave property. Bank appraisers, hot and sweaty after slogging through the slave quarters, would be sumptuously dined and wined with the choicest liquors the plantation had to offer. Conviviality having been established, some more human property would be paraded out for evaluation. The appraisers, feeling no pain, would not notice that these were the same old slaves, slightly rearranged and instructed to answer to different names. Neighboring planters also cooperated by lending slaves on appraisal day.

In booming times such discrepancies were not too closely examined. Instead of involving themselves in needless muckraking, people were occupied with buying the latest gewgaws and fripperies, to show that civilization had indeed arrived on the Florida frontier.

Achille Murat was not slow in learning the art of borrowing to the hilt. In addition, he was paid $5,000 a year for his services as a director of the Union Bank—more than he received from his other jobs combined. Convinced that he had finally found the road to wealth, he encouraged the richer Bonapartes to invest their money through him for the mutual benefit of the clan, himself in particular.

For its role as fuel to the engine of wealth, the bank won unstinting praise from those within its charmed circle. "It is the best thing afloat," boasted one planter. "A man can go to sleep and wake up rich."

Andrew Jackson, stormy idol of an age and first American governor of Florida.

The Marquis de Lafayette, hero of the American Revolution and pioneer Florida land baron. (*National Archives*)

Tallahassee—capital and heartland of the first Florida boom—as depicted in a sketch by the Comte de Castlenau, a French nobleman who visited in the late 1830s.

When the Seminole leaders were asked to sign a treaty in 1835 calling for the removal of their people to the west of the Mississippi River, Osceola plunged his knife into the document and announced defiantly: "This is the only way I sign." Seven years of war followed.

General Peter Sken Smith built this mansion on the Plaza in St. Augustine with materials shipped from his native New York. The photograph was taken in 1864 when the building served as post headquarters for the occupying Union soldiers.

The 1841 Union Bank building in Tallahassee has had a checkered career. Home of a Freedman's Bank after the Civil War, it was used in subsequent generations as a feed store, art shop, and dental laboratory. In 1984, moved to a site across from the state Capitol, it was undergoing restoration.

Francis Wayles Eppes, grandson of Thomas Jefferson, early Florida planter, staunch Episcopalian, and long-time mayor of Tallahassee. (*Thomas Jefferson Memorial Foundation*)

Princess Murat made her home at Bellevue after the death of her husband. In 1967 the building was moved from its original site and restored for a museum.

THE MAN WITH NO EYEBROWS

•

Florida, more than most places, owes a significant share of its development to those who amassed fortunes elsewhere, then headed south to spend them.

General Peter Sken Smith was one of these: perhaps a model for the breed. His story, accordingly, takes on aspects of both fable and road map for the future. He has been unduly forgotten, to the detriment of those who followed in his footsteps and could have profited from his experience. Ignorance of his history has condemned others to repeat it.

It was as part of the invalid army that he first landed in St. Augustine, on December 6, 1834. The Ancient City, with its endless orange groves, was a pleasing sight—doubly pleasing since he had nearly lost his life on the voyage down.

The local invalid population of two or three hundred included several friends from his home state of New York. He found a congenial physician in Dr. Seth Peck, formerly of Connecticut, who, after probing and poking the general, announced that the liver ailment which had launched him on his southern journey had now settled in his lungs. This was good news, because the local climate was more renowned for curing lung than liver ailments.

It didn't take an acute practitioner of medicine like Dr. Peck to see that something was wrong with the patient. The signs were all too evident, not so much in the presence as in the absence of things: the general's ailments had left him with no hair, no eyebrows, and no fingernails.

A student of human nature could have done as well as the worthy Dr. Peck in understanding the symptoms as a result of recent—and not so recent—trials and tragedies in the general's life. At the age of thirty-nine, he had recently been widowed, and was more recently threatened with death himself. A chronic inebriate for some years, he had failed in countless business ventures and been passed over, in favor of a younger brother, for managing the family fortune. This was quite a collection of burdens to bear. Yet things were on the upswing, for he had recently given up drinking, fled the cold northern winter for the warmth of Florida, and found religion after years of impiety. These were matters of relief—if not amazement—to his family.

• • •

"Peter Smith" is a common enough name. Countless thousands have borne it and have probably embraced all the known varieties of saintliness and wickedness, vice and virtue, in the human race. Some were commonplace, some extraordinary; far from the blandest of the lot was the Peter Smith who fathered the general with no eyebrows.

Smith senior had gone into business at the age of twenty-one with another enterprising young man, named John Jacob Astor. Their business was buying land, vast quantities of it, in the newly opened frontier of New York State.

Peter Smith had just made a very advantageous deal with the Oneida Indians when his firstborn son arrived, in 1795. He honored the Oneida chief, Skenandoah, by christening the boy Peter Skenandoah Smith, a name that not only served to distinguish him from all other Peter Smiths, but also was a permanent reminder of the bedrock of the family fortune.

That fortune grew. As it did, Peter Smith the elder allowed himself a few vanities and distinctions. He built a mansion in a village he named Peterboro, in a township he called Smithfield, and ever after he signed himself baronially as "Peter Smith of Peterboro."

But his was not a simple case of rising from rags to riches. There was that in it, but the journey as a whole was far more tortured and complex. Though he became one of the nation's largest landowners, he was not at peace with himself. He fretted excessively over the condition of his soul and worried constantly about the likelihood of damnation. While acquiring land with one hand, he began distributing religious tracts with the other.

The death of his wife in 1818 left him bereft. He decided to give up business entirely and devote his remaining years to propagating the faith—the words of an angry God as interpreted by a cranky man.

It took years to make an inventory of all the property he had acquired, which amounted to nearly a million acres in all but six of New York's counties, and in other states as well. To look after this property in trust he chose not the eldest son but, rather, the second son, Gerrit. For Peter Sken it was a heavy blow, in this era not long removed from primogeniture. But it was a pattern that kept recurring in his life: playing second fiddle to the second son.

Peter Sken's share of the bounty was an annuity of $350 a year, to be increased by $150 should he "choose to become a student in some respectable seminary of learning." This was a sore point in the family: Peter and Gerrit had gone off to school together in 1813, but the older brother soon dropped out, while the younger one stayed on to become valedictorian of the class of 1818 at Hamilton College.

Peter was not lured back to school by the sum of money

offered, but he did take advantage of a second provision: when he married the annuity increased to $700 a year. That was enough to live on, though not in the style to which he would have liked to become accustomed.

A scapegrace aura clung to him as he failed in business ventures and was defeated in bids for public office.

He succeeded best as a soldier. This was an area where he faced no competition from his younger brother—who for many years would be the backbone of the American Peace Society. Peter Sken was good at organizing riflemen into brigades and getting elected their leader. He rose in rank from lieutenant to major general of the New York militia.

Soldiering was not necessarily the best occupation for a man with a drinking problem. The conviviality posed more of a threat to him than bullets, and the toll clearly showed. It almost killed him—and would have, if not for a little divine intervention. A wave of religious revivals swept the part of New York where the Smith domains extended. So intense and frequent were they that the area became known as "the burnt-over district." When the general caught the spirit and traded in his bottle for a dose of religion, the change was breathtaking. The black sheep became an elder of the church; the tippler became a temperance lecturer.

As Peter Sken Smith "firmly set out in the caus of religion and servise of the Lord," he sought to repair his ravaged body by making a journey to the Ancient City, which had already acquired a reputation as the health resort of last resort for invalids and near-corpses. In a triumph of the will he gathered together the shards of his life and sailed south, his pockets stuffed with Bible tracts and his mind filled with thoughts of salvation.

• • •

The Florida he arrived in was bursting at the seams with get-rich-quick schemes, dreams that could come true if only a little capital was invested in the right places. To the spinners of dreams, this northern invalid with the proud title, wealthy family, and disfiguring ailments looked like an easy mark.

Although he publicly disclaimed interest in their ventures—he was there just for his health—in letters to Gerrit he took the measure of the place, noting the prospects for orange groves and mulberries and hotels and railroads and canals and steamboats and all the other things that could be done if only a little northern enterprise rather than native laziness were added to the natural conditions of the locale.

He rapidly became a booster, if not yet an investor, writing letters that were printed in the Albany newspaper about the charms and virtues of the place. Some of his observations were standard tourist fare, not much changed from that time to this. But he dealt with thorny problems as well, in a spirit of charity to his temporary abode. In February 1835 a disastrous freeze hit the citrus trees of North Florida, destroying the efforts of a decade in a handful of unreasonably cold nights. It was the beginning of the end of citrus growing that far north in the peninsula, but Smith played down the seriousness in his letters, describing it as just a temporary setback. Then there was the question of slavery. Revolts like Nat Turner's, although quickly suppressed by the slaveholders, made many northern invalids uneasy: they were not anxious to court any more danger than their frail health already provided. Smith took up his pen to advertise the "perfect order" found in St. Augustine, which should set these worries to rest. Though he avowed he would never own a slave himself, and looked forward to the day of universal emancipation, still he reserved some fire for the abolitionists, who were raising troublesome questions that could only lead, "God forbid," to civil war.

As he sent his letters to Albany for publication, Smith supplied copies to the *Florida Herald*, which approvingly reprinted them to show how the Ancient City was being promoted in distant places.

It was altogether a pleasant situation for the general. The balmy climate soothed his ailments and he basked in the unaccustomed luxury of a good reputation. When winter, spring, and summer had passed, a much-improved Peter Sken Smith made his way back north.

• • •

By departing he missed an event that stood his peaceful utopia on its head: the outbreak of the Seminole War at the end of 1835.

After years of being pushed back from their best lands by the onrush of white settlers, the Seminoles were faced, finally, with deportation beyond the Mississippi. They found in Osceola a leader who would resist and lead them on the warpath.

The Seminole War did not destroy the Florida economy, but it certainly reshuffled it. What was disaster for some was opportunity for others. The immediate effect of Indian raids was to render the outlying plantation areas worthless. Dispossessed planters and their families fled to cities for safety in numbers and protection by U.S. troops. By the law of supply and demand, rents and prices in the cities shot up. Storekeepers could not stock up fast enough. Never had the flow of federal dollars come so rapidly into Florida coffers. General Zachary Taylor made himself unpopular by suggesting that the territorial economy was based on continuing the war rather than ending it. But he had a point.

It was a tricky situation. Lives could be lost. Yet a man who knew his way around could profit even in the midst of unpleasantness. Peter Sken Smith knew his way around. Not only that, but for the first time in his life he had the means at hand to do something about what he knew: old Peter Smith of Peterboro, after years of fretting and complaining and damning his relatives and handing out religious tracts, finally shuffled off to whatever reward awaited him on April 13, 1837. Unable even in retirement to avoid the lure of land speculation so deeply in his blood, he had managed during his last years to acquire another half million acres in addition to the kingdom he had previously passed on to Gerrit.

With the settlement of the estate, Peter Sken got a nest egg of $46,000 and an income of $8,000 a year for life. Adequate and then some for the times. Less than a tenth of what Gerrit wound up with, but still good money. And it could grow.

Peter Sken did not wait to spend it in New York, the scene of so many previous failures. He headed back to St. Augustine, this time to settle down, not to recuperate but to invest. He was welcomed with open arms.

The first thing any city does with wealthy newcomers is invite them to contribute to its charities. Thus did the general become in short order a trustee of the fledgling Southern College and an elder of the First Presbyterian Church. For the school he acquired a principal and for the church a minister. He covered for the financial embarrassment of his coreligionists by paying half of the preacher's salary out of his own pocket.

Charity was fine, but Peter Sken Smith was bent on increasing, not decreasing, his wealth. Opportunities presented themselves left and right. He soon became chairman, director, president, or proprietor of the St. Augustine and Picolata Railroad Co., Florida Peninsula Rail Road and Steam Boat Co., St. Johns and St. Augustine Canal Co., North City Wharf Co., and Southern Life Insurance and Trust Co. This last was the most important since, as Florida's second-largest bank (and first insurance company), it provided him with a line of credit to pursue his other ventures.

He bought up land surrounding the developed part of St. Augustine and promoted the city's first suburb, North City. (He described crabgrass as "one of the best native grasses," which grew "luxuriantly"; its uprooting had not yet become a suburban obsession.) North City met the security needs of the day by hugging close to Fort Marion—so closely, in fact, that it encroached on government property, for which reason part of it was later repossessed. In the meantime, however, no place was safer from Indian raids, and lots sold like hotcakes.

For those who wanted to make fortunes in oranges and mulberries, the general offered choice plots in the putative "Town of St. Johns, E. Florida," whose virtues, it would appear from the ads, were unmatched by any place short of the Garden of Eden.

If you didn't want to buy his lands, he would sell you other people's, from the land office he established. He also practiced law. He advertised his expertise at adjusting and collecting debts —skills acquired, no doubt, on the other side of the fence, during his years as a ne'er-do-well.

He was a one-man boom, the likes of which Florida had never seen before.

Such a man must have a suitable residence, so he acquired a prominent corner lot on the town plaza and had fine materials shipped in from New York to build the largest mansion the Ancient City had ever seen, surpassing even the Smith mansion in Peterboro which brother Gerrit had inherited.

Not bad for a year's work.

• • •

Having thus made his mark in the Ancient City's financial, religious, educational, and social circles, he took the next logical step and—with the backing of his fellow New York émigrés—offered himself up as a candidate for political office. In the election of 1838 St. Augustinians were given the double treat of voting for him as representative and as delegate to the Florida constitutional convention.

Among the qualifications cited by his supporters was that he was "a gentleman of fortune, and consequently above a bribe." But here he stumbled. People who had been glad to accept his charity looked a bit more closely when he offered himself as their leader. Local politics had not cooled down any since the previous decade, when Alexander Hamilton, Jr. (a relative of Smith's by marriage), had gotten so hotly involved.

Even in this distant outpost, the general was done in again by younger brother Gerrit. Throughout his life, Gerrit seemed to have the Midas touch with money, but that was not what really stirred his soul. His true passion lay in the cause of reform. He embraced its successive waves, from temperance (one of his investments was the Peterboro Temperance Hotel, which went bankrupt for failing to slake the thirst of travelers), to dress reform (his daughter designed the original bloomers), to woman suffrage (in which he was egged on by his cousin Elizabeth Cady Stanton). The reform of the hour, which Gerrit discovered just about the time his brother discovered Florida, was the abolition of slavery.

When Gerrit embraced a reform, he did not do so quietly. He went out and made speeches about it; he paid to have these printed as pamphlets; then he cast them to the winds, as old Peter Smith of Peterboro had done with his religious tracts. Similarly, Gerrit did not merely become a member of an organization. He became its financial angel, chief publicist, and most visible spokesman, as befitted one of his wealth and achievements.

Abolitionism was the ultimate heresy in Florida.

Peter Sken's political opponents did not fail to pick up on this. They loudly condemned the older brother for the activities of the younger. The general, they said, wanted to drive the slaveholders out of East Florida, replace them with northern abolitionists, and carve an antislavery state out of this geographically inhospitable region.

Heresy! People were tarred and feathered, run out of town on rails, for lesser sins than that.

Smith fought back as best he could. At a public meeting he denied the charges, clearly differentiating himself from his brother: "He is one man—I am another. I openly opposed his

Abolition sentiments at the North; and I as openly oppose Abolition, in all its phases, in the South."

As to the letters to the Albany paper he had written during his first sojourn in St. Augustine, avowing a belief in universal emancipation, he explained them away as the sentiments of a northern tourist. Now that he had settled in Florida and invested his money there, his views had changed accordingly. He had remarried, to a southern woman who brought slaves as part of her dowry. How, he asked in triumphant logic, could he be both a slaveholder and an abolitionist? How could he want to destroy the basis of his own wealth?

Perhaps some were convinced by his arguments, but not enough. He lost the election.

The charges against him had been made most damningly in the local newspaper, the *Herald.* He thought this a particularly low blow, since he was one of the largest advertisers in its columns through his various business ventures. Why should he underwrite his own condemnation? The newspaper monopoly in St. Augustine was broken with the establishment of a rival journal, the *News*, to which his advertising was switched. The *Herald* would ever afterward insist that Smith was the "secret editor" of the *News.*

The two papers slugged it out in print, trading insults, facts and fictions. The opposing journals referred to each other as sewers and slop tubs, while their owners were flatteringly described as liars, scoundrels, vipers, and demoniac characters. No one attempted to be polite.

On rare occasions the bludgeon was traded in for the needle, with telling effect. A poem entitled "Peter Sken Smith" and attributed to "Dryden" appeared in the pages of the *Herald*; it portrayed the general as:

> *Stiff in opinions, always in the wrong*
> *Was everything by starts, and nothing long;*
> *But in the course of one revolving moon*
> *Was chemist, fidler, statesman and buffoon.*

It was enough to make a man tear out his hair. If he had any.

The rivalry that started in politics and continued through journalism and verse then made its way to the inner sanctum of the First Presbyterian Church. There Smith showed his muscle by having the owner of the *Herald* removed as an elder. When this did not stop the brickbats, the man's son was excommunicated for good measure. The Episcopal Church thus picked up a couple of new members, but the war of words did not quiet down at all.

• • •

This cacophony took place against the national background of the Panic of 1837. Banks stopped paying out their precious gold and silver, paper money plunged in value, 90 percent of the country's factories closed their doors, and there were bread riots in the big cities.

The Panic of 1819 had contributed to the development of Florida. That of 1837 decimated it. It was strike three for the territory, which had managed to survive the blows of the orange freeze and the Seminole War.

Strikes one and two had been offset by the introduction of new crops and the injection of massive government funds. But the banks were at the heart of all development schemes, and when they collapsed they brought everything else clattering down around them—almost including Florida itself, which had unwisely backed the bonds of the banks with its faith.

The backlash was swift. Bankers, once lavishly praised, now became pariahs. The 1839 Florida constitution provided that "No president, director, cashier, or other officer, of any banking company in this State, shall be eligible to the office of governor, senator or representative to the General Assembly." Politicians had a field day damning the bankers for "the mischief and injury they have brought upon the country."

Investigations uncovered the seamy side of bank operations. Swindles were widely publicized. Forced sales revealed how overvalued properties had been: one parcel appraised at $13,000 could fetch no more than $900 when auctioned off.

The distress of the plantation aristocracy was compounded by the collapse of cotton prices. Salvation was sought by switching to the higher-priced crop of tobacco. So many switched that the tobacco market was flooded and nearly destroyed. Nature continued the decimation by presenting the area, in rapid-fire succession, with drought, yellow fever, and hurricane. The canal projects, which had sold stock to raise money in better times, now collapsed, having dug scarcely a ditch.

Mulberry fever survived until 1839, following the classic pattern of overheating, then completely collapsing. One day everyone was buying; the next, no one could sell. Nothing since Holland's tulipomania centuries before had been quite so dramatic or disastrous. Then a mysterious ailment destroyed the silkworm population of Florida, and in 1844 a general blight killed off most of the Chinese mulberry trees in the country. By that time most people preferred to forget them anyhow. "Silk" was a dirty word for a long time.

There was a last desperate hope that the spring of 1840 would bring the orange trees back to blossom, having recovered from the freeze damage of five years before. This would not restore prosperity but would at least put something in the pockets of the hard-pressed growers.

Peter Sken Smith, banking on a reversal of fortunes, even set out some new imported varieties in his groves. Unfortunately, they were infested with the coccus or scale insect. Placed in a new location, they feasted on all of Smith's trees, then spread to his neighbors'. The resulting plague was so widespread that it wiped out the prospects for East Florida growers for years to come.

Those who had ridden high were broke and discredited. Bad luck dogged their footsteps. It would be a long time before anyone entrusted a dollar to them again.

Prince Murat, one of the leading debtors of the failed Union Bank, gave up hope of "waking up rich" and slipped into decline, becoming an invalid. He had always considered American whiskey to be one of the finest native products and his consumption of it—always impressive—now became truly prodigious. He rediscovered religion, as Frenchmen are said to do on their deathbeds, though he resisted the suggestion of his priest that he will his property to the Church, for lack of a son and heir. It was just as well, since his holdings were heavily encumbered.

Murat was only forty-six when he died in 1847, just before his fondest hope and dream came true: the restoration of the Bonapartes to power in France. His cousin Louis Napoleon took the reins of government in 1848. This was the economic salvation of the widowed Princess Murat: the heavy burden of Achille's debts was lifted from her shoulders by the charity of his newly prosperous cousin.

Florida had completed a cycle. A pattern of boom and bust had been established that would be repeated again and again. Names would change; technology would be updated; inflation would add extra zeros to the amount of cash in the pot. But the spirit would be the same. Easy money and good living would go soaring off until the inevitable crash. As the lessons of the past were forgotten, each generation would see them repeated.

New leaders were called in to pick up the pieces. One was a man who, despite his heritage (or perhaps because of it), had sedulously avoided political involvement in the past: Jefferson's grandson, Francis Eppes. His efforts had been devoted to running his plantation, fathering thirteen children, and building up the Episcopal Church. But as a responsible citizen he could no longer avoid public duty, and in 1841 began the first of several terms as mayor ("intendant," it was originally called) of Tallahassee. It was fitting that a churchman was called in to clean up the capital, whose reputation as a den of iniquity had spread far and wide.

Eppes was an activist at the helm. He damned the general lawlessness and lit out after the racetrack, in particular, as "a public nuisance, a hotbed of vice, intemperance, gambling and profanity." With an assist from the hard-times economy, it closed down.

A society brought up on the story of Sodom and Gomorrah was quick to see divine judgment in visitations like the great fire that swept Tallahassee in 1843, reducing the business district to ashes and cinders, or the yellow-fever epidemic that caused one visitor to write that "out of a population of 1600 inhabitants God has seen fit to take away 450 of them composing most all of the Gamblers and Blacklegs of the place."

Tallahassee's wickedness had grown up as a by-product of the first Florida boom; outsiders saw it as "riotous, immoral and disorderly." Now, with the collapse, it was a chastened place. The effects of the Eppes reforms were such that even a proper Charlestonian would, a few years later, describe Florida's capital as "one of the most refined and elegant cities of the South."

• • •

And what of the man with no eyebrows?

Watching his many schemes for wealth crumble around him, Florida's first great developer became adept at dodging subpoenas as one after another of his ventures were subjected to investigation. He even faced the indignity of arrest by his creditors. He put his ostentatious mansion up for sale, noting that it was "new and commodious, and well calculated for an Hotel, or for Offices, and for the accommodation of several families." His advertisement ran for two years in the newspaper without finding a taker. He looked on helplessly as his Florida properties fell before the auctioneer's gavel for nonpayment of taxes—bringing only a fraction of the money invested in them.

Peter Sken Smith had come to Florida for his health, and

left for the same reason—one step ahead of a lynch mob. He fled to Philadelphia, which was not hitherto noted as a health resort, but had the advantage of great distance from his enemies.

In the election of 1840, Smith pitched himself into the campaign of General William Henry Harrison for president. For once he guessed right, but Harrison died after only a month in office, before rewarding his fellow general with a political appointment. His successor, John Tyler, showed little inclination to put Smith on the public payroll. And although Smith diligently pressed each new president for an appointment, he was always unsuccessful.

Settled in at Philadelphia, Smith could once again forget his past failures and trade on his name and title. He embarked on a crusade against the foreign immigrants flooding into the country, which became the obsession of his final years.

He started a newspaper, the *Native Eagle and American Advocate*, to promote his views. He took the lead in founding the Native American Party, which demanded a twenty-one-year residency before immigrants could gain the right to vote. Then, becoming even more frenzied, he helped to split and destroy that party when it failed to agree with him that only birth upon the soil could make one an American citizen.

His old St. Augustine nemesis, the *Herald*, continued to flay him from time to time as a wily, broken-down political hack—though any notion that he was an abolitionist should have been laid to rest when he tried to convince South Carolina's John C. Calhoun to run for president in 1848.

In the end the family affliction of insanity caught up with him. *The New York Times'* report of his death in 1858 attributed it to "a complication of brain and heart disease." He was sixty-three years old.

By that time the *Herald* had ceased publishing, and Smith was mainly remembered as a complicating factor in Ancient City real-estate transactions. Periodically people would inquire about his whereabouts in attempting to remove a cloud from the title to their property.

In 1859 John Brown led his raid on Harpers Ferry to free the slaves. The guns for that venture had been purchased with money provided by Gerrit Smith.

Florida newspapers fanned the flames of dissension, charging prominent northern politicians with conspiracy in Brown's raid. But none remembered that wily politician, so recently laid away, who had been charged twenty years before with plotting the abolitionist overthrow of Florida.

Too bad the *Herald* was no longer around. They really would have had a great time with that one.

GOLDEN APPLES

•

Florida advanced from territorial status to full statehood in 1845. A decade and a half later it pulled back out of the Union. With the Civil War in the offing, the southernmost state cast its lot with the Confederacy.

If Florida's settlement had been a star-spangled affair, its departure was no less so.

Patrick Henry's grandson was a delegate to the convention that voted to secede, though he left no such memorable words as "Give me liberty or give me death." George Washington's grandniece, Princess Murat, was given the honor of firing the first cannon. Thomas Jefferson's great-granddaughter was entrusted with binding the holy ordinance of secession.

Young hotheads, proud of their passion, went off to razz the aging Richard Keith Call, who had been secession's most visible and vocal opponent. Like his mentor Andrew Jackson before him, he saw the course as nothing short of "high treason."

"Well, Governor," they shouted jubilantly, "we have done it!"

The old man stood his ground, shaking his cane at them. "And what have you done? You have opened the gates of Hell, from which shall flow the curses of the damned which shall sink you to perdition."

Call was prophetic.

By 1862 General Robert E. Lee had decided that coastal Florida was indefensible. Towns fell, almost without resistance, to the Union navy. In 1865 Governor John Milton killed himself rather than preside over surrender. His suicide didn't cause the Union juggernaut to miss a beat. The old order had passed, and Reconstruction was on the land.

Francis Eppes had sold his plantation just before the final defeat—for Confederate money. Now he was ruined: his land gone, his money worthless, his slaves freed. He served another term as Tallahassee mayor during the Union occupation, then in 1867 headed out for the wilds of central Florida. At sixty-six he again became a pioneer, one of the early settlers of Orlando. Ever the churchman, he organized the area's first Episcopal services in his home and watched with pleasure as the congregation grew. Death finally claimed him in 1881.

Princess Murat was not so flexible. Before the war she had raised money to buy her ancestor's home, Mount Vernon, and preserve it for the public as a historic shrine. But that charity, dear though it was to her, had to be abandoned temporarily as she pitched in heart and soul to support the Confederate cause.

She lobbied with her husband's cousin, now ruling as Emperor Napoleon III, to seek French intervention on behalf of the rebels. This he would not do, fearing riots in the streets of Paris. But he did come to her aid personally, as he had done before in time of need. Hearing of her distress and impoverishment after the war, he gave her a pension that eased her final years. Disoriented and disheartened by defeat, she fell victim to a stroke and died in 1867. She was buried by the side of her colorful prince. Past all worldly cares, they became legends in Florida's history.

• • •

Nature abhors a vacuum. One person's distress is another's opportunity. Even as the old order was being crushed, the new was coming to life—if only as a gleam in the eye of occupying troops.

The Union soldiers stationed in St. Augustine found it by far their most pleasant assignment. Food was good and plentiful, the climate sublime, and young ladies were available for dancing, if not more. Far from being hell, that theater of war was so enjoyable that some thought to make it home. Their numbers were increased by those who heard of Florida by word of mouth and thought it worth trying in the postwar years. The Johnnies who went marching home again had to find a livelihood, and their quest led some of them back south, this time as civilians.

Word of mouth brought in the dribbles. The flood began with the work of the professional publicists. And an unlikely crew they were!

There was Harriet Beecher Stowe, whose antislavery novel *Uncle Tom's Cabin* was so influential that Lincoln called her "the little woman who wrote the book that made this great war." Seeking to help the freedmen (and provide an occupation for her war-wounded and alcoholic son), she purchased Laurel Grove cotton plantation and followed Lafayette's path of establishing a model colony. Like that earlier venture, it was a conspicuous failure.

Mrs. Stowe was distressed, when she visited, to see the results. But she fell in love with the area and bought a winter home at Mandarin on the St. John's. It was a picturesque Carpenter Gothic cottage whose verandas she extended around a huge live-oak tree. Set in a scenic orange grove, it became Florida's most famous tourist attraction. Steamboats landed at the dock and curious tourists made themselves a nuisance by picking her orange blossoms, peering in her windows, and complaining loudly if the famous authoress was not visibly at work with her pen. Her exasperated husband occasionally shooed them off with his cane or locked the gate at the wharf. But each succeeding boat brought a new crowd, and the Stowes resigned themselves, more or less, to a life of celebrity in a part of the country where a decade before they would have been quickly mobbed and lynched. Times had changed.

Mrs. Stowe continued her writing to pay the bills. Her publisher hoped for another novel, but her thoughts dwelt instead on the loveliness of her surroundings. She wrote articles about Florida, which ran first serially in the *Christian Union* and then were bound together as *Palmetto Leaves*, published in 1873. The number of tourists visiting Florida increased dramatically.

She also testified to the warm hospitality she received in her winter home, and her remarks were widely quoted as a counterweight to some of the atrocity tales then current. One editor, recently a Confederate soldier, remarked archly: "We are glad that Mrs. S. has done this little to repair the world of evil for which she is responsible in the production of *Uncle Tom's Cabin.*"

In fact, the picture she painted was so idyllic that it was widely rumored she had retracted her antislavery sentiments. That charge she branded a "vile slander."

• • •

Another Yankee, less celebrated but even more enterprising, figured prominently in the postwar publicizing of Florida. His name was John Whitney and he was a grandson of Eli Whitney, whose invention of the cotton gin had simultaneously rendered slavery profitable and civil war inevitable, according to many historians.

John Whitney's contribution to that war was a company of volunteers for the Union Army that he raised and equipped at his own expense, with money he had made as a newspaper publisher in Boston and New York. Rising in the world of politics, he was elected mayor of Rahway, New Jersey, in 1868.

When the Civil War had ended he bought an island—

christened Whitney's Island—in St. Augustine's San Sebastian River and built a winter home. Not one to keep a good thing to himself, he bought large tracts of land and became a developer. Building lots were offered at $25 each—to northerners only. Streets were laid out and named for the members of his family. To promote sales he published a pamphlet with the backbreaking title *A Brief Account of St. Augustine and Its Environs. Its advantages as a winter residence for Invalids and Northern Tourists. Productions, Resources &c, &c.* This was successful enough to go into a second edition.

An even larger venture was his launching of the *St. Augustine Press.* The first issue of this newspaper had the enormous press run of a quarter of a million copies. Their distribution around the country helped rekindle the Ancient City's tourist trade.

To accommodate the visitors, Whitney went into the hotel business. He and his son-in-law, W. W. Palmer (whose Union veteran father became postwar mayor of St. Augustine), were partners in one of those great wooden Victorian tinderboxes whose fiery ending was almost preordained, awaiting only the spark of a sleepy smoker or gnawing rat or creosote-clogged chimney. They were glorious when they went, but the insurance was seldom enough to make them profitable if their life span had not been sufficiently long to amortize building costs. Whitney's lasted longer than most, but took a good part of the downtown with it when it burned.

To entertain those who stayed at his hotel and perused his building lots, Whitney went into the tourist-attraction business as well. One of the bubbling sources of the river that surrounded his island home he called "Ponce de Leon Springs" and promoted as the city's first (but not last) fountain of youth. His son later added a dancing pavilion and alligator farm to the site, to keep it competitive with other attractions.

Two generations of tourists were hauled out the long sand road to take a sip of the waters. The carriage drivers who hauled them were rewarded with a stiffer kind of drink for their services.

Eventually the health department closed down the springs—shortly before national prohibition would have rendered the drivers' thirst quenchers illegal as well.

Another entrepreneur meanwhile discovered another fountain of youth closer to the downtown hotels, and Whitney's pioneer tourist attraction became a thing of history. By that time its promoter had gone on to his reward.

• • •

Then there was that rarity, a publicist whose background was with the Confederacy rather than the Union. But Sidney Lanier had a fairly ethereal military career with the Lost Cause—nothing to compare with his solid reputation as the best flute player in Georgia. His passions ran not with the rifle and cannon, but rather with the music and poetry he combined to gain a certain immortality in literature and a niche, as pride of the South, in the Hall of Fame.

Lanier worked against two problems: time and money. Suffering deeply from tuberculosis picked up in a prisoner of war camp, he was not slated to have a long life. And he had the perpetual poet's complaint of poverty. Lines that would live a thousand years did not earn enough to put food on the table for a single week. He just scraped by.

One day a letter came from an official of the Atlantic Coast Line Railroad. What did a railway want with a poet? Lanier explained to his wife: "he wisheth me to write a—, a— (choke, choke, choke) a— ch— (gulp, gulp, gulp) a Guide book to Florida Travellers. He proposeth, By Pegasus, to pay my hotel-bills and travelling expenses, and to give me one hundred and twenty-five dollars a month— By Croesus, in addition thereto."

The impecunious poet could not afford to pass it up. South he went, in April 1875, to write "a guide-book which should be also a poem."

In addition to flora and fauna and ancient landmarks, he

described such newer attractions as Mrs. Stowe's cottage and Whitney's Ponce de Leon Springs. Though some of the information was second-hand, part of it came from direct observation; most personal of all was the section of advice for consumptives who sought relief in Florida. As he wrote and corrected proofs for the book, Lanier was periodically laid low by his own hemorrhaging lungs.

Though he compared the pleasure of doing the work to "being stabbed with a dull waepon," it met with greater success than did any of his other works during his lifetime. Published in 1875, it was reissued in 1876, 1877, and 1881. Chapters from it appeared in *Lippincott's* magazine and were reprinted elsewhere. A century later it was still in print—as history rather than Baedeker.

Lest his authorship be seen as tainted by pecuniary motivations, it should be noted that he was sincere enough to take his own advice a year later when his lungs acted up again. He spent the winter of 1876–77 in Tampa, which he described (in not exactly guidebook prose) as "the most forlorn collection of little one-story houses imaginable." But the weather was "perfect summer" and he found himself bubbling with song. He wrote a number of poems, one of which fetched double the previous rate from *Scribner's*. Though the money was welcome, his physical relief was only temporary: in 1881, not yet forty, Lanier succumbed to his ailment. The Florida guidebook was still in print, encouraging southward migration for the great postwar boom.

To Lanier and Whitney and Mrs. Stowe should not go all the credit as publicists. In fact, the rarity in those years was a Florida immigrant who *didn't* write a book, pamphlet, or at least a letter to the old hometown newspaper expatiating on life in the sunshine. There are enough dating from that period to fill a library shelf, running the gamut from sober fact to wildest fancy.

One pamphlet published by the state was frank enough to admit that "roaches, like the poor, will always be with you." That deserved three stars for honesty, as against the booster who asserted: "Insects are neither numerous nor troublesome." (This same fictioneer pronounced the area exempt from tornadoes and hurricanes, and when asked "Do people ever die there?" replied, "Hardly ever. When we want to start a graveyard, we kill a man.")

Two threads run constantly through the literature of promotion. One is defensive assertion, such as "The country is full of gassy, brassy, impertinent, addle-headed detractors of Florida." The other is a warning to newcomers: "Beware of falling, through a spirit of imitation, into any of the untasteful, slack and unthrifty habits of the native."

• • •

Florida's remarriage to the nation was marked by things old, new, borrowed, and Blue.

Old were the ideas of crops, of tourism, of providing a haven for invalids. Even previously discredited notions had a rebirth. The first pound of Florida coffee was given a cash reward by the Department of Agriculture, with great hopes expressed for future pounds to come. Richard Call's daughter wrote a new manual on silk cultivation and produced enough of the fabric herself to make a state flag, though not much more. Dreams of a canal across North Florida came back with sufficient strength to launch yet another survey by the Army Corps of Engineers.

New was the order of priority placed on various schemes for wealth. While the invalids—long the staple of business—still came, it was on the healthy tourist that attention increasingly focused. A spiritual successor to the "Americanus" of 1821 assured St. Augustinians of 1866 that the upper crust could be lured there. If only an enterprising man such as Phineas T. Barnum could be gotten to back the work, "he could soon build up a city far superior to Newport."

Among the crops, cotton was no longer king. Its regal position was taken by the orange, which made a dramatic comeback from the freeze and pest damage of a generation before, aided by time, clime, and ladybugs, which proved to be natural predators of the scale insect. Lumber was growing in importance, and virgin forests would soon be a thing of the past. Indeed, such a wide swath was cut in the green belt from Georgia southward that within a few years it would be blamed for altering the climate.

The focal point of the state was no longer the Middle Florida plantation belt but, rather, the towns along the St. Johns River. There the steamboats reigned haughtily until the revolution of the railroads altered the picture so drastically as to give literal meaning to Thoreau's remark that "One generation abandons the enterprises of another like stranded vessels." Fittingly, one of the prominent destinations for the steamboat traffic was the now vanished resort town of Enterprise.

The borrowed part of the equation was northern energy, capital, and immigrants. As orange fever gripped the nation, there was a rush to Florida rivaling the migration when the territory first came into the American orbit.

Once again there was a large group of displaced people looking for opportunity. Few places (thanks to the talented pens employed, and tall tales told, in its behalf) sounded as good as the Sunshine State, where bountiful crops would spring up without fertilizer, where there were no insects, no freezes, and never a drop in the market price of the main commodity. Moreover, the family cat could go out and catch game for the family supper. It sounded like paradise. Some people believed anything. Horace Greeley is best remembered for telling young men to go west, but in 1866 he was advising them to go to Florida. And they went.

The something Blue was the residual tint of Union uniforms. Veterans, ranging from private to general, were the most conspicuous group of immigrants, and the southernmost state sprouted chapters of the Loyal Legion and the Grand Army of the Republic. Later, as the years took their toll, retirement colonies of Union veterans would be established in Florida. Towns like Lynn Haven can boast of that southern rarity, a monument to those who fought to crush secession and save the Union.

• • •

Orange and blue were the royal colors, and no one wore them more conspicuously in the 1870s than General Henry Shelton Sanford. During the postwar decade he was the closest thing Florida had to a king.

Kings were nothing new to Sanford: he had known many of them, and King Leopold of Belgium was godfather to one of his children. He was not born to such royal familiarity, but had acquired it by consciously applying wealth and political influence to the international scene.

Henry S. Sanford was a Connecticut Yankee, born in 1823 to a family whose fortune had been made in the manufacture of brass tacks. Diplomacy, rather than industry, was his chosen field, and the world, not just Connecticut, was his oyster.

In 1861 President Lincoln appointed him minister to Belgium, and throughout the Civil War entrusted him with important secret missions in Europe. It was Sanford who conveyed the offer of a generalship to Giuseppe Garibaldi (the Italian liberator turned it down, uninterested in anything less than the post of commander-in-chief of the Union Army). Sanford also worked behind the scenes to prevent France and England from selling weapons to the Confederacy.

While performing these delicate missions, he did not forget the boys on the homefront. Impressed with the valor of her volunteers at the Battle of Bull Run, he presented Minnesota with a battery of cannons in 1862. The governor returned the compliment by naming Sanford a major general in the state militia. Despite the honorary nature of the title, Sanford showed no embarrassment in using it ever afterward.

At the same time he presented a fine Krupp cannon to Connecticut, but his native state was not gracious enough to reward him with a generalship.

Sanford's money, far from lying idle or being limited to brass tacks during those years, was invested wisely. Along with his uncle, he was the largest stockholder in Scovill, the famous Waterbury brass company that prospered mightily as shells were lobbed and bullets rained on enemy troops. He also had a large and profitable stake in the Wheeler & Wilson Sewing Machine Co., which was outproducing Isaac Singer's rival firm by two to one in those days. Every new uniform stitched was good for business.

When the war ended and Sanford toted up his wealth, it came to a cool million. Not a bad stake, but he had increasing personal responsibilities to deal with. During the war he had taken a bride, Gertrude du Puy, nearly twenty years his junior and reputedly the most beautiful American woman in Paris. She had expensive tastes, and presented him with eight children.

Just as his expenses increased, the return on his investments dwindled. The valuable patents of Wheeler & Wilson expired, and the $80,000 a year he had been raking in from them plummeted accordingly. Scovill proved less a bonanza in peacetime than it had in war.

Looking at the situation, Sanford saw that the obvious place for his capital to migrate was to the South. There "property could be bought for 1/10th of its former values & should produce as great or greater returns than before the war." He proceeded to marshal his capital and attack on many fronts at once. First came a modest investment in an orange grove and house at St. Augustine that had been acquired through tax sale during the war by Abraham Lincoln's private secretary, John Hay.

The transaction was from one presidential agent to another, for Hay had been on a secret mission when he paid $500 for the grove in order to qualify as a Floridian. The scenario, one of many rehearsals for Reconstruction, called for Hay to be sent back to Washington as Florida's congressman. This never came to pass, but the grove might still have proved a good investment, since it produced $2,500 worth of oranges in a season. Hay complained, though, of being eaten up by "incidental" expenses and never seeing a penny in profit, so he was glad enough to pass it on to Sanford in 1867 for five times the original purchase price. Two years later the general had to pay another $1,500 to clear the title, the former Confederate owner having raised a stink about the legality of the Union tax sales. Still, the house was a convenient winter residence, and Sanford turned down an offer to double his money by selling it the next year.

If he had no cause for dissatisfaction with this first Florida venture, his other southern investments did not turn out so well. In 1868 he leased a cotton plantation on South Carolina's Barnwell Island. A plague of caterpillars promptly swept in and destroyed the crop. Then he bought a sugar plantation in Louisiana and built a refinery on it. The refinery burned and the plantation was flooded out by the Mississippi River.

Taking his patronage where he was best treated, he plunged into Florida in a big way in 1870. He bought a 12,500-acre tract of virgin land on Lake Monroe, a large basin that formed the navigable head of the St. Johns River. Accessible by the steamboats, which were then in their heyday, it offered excellent possibilities for opening up to development a vast and still largely unknown part of the peninsula. His settlement was called Sanford, and to burnish its strategic location in the mind, it was nicknamed the Gate City.

There was a touch of historic irony in the transaction. Sanford's first Florida purchase had come from a well-connected Union official. This next, much larger, deal was between the honorary Union general and Florida's greatest Confederate victor, General Joseph Finegan, whose success at the Battle of Olustee was one of the few southern triumphs in the state's rather meager Civil War history.

If in some places southerners were taking it on the chin in dealings with Yankee investors, at least in this particular instance the old Confederate managed to turn a profit. He had bought the tract at courthouse auction before the war for only $40; now he sold it to Sanford for $18,200. Not only that, but Finegan, who had become a Savannah cotton broker, stood to make additional commissions from handling some of the crops grown on the land and for peddling some of the lots. The two generals, despite past differences of allegiance, settled into an amicable synergistic arrangement.

Plunging into his role as city father, Sanford arranged for the laying-out of lots and grove sites and ordered the construction of necessary buildings. A large dock accommodated steamboats to bring in supplies and settlers and carry out the crops that would make everyone rich.

To guard the morals of his flock, Sanford provided free building lots for churches and stipulated in deed restrictions that the town remain dry, lest its labor be dissipated by the demon rum. This was, perhaps, a strange insistence on the part of a man who had once invested in a redistilling process designed to turn cheap liquor into something more expensive. But as city father he had a vested interest in sobriety—and his alcoholic investment had not panned out anyhow.

• • •

Florida, having lured him in, now began to act up on him.

When he brought in blacks to clear the land, native white crackers attacked them with guns. Some were killed, some wounded, and the rest driven off. Turning to the international labor market for replacements, Sanford brought in a colony of Swedes, who formed the settlement of New Uppsala. Later he brought in some Italians with citrus experience and projected a settlement called Sicilia for them.

The caterpillars, which had plagued Sanford's South Carolina investment, migrated south just in time to decimate his fledgling Florida cotton crop.

Then the rains came. Back-to-back hurricanes in August 1871 battered the settlement. New houses were blown from their foundations. The slaughterhouse was leveled, fences uprooted, the wharf inundated and torn apart. In the midst of it all, two of the Swedish women gave birth to children.

But this was nothing compared with the damage caused by the Panic of 1873. The general, like others, had gone in heavily for the glamour stocks of the day: railroads. He might as well have become a philanthropist. When the panic hit and the water drained out of the stock, he was left with about two cents on the dollar.

His wife obliged him in those trying times by continually overdrawing accounts and sending a flood of complaints from their European home (she refused to come back and live in the crude and vulgar United States) that their carriages and cotillions were not fine enough to keep up with their noble neighbors.

There was nothing for Sanford to do but liquidate elsewhere in order to hold on to his Florida properties, hoping they would weather the storm. He forged ahead as city father, building a hotel, establishing a bank, and—though he must have done so warily—investing in a railroad to make his landholdings accessible as the age of the steamboat passed.

Buildings and institutions may seem like fairly permanent monuments, but fires and changing tastes can sweep them away overnight. Henry Sanford's most lasting contribution came in a much more perishable commodity: citrus.

Owning a Florida orange grove became a status symbol for northern politicians after the war. They prodded the Department of Agriculture into researching remedies for the ills that afflicted their groves, from pests like the white fly, red spider, and rust mite to diseases like sooty mold, foot rot, and orange blight.

This helped some, but there was a larger problem. Citrus had been a vanished crop for so long that the whole body of knowledge acquired through practice had died off with its holders. There was no shortage of advice available, but much of it was contradictory. One farmer would pick the fruit. Another claimed that bruises could be avoided only by clipping it. One would fertilize his grove. Another pronounced fertilizer death to the trees. Yankees would painstakingly grub the field before laying out their groves. Crackers would quickly burn theirs off instead. Both loudly proclaimed the superiority of their methods, and were willing to fight about it.

What was needed was a little careful experiment, and that was what Sanford provided at his famous Belair Grove. Citrus was something for which he had real care and concern. If anyone should be considered the father of the modern industry, it is he.

He had become familiar with citrus and tropical fruits during his travels in Europe, Africa, and South America. Having discovered pineapple on the slopes of the Andes in 1857, he brought it to Belair to see if it would thrive in Florida. Two hundred kinds of grapevines, a hundred varieties of citrus, several figs, olives, almonds, and mangoes gathered from around the globe were tested at his private experiment station. He pioneered the introduction of lemons into Florida almost single-handedly. He even had a still built—not for moonshine, but to distill perfume from flowers.

Nor did he keep the results to himself: other grove owners secured their stock from him, often at no cost, thus multiplying Belair's influence many times over.

He engaged in that favorite prerogative of growers, presenting boxes of fruit to friends. Given his international sphere of activities, the friends were sometimes highly placed. One year Otto von Bismarck delighted in a box of oranges from Belair Grove.

For his experimental and promotional activities, Sanford could hear his praises sung from one end of the St. Johns River to the other. When election time came around he was regularly proposed for either governor or senator, though never successfully. There was some resistance to electing a man whose primary residence was in Europe.

But through his Washington contacts, the general was able to keep a tight grip on the distribution of federal patronage in Florida. He played gracious host to these contacts when they visited, even getting Ulysses S. Grant to turn the first shovel of earth for the South Florida Railroad that was to link the Sanford domains with more inhabited parts of the state. He was disappointed, however, in his cherished hope of getting another diplomatic appointment. Because he had riled some powerful senators, they blackballed him every time a president submitted his name.

In the balance, frustration outweighed success in Sanford's first Florida decade. He had, in truth, bitten off more than he could chew, and his sense of timing was execrable. Natural difficulties plus the national financial depression left him continually strapped for funds. "If I could," he wrote his wife, "I would get out of Florida & never put foot on it again, so disgusted am I."

But so many of his eggs were by then in the Florida basket that getting out was not an option. He could, however, get others to share the burden. From among his diplomatic contacts he recruited a group of British and European investors, and in 1880 formed the Florida Land and Colonization Company, Limited, with offices in London. Sanford put in his 23 square miles of Florida and became president and major stockholder.

It rapidly turned into a nightmare. The freewheeling man of vision no longer faced collapse with the due date on his next bank note, but now he risked being niggled to death by his board of directors. Feeling himself like Gulliver restrained by Lilliputians, Sanford freely vented his spleen. When he demanded boldness, the directors called for caution.

"In England we move slowly and with more caution than you are accustomed to in America," they explained. He fumed. They forbade. The partnership devolved into two camps of mutual suspicion and hostility. Mrs. Sanford delivered her ultimate insult when she accused the directors of "being rude & aggressive to us in such ways as only the vulgar are capable of."

Sanford lost the battle. Disgusted, he turned his attention to Africa, where his friend King Leopold had a colony in the Congo that just cried out for a Yankee entrepreneur to develop it. He tried, but his time had passed: he never made enough in Africa to sever the uneasy ties that bound him to the Florida Land and Colonization Company, Limited.

He was just returning from a trip to Florida in the spring of 1891 when death overtook him at Healing Springs, Virginia. It was an appropriately ironic place of departure for this man whose bittersweet life had been as rich as his mangoes and as tart as his lemons. The millionaire who had sought southern properties at one-tenth their value was skirting bankruptcy at the end of his days.

A year after his death the Florida Land and Colonization Company gave up the ghost and liquidated its holdings. Mrs. Sanford showed as little interest in the Florida properties as ever, allowing them to fall to ruin. In 1902 an April Fool's Day offer of $1,000 for the once-magnificent Belair Grove was accepted, and the property passed forever from the hands of the Sanford family.

LONG LIVE THE KING

•

One feature of the second great Florida boom was that it did not center on a single event, crop, location, or personality. It survived the collapse of the things that had launched it and the promoters who had egged it on. It was a traveling enthusiasm, a spirit of boom with great comeback powers—a series of boomlets, actually, laid out serially over several decades and having several major figures.

No sooner was one king dead, literally or figuratively, than another was crowned in his place. Sometimes rival kings contended and divided up the turf. They were always cheered on as long as they had money to spend and cast off as soon as they went broke, praised extravagantly and forgotten quickly. Fate was cruel, but men still lined up to ride the whirlwind.

The crown slipped from Henry Sanford's brow about the time he had to seek out foreign investors. Almost immediately there was another claimant whom a chorus of voices hastened to proclaim king. He didn't come to Florida with that in mind, but his entrance was so spectacular that nothing else could possibly have happened. His name was Hamilton Disston.

It was as a sports fisherman that the Philadelphian first surveyed the Florida scene in 1877. He was enjoying the hospitality of his friend General Sanford, who convinced him there was more to do in the state than cast a lure and kill the wildlife. He thought it over, talked it up with friends back home, and in 1881 made his mark by purchasing 4 million acres of Florida and becoming the nation's largest landowner.

Who was Hamilton Disston—besides land baron nonpareil? By profession a saw manufacturer, by inclination a *bon vivant*, and by his land purchase the seminal benefactor of phase two of the second great Florida boom.

His profession was his birthright. Born in 1844, he was the son of Henry Disston, an English immigrant whose mechanic father had died just three days after their boat docked in Philadelphia. The teen-aged Henry apprenticed himself to a sawmaker, then went into business on his own. A technical innovator, he managed to produce the high-quality steel needed for saw blades and thus freed himself from reliance on imported materials. Then he turned the tables by becoming an exporter: Disston Saws acquired international respect and conquered world markets. When the Civil War came, he retooled his factory to meet military needs and reaped another bonanza.

Hamilton Disston grew up in the family business, working in the factory from his youth and winning the friendship of the employees. He inherited the presidency when his father died in 1878, though ownership of the firm was shared with his brothers. Freed of parental restraint, he was in an ideal position to be bitten by the Florida bug.

His friend Sanford assured him there was money to be made in draining off swampland. Disston got together a group of investors and struck up a deal with the state: if they drained the publicly owned land at their expense, they would in return be given title to half the high ground created. There was only one problem. The state could not keep its part of the bargain, because it was being sued by creditors who wanted to force the sale of all public lands to satisfy their debts. A million dollars was needed to forestall this disaster. Florida's fate hung in the balance.

Disston came to the rescue. For 25 cents an acre he bought 4 million acres of public land and gave the state the million dollars it needed to get out of debt and out of court. Carried out just in the nick of time, this was a chapter of government finance as thrilling as an episode of the silent screen cliffhanger *The Perils of Pauline.*

It was the era when the promotion of railroad construction by land grants—so many acres for each mile of track laid—was standard operating procedure. If Florida had been forced to sell her public lands, she would have been unable to compete in luring the railroads, so badly needed to open up the vast interior to settlement. She would have been condemned to stagnation while states all around freely dispensed the public domain and reaped the benefits.

The lure of benefits exercises a Svengali-like influence on the public mind, whereas problems are usually perceived only after the fact. A few decades later both parties to the deal might have acted differently, since the great land giveaways resulted in a whole new set of woes. But in 1881 Hamilton Disston was the man of the hour, and Florida gave him the royal treatment. General Sanford, who had financial problems dealing with a mere 23 square miles, was shunted aside in favor of this new Midas, whose kingdom embraced 6,250 square miles of some of the wettest land in Florida.

• • •

Hamilton Disston was a pioneer in creative financing. He didn't have the million dollars with which he was rescuing Florida from underdevelopment, but he knew how to get it. After scraping together the down payment himself, he sold half the acreage to a British syndicate for $600,000. The money came just in time to prevent foreclosure of the whole deal.

British, British everywhere.

Orange fever was rampant in England as it was in the United States. Several books about Florida were published in London, complete with advertisements for pith helmets and other necessary supplies. More than a dozen British companies were chartered to invest in the Sunny South. In addition to Sanford's Florida Land and Colonization Company, they included the East Florida Land and Produce Company, Florida Southern Land and Finance Syndicate, Southern States Land and Timber Company, and Florida Orange and Grapefruit Groves. The shareholders and directors of these concerns included prominent figures in the political, financial, and social world.

The Florida map was dotted with settlements like Ruskin, Acton, and Avon Park that clearly showed their origin. The duke of Sutherland, Queen Victoria's cousin, established a home at Tarpon Springs, on the Gulf Coast.

Prominent among settlers were the remittance men—second and third sons of well-to-do families whose place in the pecking order meant they were not slated to inherit the family fortune. As consolation prizes they were given Florida orange groves, a small stipend from home, and best wishes for success in the New World.

Veteran Florida citrus men found they could make a living by taking on these remittance men as students, charging good prices to teach them the tricks of the trade.

The syndicate Disston sold to, the Florida Land and Mortgage Company, was headed by Sir Edward J. Reed, a naval designer, shipbuilder, editor, author, poet, and long-time member of Parliament. The company planned to promote immigration, develop settlements, and sell land. Its investors did not prosper, but Hamilton Disston had turned his first profit in Florida.

He had plenty to spend it on. Though canals had a checkered past in the state, Disston had double incentives for building them: his land was both swampy and isolated. Canals would drain the swamps and provide transportation to the dry land created. An avid yachtsman, Disston was betting that waterways would be the dominant arteries of travel and commerce in the peninsula. He invested in dredges and steamboats and a factory to make and repair them.

As water was siphoned off the land, sugar cane was planted. The rich muck was a tremendous fertilizer, and Disston's cane won first prize at an exposition in New Orleans, competing with the established varieties from Louisiana, Cuba, and Mexico—a sweet victory against stiff competition. He built a sugar mill on his property, and tourists were told that failing to see Disston's St. Cloud Plantation was "like going to Rome without seeing St. Peter's."

He provided the political clout and the land for the Department of Agriculture to set up a sugar-cane laboratory and do his experimental work for him.

In 1890 an attempt was made to free the United States from imports by giving a federal bounty of 2 cents a pound for domestic sugar. Disston expanded rapidly to collect these pennies from heaven, taking on partners to help finance it who shared his love of money but not his feeling for Florida or his personal satisfaction at empire building. Their concern with profits turned the whole thing into a speculation rather than an agricultural venture. Sparks flew in the Philadelphia office and changes of command were frequent.

The friction couldn't have come at a worse time. Nature was taking its toll in Florida, as canals were silting up and causing drainage problems; excessive rainfall left large acreage under water; and cane borers attacked the crop. The Department of Agriculture closed its experiment station, announcing that the proper land for sugar cane was farther south in the peninsula. Experiments in cultivating rice were a failure.

The Panic of 1893 hurt deeply. Desperate for cash, Disston peddled what he could to better-heeled investors and mortgaged the rest of his Florida holdings for $2 million.

Then the Congress took away the sugar bounty. Florida

real-estate values dropped. After July 1895, the Disston Land Company could no longer meet its mortgage payments.

Faced with ruin on all sides, Hamilton Disston sat in his bathtub on April 30, 1896, and shot himself in the head. It was announced merely that he had "died suddenly." He was fifty-one years old.

The family, which had never been enthusiastic about Florida, was left to liquidate his ventures. Some of his land was purchased by a Shaker colony. The would-be metropolis of Disston City was rechristened Veterans City and peddled, along with St. Cloud, as a retirement community for Union veterans. The yacht *Hamilton Disston*, which had ferried the former king through his watery domains, was stripped of its machinery and abandoned. When the government had taken its share in taxes, the remainder of the vast empire was sold for $70,000. The Disstons wanted out of their unhappy paradise, even at a tremendous loss.

A much younger brother, Jacob Disston, kept the faith in the decades after Hamilton's suicide, to the extent of investing another million dollars in various improvements on the Gulf Coast between St. Petersburg and Tarpon Springs. Though it did not ruin him, neither did he meet with any success. Ventures that a few years earlier or later would have prospered tremendously instead wound up auctioned off on the courthouse steps.

The Disstons were not destined to increase their wealth in Florida.

• • •

It was Hamilton Disston's great misfortune to bet on sugar and canals in what proved to be an age of oranges and railroads. He was both ahead of and behind the times. Like his friend and predecessor Sanford, he suffered from a shortage of capital at the worst possible moments.

But it would be a mistake to dismiss or downplay his contributions. Through his development efforts he extended the frontiers of civilization ever southward into the peninsula; others would follow, for it was the right direction to go. He proved, on a larger scale than ever before, that drainage canals could transform Florida swamps into dry land. He also showed, through negative example, that such works required constant maintenance to keep nature from reclaiming its own. He pioneered sugar growing on a large scale—only in the wrong place. Others, following the advice of the Department of Agriculture, would plant farther south and reap great fortunes.

Most of all, he greased the wheels for development from which others profited far more than he. By rescuing Florida's public lands from forced sale, he enabled the state to be competitive with its neighbors in dealing out the public domain as incentives to railroad building.

An orgy of track laying followed in the wake of his purchase. More than five hundred railroads were chartered by the state, each with the promise of generous land grants for mileage completed. By 1885 over 10 million acres had been thus dispensed. Reality was left behind in succeeding years as obligations exceeded available land by over 3 million acres. But Florida, which had ranked last in the South in railroads, wound up leading the nation in mileage per capita.

Incentives could be used for other developmental purposes as well. A canal company proposed to scoop out the remaining barriers between the coastal chain of islands and the mainland, to create a protected intracoastal waterway down the peninsula as far as Dade County, where a handful of hardy pioneers made arrowroot starch to sell for what they could not grow or catch in that semitropical wilderness. For every mile completed, the company received 3,840 acres. That came to over a million acres for 268 miles of waterway—which deteriorated rapidly for lack of maintenance once the official inspection to approve the work was over.

But the railroads were treated best of all. It was an age that waxed lyrical in predicting that "the iron horse, with bowels of fire, muscles of steel and breath of steam, with a shriek and a snort, will rush over the metallic track and annihilate time and space so rapidly that the Atlantic and Gulf coasts will be within a few hours of each other."

Their time in the sun had come.

• • •

No one basked in it more than a shrewd and canny Connecticut Yankee named Henry Bradley Plant.

In the dismal parade of rich men who lost their fortunes in Florida, Plant constitutes that pleasant relief of someone who left wealthier than he came. "I made a careful survey of the situation, calculated upon the prospects and concluded to take advantage of the opportunity," he told a reporter who inquired about the key to his success.

Plant had acquired the wisdom of age by the time he took his Florida plunge: he was old enough to be Hamilton Disston's father or Henry Sanford's elder brother, though he outlived both of them. He prospered from their mistakes, having had long experience in turning other men's difficulties to his advantage. He was no stranger or newcomer to Florida. He had watched it—like a hawk—for a quarter of a century, through good times and bad, before he started investing his own money in a big way. He knew what he was getting into.

Henry Plant came by his shrewdness the hard way. He was born with neither silver spoon in his mouth nor brass-tack fortune in his pocket. At the age of six he lost both father and sister to typhus and barely escaped death himself. Never inclined to bookishness, he ran away from his first day at school, and later declined an offer from his grandmother to pay for his education at Yale. She hoped he would study for the ministry, but his outlook was more worldly. He plunged into business right at the bottom, swabbing decks on a boat that ran between New Haven and New York. Advancing through the ranks, he was placed in charge of freight handling and won praise for the good care he took of other people's property. After five years he was offered a captaincy. Instead, he quit, to apply his freight expertise to land rather than water travel. Roads were improving, railways were being built, and his switch was made with perfect timing. He rose in the ranks of the Adams Express Company.

In 1853 his wife suffered congestion of the lungs, and doctors prescribed an immediate rest in Florida. The journey south took eight days and the lodgings they found at Jacksonville were primitive. Fortunately that didn't kill the patient before the climate could work its wonders. Plant returned winter after winter with his ailing wife, and the accommodating express company placed him in charge of their southern operations so that he could keep his wife in the sun.

With the outbreak of the Civil War, Adams Express feared that its southern properties would be seized. To avert this, title was transferred to the newly organized Southern Express Company, with Plant in charge. The Yankee freightmaster was entrusted with delivering Confederate military payrolls. Plant threw himself into the work, partly to overcome his grief at the loss of his wife: Mrs. Plant finally succumbed to tuberculosis on February 28, 1861, just a week after her fortieth birthday.

Plant worked himself into a breakdown by 1863. Leaving the business in the hands of his associates, he took off for Europe to recuperate. He returned through Canada and was in New York when Lee surrendered and John Wilkes Booth shot Lincoln.

The South lay prostrate—but such situations were always Henry Plant's opportunities. Few knew the area as well as he, from his freight operations. After the Panic of 1873 had virtually destroyed the southern railways, Plant went in buying—at bargain-basement rates. He gathered together a group of investors with confidence in his judgment, covering the spectrum of old money and new, north and south. They included honorary

Union General Henry Sanford and former Confederate Secretary of the Treasury Christopher Memminger. Newly rich oilman Henry Flagler invested alongside aristocratic railwayman James Roosevelt. Plant sniffed out the properties and his partners put up the money.

His personal fortune grew, with Southern Express at its base. After the war, Adams Express had asked him to give it back. Nothing doing. What had been a wartime subterfuge threatened to become permanent. They took him to court—and lost. Plant had branched out from there.

At first the partners merely bought bonds, but then it became clear that the most profitable thing to do was buy distressed lines, reorganize them, and operate them. Plant was in charge. Starting in 1879, he bought more than a dozen lines, combined and improved them, built the necessary tracks to link them up, and soon had an impressive empire extending south from Charleston and Savannah into Florida.

The informal partnership was incorporated in 1882 as the Plant Investment Company. One insider described it as "Mr. Plant and his friends who have money, cash, to invest. When it is decided to do a certain thing, build a piece of road for instance, they figure out what each is to pay and send in their checks for the amount. They have no bonds, no indebtedness, no interest to pay; they build railroads to operate them and not for bond and stock speculations."

In addition to buying old railroads and building new ones, Plant operated steamboats on the St. Johns, Apalachicola, and Chattahoochee rivers. The company had vast quantities of real estate to develop and sell as a result of land grants received for laying track. Their own network of telegraph lines linked the empire together.

Then Plant discovered Tampa.

With his usual clairvoyant eye, he saw more to it than Sidney Lanier's forlorn village. "I found Tampa slumbering as it had been for years," he later recalled. "It seemed to me that all South Florida needed for a successful future was a little spirit and energy, which could be fostered by transportation facilities."

Plant had a special incentive to foster those facilities. There was a small railroad that had an unbelievably generous land grant to build a rail line to Tampa. Strapped for funds, it was just about to miss the deadline and lose the grant. Plant stepped in, bought the line, completed it in record time, and added a large chunk to his domains.

In the decade before Plant came, Tampa's population had declined by 10 percent. In the decade after he arrived it shot up more than 1,000 percent. By 1886 it was possible to get there all the way from New York without changing trains. Tampa grew from backwater to vital link: Plant built Port Tampa nearby and ran a steamship line that connected his railroad to Key West and Havana.

Exiled Cuban cigar makers set up shop in Tampa, and the port leaped to dominance in the importation of tobacco. When phosphates, a rich source of agricultural fertilizer, were discovered nearby, Tampa became their main place of export. Customs receipts, which had totaled only $75 in 1885, were in excess of $100,000 five years later.

Henry Plant's timing was once again flawless. He had waited for years and served many other masters, but now he was a tycoon in his own right. *Success* magazine didn't hesitate to crown him "King of Florida."

• • •

A century before, America had broken with the pattern of royal rule and waved the republican banner in the face of an often hostile and uncomprehending world.

But in the gilded age that followed the Civil War, there developed an almost insatiable thirst for things noble, regal, and titled. Those who had acquired fast fortunes could scarcely wait to separate themselves from the horde, the masses, the common people—those who had a few short years before been brothers and sisters, uncles and cousins, customers and fellow workers.

These rich, and no longer common, people gloried in recognition of their status and titles, whether they were oil kings, merchant princes, cattle barons, tobacco dukes, or traction czars. Many of them purchased bankrupt European noblemen as husbands for their daughters—a *quid pro quo* arrangement that would later acquire an exceedingly bad name but at the time satisfied the divergent needs of those on both sides of the Atlantic.

All of them, stay-at-homes and go-abroads alike, built suitably grandiose palaces to advertise their station in life. America's first professionally trained generation of architects was blessed with rich clients who not only could afford all the trappings but actually demanded them. Wedding cakes were no more ornate than some of the resulting architectural confections.

The ritualistic grand tour of the continent provided inspiration for countless castles and châteaux in New York, Chicago, Newport, and elsewhere. Florida was architecturally deprived by comparison. Fantasies there mostly concerned foliage and wildlife and winter climate. But the built environment was staid. It ran from primitive log or board-and-batten cabins to the plainer run of Victorian houses graced, here and there, with a tower or mansard and a little gingerbread trimming the veranda. Hotels and public buildings were larger, but not much more ornate. Although some were brick, most often the abundant native heart pine, so resistant to rot and termites and so susceptible to flame, formed both frame and siding.

Florida's architecture was not the stuff of which dreams were made. Until Franklin Smith came along. This Boston hardware merchant seethed with visions that would have condemned a lesser man to the lunatic asylum. But not a wealthy resident of Beacon Hill whose great-grandfather had been president of Harvard and whose father occupied the respected post of collector of the port of Boston.

Moreover, Smith's ideas were not mere daydreams, for he always sought to render them concrete—and always took himself very seriously. He was not trained in architecture—hardly anyone was in those days—but it was an avocation, a passion, that appeared early and stayed with him all his life. Perhaps the first indication came as a boy when he carved a bird cage in such perfect Gothic design that he never tired of displaying it to the public, even in his dotage.

He was twenty-five years old, in 1851, when a visit to London's Crystal Palace Exposition further fired his interest. The display of architectural styles from around the world struck him as particularly educational and worthy of repetition. His favorites he copied as clay models in exact scale and added to the collection with his Gothic bird cage.

When he was called upon, back in Boston, to raise money for the fledgling YMCA, the Crystal Palace experience inspired him to plan a world bazaar. The inside of Tremont Temple was lined with façades of buildings from the corners of the globe. Executed as carefully as any Hollywood set, these facades were peopled by prominent Bostonians costumed in native dress and hawking wares specially imported for the affair. It broke records as a fund-raising event, and for years after, Franklin Smith's portrait hung in the Boston YMCA.

Smith also lent his support to the antislavery cause and enrolled quite early in the Republican Party. He attended Lincoln's inauguration in 1861, and his wife of just a week was one of the conspicuous belles of the inaugural ball.

Smith Brothers Hardware enlisted in the Civil War by supplying material for the Union forces. It sickened Smith, as an honest and upright merchant, to see the amount of fraud and chicanery in the letting of government contracts. Like that other reforming Smith, Gerrit, he took the path of oratory and pamphleteering to try to correct the abuses. His revelations did not sit well with those in the Navy Department whose lack of integrity was being spotlighted.

A wartime measure had been adopted providing that government contractors could be subjected to military justice. To silence the squawking Brahmin, naval officials swept down in 1864 and hauled the Smith brothers, Franklin and Benjamin, off to a military jail, where they were held incommunicado on $500,000 bail and scheduled for court-martial on charges of defrauding the government. Justice took its course, and they were sentenced to two years in prison and fined $20,000.

The Smiths had a powerful advocate in Senator Charles Sumner of Massachusetts. He pointed out that the fraud charged on sales to the government amounting to 1,205 pages of transactions, totaling over $1.2 million, represented a minuscule proportion. "If a mountain in labor ever brought forth a mouse, it is this mountainous prosecution, whose only offspring yet crawling on earth is an allegation of loss to the United States of one hundred dollars!" he wrote after reading the Navy Department's lengthy report on the case.

Abraham Lincoln agreed, noting: "I am wholly unable to believe in the existence of criminal or fraudulent intent on the part of one of such well-established good character as is the accused." And he exercised executive clemency: "The judgement and sentence are disapproved and declared null, and the accused ordered to be discharged."

That was on March 18, 1865. Less than a month later Lincoln was dead from an assassin's bullet. Franklin Smith presided over Boston's memorial service to the martyred president. Then he prepared a hundred-page pamphlet titled *The Conspiracy in the U.S. Navy Department Against Franklin W. Smith of Boston, 1861–1865. A record of flagrant abuse of the war power in the late civil war.* He kept it in print for the next quarter of a century.

In 1869, he took up his pen to write *Wooden Ships Superseded by Iron. Cheap Iron Indispensable for the Revival of American Commerce.* Then, a decade later, as financial panic and depression swept the country, he entered the public debate once again with *The Hard Times. Agricultural Development the True Remedy.*

All through those years he regularly sallied forth from the Hub of the Universe to places like London, Paris, Rome, Athens, Cairo, and Constantinople, imbibing culture and wondering how he could best share it with his less fortunate countrymen.

His wife's family, prosperous Baltimore Quakers, had established a winter home in a Florida orange grove after the Civil War. Smith visited them in St. Augustine, enjoyed the Ancient City, and decided to build there himself. A European tour provided inspiration for both the style and building material of a winter residence that would set a new standard in the Sunshine State. No Victorian cottage, no simple mansard for this hardware millionaire and missionary of culture. Nothing less than a landmark would do.

Clay carvings, bird cages, and façades had been fine when that was all he could afford. "But miniature models only stimulated an impatience for architectural reproduction on a full scale," he wrote. Now he was in a position to gratify that impatience.

Traveling through Spain in 1882, he savored the legendary Alhambra, a relic of Moorish times that had been popularized for Americans by the pen of Washington Irving. Smith had found his model.

His winter home in St. Augustine would not be a strict reproduction but, rather, an inspiration. He called it Villa Zorayda, after one of the princesses in Irving's *Tales of the Alhambra.*

The Smiths ransacked market places in Granada, Tangiers, and Cairo for suitable furnishings and decorations, picking up a few additional design ideas along the way. Tiles for the floor and wainscoting were specially made in Valencia. Balustrades and window lattices were copied in Cairo, a fireplace in Constantinople. The Kensington Museum yielded up molds for the intricate arabesque traceries that cover the walls of the Alhambra.

Villa Zorayda became a veritable textbook for an architectural style variously called Islamic, Oriental, Hispano-Moresque, or, most appropriately, Moorish Revival. The effects were striking—and fitting, thought Smith, given the Ancient City's Spanish background and warm climate. It was a design "which the experience of centuries had proved desirable in semitropical countries."

Moorish Revival became the rage, and a host of the less imaginative rushed to copy. Equally significant as Smith's popularizing of an architectural style was his introduction of an experimental new building material. After deciding on his design, he had puzzled over what to build it with. "An oriental house of wood would be an anachronism; yet there is no stone in Florida. To freight it from the north would be an extravagance." A trip to Switzerland provided the answer. On the shores of Lake Geneva he watched the construction of a château poured from concrete into molds and hardened. He marveled as sand, cement, and leftover building rubble were transformed by cheap and unskilled labor into graceful Grecian balusters and solid castle walls. "The problem was solved. I saw henceforth an age of stone for St. Augustine instead of pitch-pine wood."

Mixing locally available coquina shell with cement, he poured his dream house, layer by layer, between wooden boards. Every other day a new course was added as Villa Zorayda raised its embattled parapets beside the mudflats of Maria Sanchez Creek.

Poured concrete wrought a building revolution. As Smith noted with satisfaction in the inevitable pamphlet that followed his triumph: "Now it is in universal use, not only for first-class and rich buildings, but for fence posts, sidewalks, chimney flues, etc., etc., and the piers beneath the poor man's cottage, formerly built of bricks from the North at double the cost."

Villa Zorayda attracted immediate attention. The volume *Artistic Homes of the United States* hailed its "curious beauty" and noted: "It must be an extremely commonplace and unimaginative person who can look up at the façade of this building and not begin to dream dreams."

A visiting reporter answered the question on everyone's mind: "I believe it is safe to say that its proprietor will have expended at least $100,000 in the gratification of his Oriental tastes when through with the castle and its grounds."

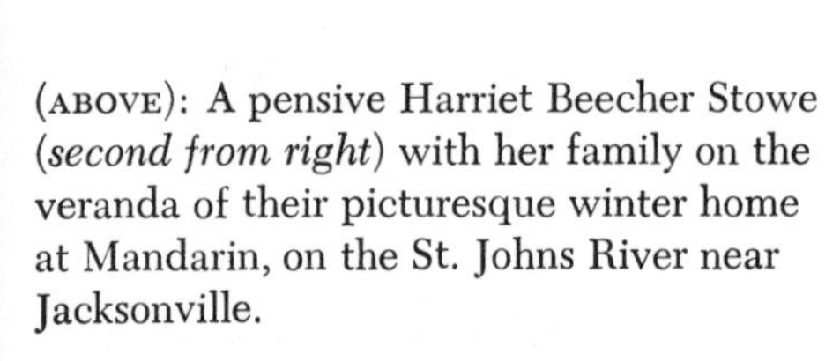

(ABOVE): A pensive Harriet Beecher Stowe (*second from right*) with her family on the veranda of their picturesque winter home at Mandarin, on the St. Johns River near Jacksonville.

(LEFT): Monument honoring Union soldiers at Lynn Haven, Florida.

(OPPOSITE, TOP): The great sport for tourists in the 1870s was to travel down Florida's rivers by steamboat and shoot the wildlife. They made a serious dent in the population of some species and aroused the ire of such pioneer conservationists as Harriet Beecher Stowe.

(OPPOSITE, BOTTOM): The impressively triple-towered Hotel Sanford was one of the investments the honorary general made in his new city.

(OPPOSITE, TOP): The freeze of 1886 was the worst Florida had experienced in half a century. It left icicles hanging from these trees in St. Augustine.

(OPPOSITE, BOTTOM): This magnificent specimen, billed in 1883 as Florida's largest orange tree, was located near Waldo in Alachua County. The owners claimed it produced an annual crop of 10,000 "golden apples."

Henry Bradley Plant, self-made tycoon who bought when prices were low and profited from the misfortunes of others.

Hamilton Disston, saw manufacturer, gay blade, and Florida's largest landowner.

Villa Zorayda, Franklin Smith's winter home in St. Augustine, launched a revolution in architectural style and construction technique.

THE OILMAN COMETH

•

The concrete had barely cured on Franklin Smith's creation when someone came knocking on the door and wanted to buy it. His name was Henry Morrison Flagler and he could afford it. He was the first president of Standard Oil of New Jersey and his annual income was larger than Smith's entire fortune. He was on his honeymoon, so the romantic Villa Zorayda may have been especially appealing.

Alas, it was not for sale. But Smith, as a missionary for the potential of St. Augustine, did not let his visitor go away empty-minded. He sketched the prospects, outlined the dreams in concrete, described a Spanish future to match the Spanish past, and drew Flagler into his web as surely as the spider did the fly.

If Smith had done nothing else but that, he would have earned his place in Florida history. As muse to the multi-millionaire Flagler, he launched a train of events whose significance to the Sunshine State was unmatched before or since. Where Smith could dream and demonstrate, Flagler was in a position to *do.* And over the next three decades he did Florida up right.

• • •

Horatio Alger might have written the life of Henry Flagler, except that he would have had to fudge on a few of the moral points.

The beginning was appropriate enough. The oilman-to-be was born in upstate New York in 1830 to a poor but honest Presbyterian minister and his wife, who had been widowed from a previous marriage. They struggled along on $400 a year, giving Henry a childhood filled with vivid examples of the hardships of poverty. In later years he declined to discuss them, averring that "my recollection of my early life is very indistinct."

By the age of fourteen he had had enough of the life of the manse, and headed west. He arrived in Republic, Ohio, with a carpetbag full of possessions and six coins in his pocket—none of them gold. One of these he saved for the rest of his life as a reminder of his escape from humble origins.

With the help of his half-brother Daniel Harkness and other relatives from his mother's earlier marriage, he obtained work as a store clerk. By the time he was fifteen he had already surpassed his father's $400 a year. He showed an aptitude for business, and prospered sufficiently by 1853 to take a bride—his mother's niece Mary Harkness.

He acquired a share of a distillery, but, plagued by Presbyterian scruples against the evils of the liquor trade, he sold it to his half-brother Dan, who worshipped at a different church.

During the Civil War, Flagler, by then the father of two children, avoided military service. He took note of the economic impact of the conflict, investing in salt mines, whose value boomed to fill traveling armies' need for the product as a food preservative. But the end of the war saw a collapse in that speculation, which left Flagler in debt. Bereaved additionally by the death of his mother and younger daughter, he sought, unsuccessfully, to recoup his fortune by peddling a better horseshoe.

Fortunately, while he had failed the Harknesses had prospered. Through deft market maneuverings and inside knowledge of impending war taxes, their liquor business had left them extremely wealthy. People who were seeking to launch businesses in the postwar years came to the Harknesses to borrow money. One man sought $100,000 to expand his operations. The Harknesses agreed, provided their kinsman Flagler was taken into the firm to look after their interest. The business was new and considered speculative. The product, which had been peddled by traveling "doctors" as a remedy for what-ails, had only recently become available in larger quantities than small medicine bottles, and its greatest uses were still decades in the future. Still, the Harknesses could afford to take a chance.

The commodity was petroleum. The borrower was John D. Rockefeller. The business that he and Flagler built up was Standard Oil. They all got rich as Croesus. Along the way they did a few things that wouldn't have made Horatio Alger proud. As years went on, people delighted in pointing that out, even writing whole books about it.

From the beginning, Rockefeller and Flagler were the closest of partners. "For years and years this early partner and I worked shoulder to shoulder," Rockefeller recalled later. "Our desks were in the same room. We both lived on Euclid Avenue, a few rods apart. We met and walked to the office together, walked home to luncheon, back again after luncheon, and home again at night. On these walks, when we were away from the office interruptions, we did our thinking, talking, and planning together."

The result of this close collaboration was the greatest moneymaking venture in American history. Years later, when a reporter asked Rockefeller whether he had conceived the idea of Standard Oil, he replied, "No, sir. I wish I'd had the brains to think of it. It was Henry M. Flagler."

They kept the habit of closeness after Standard headquarters moved from Cleveland to New York in 1877, and the two occupied neighboring townhouses just off Fifth Avenue.

It was, they were both fond of saying, a "friendship based on business," which they proclaimed far superior to a "business based on friendship." The exact meaning of this may be inferred from Flagler's unguarded but vehement remark to muckraker Ida Tarbell at the turn of the century about his friend and partner of many decades standing: "He would do me out of a dollar today," said Flagler, smashing his fist on the table. "That is, if he could do it honestly, Miss Tarbell, if he could do it honestly."

The love of money was something they shared, and from the beginning of Standard Oil, as Flagler liked to say, "we were prospered."

• • •

Money can't buy everything, though it took Flagler a long time to learn that and he fought against it every step of the way. Money can't buy health and, as the songwriters say, it can't buy love.

All through the years the Standard Oil millions were piling up, Mary Harkness Flagler was suffering, a semi-invalid whose lack of robustness kept her husband home nights but didn't distract him from business. The years and the move to New York did nothing to help her, and by the late 1870s her bronchial condition was so alarming that doctors recommended she be taken to Florida to escape the harsh winter. The dutiful husband took his wife to Jacksonville, then accompanied her on the boat down the St. Johns River to Tocoi, where a small train hauled them the rest of the way to St. Augustine.

The accommodations were bad. Their fellow visitors were mostly consumptives, coughing away, filling street and hotel with the sounds of their ailment. Flagler did not like it a bit. He caught the next train back to Tocoi and the next boat to Jacksonville, where the rest of the sojourn was passed.

Mary Flagler's condition improved, but her husband was

anxious to get back to work: he had a little business in Florida, through his investments with Henry Plant, but not enough to keep him occupied for long. So they headed back to New York.

In succeeding winters, Flagler urged his wife to go off to Florida without him. He would work while she recuperated. Nothing doing. She stayed at home and suffered.

On May 18, 1881, she died.

Flagler grieved. All his money had not been able to prolong her life. His daughter, Jennie, had married and left home, but his son, Harry, was just eleven and needed someone to look after him. Carrie Flagler, Henry's half-sister, was brought to New York for that purpose.

To provide a change of scenery, a forty-room house on 32 acres jutting into Long Island Sound at Mamaroneck was purchased, for $125,000; another $330,000 went into renovations. The resulting estate was rechristened Lawn Beach, by Flagler the minister's son, from its original name of Satan's Toe.

Flagler mourned, but not forever. On June 5, 1883, he married the nurse who had cared for his wife during her final illness. Although the family was not enthusiastic, Flagler was determined, as usual, and Ida Alice Shourds was ecstatic to be his bride. Alicia, as she was known, was a flaming redhead, eighteen years his junior, whose aspiration to be an actress was at variance with her background as a minister's daughter. Like Flagler before her, she was anxious to leave poverty behind. She loved the status, privilege, and spending sprees afforded by her new husband. He was too busy to take time off for a honeymoon, but when his liver became "disorderly" that winter, he decided a trip to Florida would be just the thing to improve it. His physician insisted that a visit to healthful St. Augustine be included, and though the patient was not too enthusiastic, he followed the doctor's orders—to his pleasant surprise.

"There had been a wonderful change in the former state of things," he noted. "Instead of the depressing accommodations of nine years before I found the San Marco one of the most comfortable and best kept hotels in the world, and filled, too, not with consumptives, but the class of society one meets at the great watering places of Europe—men who go there to enjoy themselves and not for the benefit of their health."

He liked it well enough to stay. It did not have the aura of sickness and death about it, which had driven him off on his first visit. Still, it was not tremendously exciting.

"I couldn't sit still all the time, and I used daily to take the walks down St. George Street, around the Plaza to the club house, and back to the hotel again. I found that all the other gentlemen did the same thing, with the same apparent regularity." It was all there was to do for entertainment.

"But I liked the place and the climate, and it occurred to me very strongly that someone with sufficient means ought to provide accommodations for that class of people who are not sick, but who come here to enjoy the climate, have plenty of money, but could find no satisfactory way of spending it."

The "someone" Flagler described was a perfect self-portrait. Money was rolling in faster than he could ever spend it. Celebrating his fifty-fourth birthday in Florida with his beautiful, much younger wife, he was in a mood to use some of it for pleasure and enjoyment.

At the beginning of 1882 the Standard Oil Trust had been formed from all the companies acquired by hook or by crook over the previous decade. By the end of the year a United States Senate committee was investigating the trust, and Flagler, on the witness stand, was bluntly told by the committee counsel, "I am trying to expose your robbery." What an indignity for the minister's son who, like his better-known partner, believed that God had given him his money.

Many of the Standard Oil partners found it convenient at midlife to step back from the firing line and count their money, leaving others to dodge the bullets. Flagler led the way. His holdings were too extensive to permit him to back out completely—he remained a vice president of Standard Oil until 1908 and a director until 1911—but after that honeymoon trip to Florida he had something on his mind besides petroleum.

• • •

The view from Villa Zorayda's tower was not much: the mud-flats of a scraggly tidal creek, and beyond that downtown St. Augustine, noted over most of the centuries of its existence for being dirty and rundown. But in the mind of the villa's creator, it was a sight to behold. He sketched it vividly for his student: palatial hotels here, landscaped parks there, the whole drawn together by a broad paved avenue worthy of the Spanish name Alameda. Old Spain would be re-created in a glory it had never had, complete with indoor toilets and electric lights.

Flagler saw the possibilities. He struck a deal with Smith. They would build $200,000 worth of hotels and entertainment facilities. Flagler, as silent partner, would put up $150,000; Smith, as public partner, would raise the rest. When Smith couldn't raise his $50,000, Flagler did it all himself. The original amount ballooned as he proved himself at least as seriously bitten by the Florida bug as his mentor.

There were two responses from the public, roughly delineated along geographic lines.

Those in the New York business world who knew Flagler as a sober, serious, successful, and somewhat ruthless trust builder were amazed and aghast. "Flagler," said one of his friends, "I was asked the other day why you were building that hotel in St. Augustine, and replied that you had been looking around for several years for a place to make a fool of yourself in, and at last selected St. Augustine as the spot."

The oilman himself liked to explain his motivation with a story. "There was once a good old church member who had always lived a correct life until well advanced in years. One day when very old he went on a drunken spree. While in this state he met his good pastor, to whom, being soundly upbraided for his condition, he replied, 'I've been giving all my days to the Lord hitherto, and now I'm taking one for myself.' This is somewhat my case. For about fourteen or fifteen years, I have devoted my time exclusively to business, and now I am pleasing myself."

In Florida people did not question Flagler's sanity or sobriety, because they were too busy trying to see how they could get a share of his money. Speculators snuggled up to every piece of property he bought, hoping some of the wealth produced by his development would rub off on them. "St. Augustinians think they have a bonanza," he wrote disgustedly, "and they are working it for all it is worth."

He was flooded with proposals to buy this or that, and developed a standard reply that all he wanted was a little piece of land for his hotel. As to speculation, he could make more on Wall Street in a week than he could in Florida in a year. When he heard that a delegation from neighboring Palatka wanted to visit to sell him on the virtues of their city, he said he would arrange to be out of town. He did everything he could to discourage those with dollar signs in their eyes. Even the land for his hotel was largely created, by filling in the northern reaches of Maria Sanchez Creek, rather than bought on the open market.

But the speculators were right to sniff a boom. Flagler was the one who didn't realize just how far he would go.

• • •

One of New York's newest and smallest architectural firms in 1885 was Carrère and Hastings. It consisted of two architects and an office boy occupying a single cramped room. Business was not plentiful, so when Thomas Hastings received a note asking him to call on Henry Flagler, he hurried right off.

Partner John Carrère held down the fort, on the off chance that a client might walk in. An hour later he heard a tremendous commotion in the hallway.

"It seemed to me as if every door was being slammed, and the first thing I knew Mr. Hastings had opened and slammed our door and was standing in the office and I saw the New York directory flying through the air at my head. I just managed to dodge that when I had to duck again to allow a T square that was flying in my direction to pass without hitting me."

Hastings was a bit nervous and high-strung, but this outburst was more than his partner had counted on. Carrère, older and graver, was not used to defending himself against a maniac. He did his best, however. "I began to pick up things from my desk and throw them at my partner, until above the din and confusion I heard Mr. Hastings shout: 'We are going to Florida! We've got a million dollar hotel to build there!' Then we simply proceeded to smash everything we could lay hands on, our office boy ably assisting us."

Hastings, the artistic soul of the firm, was just twenty-five years old. Carrère, its chief diplomat and businessman, was twenty-seven. They had studied at the Ecole des Beaux-Arts in Paris, returned to the United States, and joined the firm of McKim, Mead and White, which was forging its way to architectural leadership in this country. Though strangers in Paris, they became inseparable in New York and soon established their own office. Their commission from Flagler was an architect's dream: a wealthy client in a mood to spend and with a yen for distinction. What a way to start a business!

It was no coincidence that they got the break. Flagler always had a soft spot for ministers' children, and Hastings's father was his pastor. The architect was descended from a long line of divines. His grandfather, an albino, was a noted composer of church music, including the classic "Rock of Ages."

Despite this heritage, Thomas Hastings never joined the church—though he did design several outstanding church buildings. The artistry the grandfather applied to sacred music was transmuted in the grandson to a skill in drawing. This was evident from childhood, when the boy practiced his art on the walls and pages of books, where it was not appreciated. He left school as a teen-ager to work as draftsman for the celebrated cabinetmaker Christian Herter, on whose advice he decided to study in Paris.

The Beaux-Arts system, an innovation in architectural training, firmly linked theory with practice and taught its students the importance of ornamentation, of relating a building to its site, and of making form follow function. The preferred styles were those of the Renaissance, but applied to modern situations, not just relentlessly copied.

Though Hastings belonged to no church, his ingrained puritanism kept him from the wild life during his student years. He could laugh at a risqué story, but most vices were beyond him. An artist, not a playboy, he was never so happy as when bent over a drafting table, drawing, correcting, discarding, and starting again, oblivious of everything save the problem he was trying to solve.

John Carrère had followed a different path to Beaux-Arts. Born in Rio, he was the son of an American coffee planter of French extraction, and received most of his education in Europe. If he lacked the particular artistic genius of Hastings, he was amply blessed with talents the other lacked. The combination of their skills made for a completeness neither could have hoped for alone—and for a successful partnership that would rise, after the initial boost from Flagler, to the heights of the profession.

• • •

Thomas Hastings and Henry Flagler arrived in St. Augustine in May 1885 to examine the site and get the planning under way. They stayed with Dr. Andrew Anderson, a physician whose famous Markland orange grove adjoined the Flagler property. Anderson, who had agreed to be the oilman's local representative, was less visionary and more levelheaded than Franklin Smith, but no less a local booster. He would soon be elected St. Augustine's mayor on a platform of helping transform the Ancient City into the Winter Newport that Flagler projected.

When he first saw the property, Hastings was dismayed to find it low and marshy, bisected by Maria Sanchez Creek. But that was nothing that hundreds of pine pilings driven straight into the ground, and tons of sand poured on top, could not remedy. The architect wandered about the city, absorbing its atmosphere. The size of the hotel meant it could either overwhelm or add to the ambience of the place. Hastings unhesitatingly chose the latter goal.

Professional colleagues followed the progress of the choice commission with interested and envious eyes. They expected something in the French style because of his training. But he surprised them. "I wanted to retain the Spanish character of St. Augustine," he recalled on a later visit, "and so designed the buildings in keeping with the architecture of the early houses here with their quaint over-hanging balconies."

The result was a graceful castle in Spanish Renaissance style, topped with red tile dome and towers, fringed with terracotta ornamentation. The building material was poured concrete with local coquina shell mixed in. Franklin Smith helped train the masons in using the material he had pioneered. Artists and craftsmen from two continents worked on the interior effects. Louis Tiffany did the stained-glass windows.

Flagler had been impressed by the San Marco Hotel and showed his gratitude by decimating its staff. Its builders, McGuire and McDonald, were put in charge of his construction, and the manager, O. D. Seavey, likewise came over into his employ.

Flagler named his hotel the Ponce de Leon, after the Spanish explorer who preceded him in quest of a fountain of youth. Associates of the middle-aged oilman with the new young wife noticed him stepping in somewhat peppier fashion and could understand his affinity for that legend.

Hastings liked to joke that in his beginning days he was afraid his buildings were going to fall down, but when he saw them later he was afraid they wouldn't. That did not apply to the Ponce, which would always give him a special sense of satisfaction. Not only was it his first major job, but it was pioneering in several other important respects: Florida's first truly monumental building, it also reintroduced the Spanish style to the former Spanish colony. Moreover, it was an experiment, and a highly complex and successful one, in poured-concrete construction on a scale hitherto untried.

The Ponce helped revolutionize hotel design around the world. Starting with no particular knowledge of hotels, the architects consulted veteran hotel men, who agreed on only two things. First was that rooms should be in some multiple of 27 inches, which was the measurement of a standard width of carpet. Second was that none of their competitors knew anything at all. After the Ponce was completed, Carrère and Hastings became the recognized experts on hotels in the architectural world.

That the thick walls were destined not to fall down was due to the skill of the architects and builders, but also to the determination of the financier. "I want something to last all time to come," Flagler said. "I think it more likely I am spending an unnecessary amount of money in the foundation walls," he told the contractors, "but I comfort myself with the reflection that a hundred years hence it will be all the same to me, and the building the better because of my extravagance."

With the oil money pouring in, Flagler could afford to indulge merely as a hobby in "a hotel that suits me in every respect, and one that I can thoroughly enjoy, cost what it may." But he was too instinctively a businessman to forget the bottom line: "I do not care whether it pays in five, ten, fifteen or twenty years, but I would hate to think that I am investing money that will not bring a return in the future."

Remembering his boredom at the gentleman's daily routine of walking downtown and back to the San Marco, Flagler resolved to provide adequate amusement facilities for his resort. Hastings thus designed the Alcazar, facing the Ponce across a tropically landscaped park. Its hotel portion was small, but the ground floor featured an arcade of shops around a courtyard where Fifth Avenue stores could open seasonal outlets for the traveling rich.

In the rear was the greatest attraction, the Casino, which included a huge indoor swimming pool (complete with a private section for ladies who declined to appear in public wearing bathing apparel) sunlit through a glass roof, with a stage and ballroom on upper levels overlooking the water. Adjacent to these were Turkish and Russian baths, a massage parlor, and a carpeted gymnasium. The most up-to-date therapeutic gadgetry was available to relieve chronic overindulgers in the multi-course dinners the hotel served.

For those of an active bent, the latest sports fads were catered to. A bicycle-riding academy and tennis courts were located behind the Casino. The green surrounding old Fort Marion, where the changing of flags had taken place in 1821, was turned into a golf course. Its moat and raised earthen fortifications were the obstacles that tested the players' skill. Nighttime saw the fort's terreplein transformed into an outdoor ballroom, decorated and lit with Japanese lanterns. A military band provided the music.

Across the bay, on Anastasia Island, the hotel maintained a beach cottage for those daring enough to engage in the nascent sport of surf bathing.

Flagler's casino was a place for gamboling, not gambling. But games of chance also appeared, for the amusement of the wealthy clientele. A young man named E. R. Bradley began a lifelong habit of sticking close to the oilman when he opened his Bacchus Club on a side street discreetly close to the Ponce de Leon, featuring fine food, drink, and gambling.

Flagler's investment expanded from the original $150,000 up into the millions. He wound up building churches, jails, courthouses, city halls, waterworks, paved streets, and all the other requirements of a modern city. Most important, he went into the transportation business.

Bringing in the quantity of material required for his buildings put a severe strain on the tiny railroad serving St. Augustine. The owners appreciated Flagler's business but were not about to make huge capital investments to suit his needs. Having

Facing the Ponce was the Alcazar. Architect Thomas Hastings always regretted that the grand colonnade he designed for the front of the hotel (shown in his sketch here) was never built.

The Ponce de Leon Hotel in St. Augustine—the first and finest Flagler ever built—was begun in 1885, completed in 1887, and opened to the public in 1888.

served as Standard's expert in dealing with railroads over the years, Flagler knew just what to do: he maneuvered them into a hard place and bought them out. It was child's play for him, a stroke of fate for Florida. South of St. Augustine lay a vast wasteland, pockmarked with a handful of settlements too isolated and distant to prosper. A railroad extending down the coast would change all that, opening the east coast of the peninsula to settlement and making the builder land-rich with grants from the state.

The same logic that led Flagler, in the oil business, to gather competitors into the fold or crush them ruthlessly, now asserted itself in his second life as resort magnate, railroad builder, and land developer.

This was his potato chip, and he couldn't eat just one. He had begun with the idea of doing something in partnership, but the partners were never rich enough to come up with their share, never quick enough to catch the drift of Flagler's thinking. He decided he would rather do it himself.

Franklin Smith had built a large Moorish-style hotel facing the park between the Ponce and the Alcazar, which he named the Casa Monica, after the mother of Saint Augustine, bishop of Hippo. It stretched his finances to the limit. After a season, Flagler bought him out, renamed the place the Cordova, and operated it along with his other hotels.

A small rail line, mainly for logging purposes, had been built south to Ormond, and two entrepreneurs had opened the seventy-five-room Ormond Hotel. Flagler bought both the railroad and the hotel. His vision of a Winter Newport expanded to a dream of an American Riviera. He improved as he went along. McGuire and McDonald were sent to double the size of the Ormond Hotel. The railroad was upgraded from narrow- to standard-gauge and incorporated into his system as it advanced southward.

Among his peers, Flagler encouraged investing. He had some success with Standard Oil partner William Warden, who had been putting his gains into Philadelphia real estate and utilities. Warden Castle, a huge Moorish-style winter residence, had grown up on the fort green as a result. Whereas Flagler had filled in the northern reaches of Maria Sanchez Creek, Warden dredged the southern end to create a lake replete with islands, surrounded by lots to be sold by his St. Augustine Improvement Company, which would build to suit. The resulting houses could be serviced by the gas-and-electric company Warden set up.

But he was the exception. Other oilmen came to visit, not to put their money into Flagler's Winter Newport. One was John D. Rockefeller, who recalled that Flagler had originally talked about investing $30,000 in an orange grove. Surveying the scene, he cackled, "I guess he's got $30,000 in here. It looks like it." But Rockefeller's involvement was limited to buying Standard Oil stock from Flagler to provide cash for the development of Florida. Flagler got a lot of pleasure from the development, and Rockefeller got a lot of profit from the stock.

FOLLOW THE CROWDS

•

Henry Plant was not idle during this time. He matched Flagler mile for mile in track laid, acre for acre in land received, and hotel for hotel in the race to become resort magnates. They worked different territory: Flagler down the east coast and Plant through central Florida and over to the west coast. They also moved in different directions from simplicity to ornateness in their hotels.

Flagler's Ponce de Leon was the finest and most distinctive he ever built. As he moved down the coast he dispensed with the services of his architects and entrusted the design and building to his contractors, McGuire and McDonald. Consequently, the later hotels were well built, competent, and huge, but uninspired. Large, bulky Edwardian structures, they lacked all the fripperies and fine points that made the Ponce de Leon such a delight to the eye. They were also constructed of wood, which proved far less durable than the oilman's initial concrete venture in the field.

Plant moved in the opposite direction. First he bought up some of the large wooden Victorian hotels along the route of his expanding railroad, more notable for size than distinctiveness of design. Then he decided to start from scratch and do something to rival the Ponce de Leon. This was no easy task, but he had the money to give it a try.

Flagler's hotel opened to the public in January 1888. Six months later the cornerstone was laid for Plant's answer, the Tampa Bay Hotel. Construction took three years, and in the meantime Plant and his wife, Margaret (he had married a second time in 1873), went on an international shopping spree. In 1889 Plant took an exhibit of southern products to the Paris Exposition, carrying away several medals that he later displayed in his hotel. He ran the first American flag up the Eiffel Tower, and expressed the opinion that that landmark would have to be demolished in not too many years because the metal used in its construction was bound to deteriorate. Plant's mind, like Flagler's, was focused on building something that would last for all time.

After the exposition the Plants traveled through Europe, spending hundreds of thousands of dollars on antiques, furnishings, and decorations for the hotel. Mrs. Plant's skills had been honed decorating and upholstering her husband's Pullman cars. Now she sent back bric-a-brac by the shipload.

The Tampa Bay Hotel had its grand opening in February 1891. Cost estimates have run from $1 million to $4 million. The figure given out at the time was $2.5 million. Whatever was spent, the results were extraordinary. The canny Connecticut Yankee had finally produced his folly.

He liked it. Two years later he described it as "that haven which has been so often described but to which no writer to my mind has done justice."

That was not because they didn't try. To one it was "the most attractive, most original, and most beautiful hotel in the South, if not in the whole country." Another went further, proclaiming it "one of the modern wonders of the world." A reporter seeking to describe it by comparison found himself at a loss and finally concluded that "it has no kind; there is none other in similarity with it."

It was huge. It was ornate. It was Franklin Smith's Moorish Revival style carried to the outermost limits. It was exactly the kind of hotel Phineas T. Barnum would have designed had he been bitten with the Florida bug.

Rising like a mirage from the sandy streets of Tampa was an elongated brick building with thirteen minarets topped by silvered onion domes and gilded crescents. A walk around it on the outside covered a mile. From behind horseshoe arches of lacy gingerbread, the quarter-mile-long front porch overlooked a lush garden, which featured the words "Tampa Bay Hotel" planted in foliage. A large live-oak tree by the riverbank gave Plant a counterpart to Flagler's Ponce de Leon legend: he claimed, contrary to all records of longevity, that Hernando de Soto had parlayed with the Indians under its overarching branches back in 1539.

The interior was no less distinctive. Boston, New York, and Grand Rapids contributed their best, while the European shopping spree had netted items traced back to Louis Philippe and Marie Antoinette. There were bronze dwarfs, silver busts, Japanese screens, old masters, marble columns, beveled glass, bric-a-brac and more bric-a-brac. It was the age of clutter. "Nothing offends the eye or the taste at any point," wrote one observer—though certainly nothing was bland enough to give the eye or taste any rest either.

Henry Plant liked music, found it restful. "It is medicine to me," he said. His tastes were catholic, running from Haydn and Handel to hurdy-gurdy. For his hotel he hired musicians from the Boston Symphony Orchestra. Their lilting strains could be heard in the octagonal dining room, where patrons munched on pastries prepared by a chef from Delmonico's.

The dinnerware was an eclectic delight, varying from course to course. "Oh! what a pleasure it is to feast from the table service," wrote one impressed guest. "They bring you beef on a bit of French porcelain, your salad on an old Vienna plate, ice on a saucer designed by Moritz Fischer and coffee in a Wedgewood cup."

Plant's trains unloaded right at the porch, where rickshaws waited to carry guests down the long hallway to the registration desk.

It is hard to think what more Plant could have done to create and present his version of paradise to the public—or, at least, such of them as could afford it. No wonder he liked the place. Fortunately he was spared the judgment of a later generation that the whole thing was "a monument to bad taste."

• • •

Henry Flagler was invited to attend the grand opening of the Tampa Bay Hotel, thus giving rise to one of the most enduring tales in Florida history.

It goes like this:

When he received Plant's invitation to the affair, Flagler asked, "Where is Tampa?"

"Follow the crowds," shot back Plant.

The story was so good that the characters have been used interchangeably, and any number of destinations substituted for Tampa. What makes it so popular is that it aptly describes the friendly rivalry of the east- and west-coast magnates. But, unless Plant and Flagler tossed the *bons mots* back and forth endlessly, most of the stories should be considered about as reliable historically as Parson Weems's tale of George Washington chopping down the cherry tree.

The two developers traded visits every year to show off their latest accomplishments. When they traveled together they did so in style, either on yachts or private railroad cars or anything else that was sumptuous and handy.

Plant practically lived in his railroad car, though his official address was his Fifth Avenue palace in New York. He liked to be where the action was in his empire, so a mobile headquarters was only natural. His famous private car, No. 100, was a familiar sight on the tracks of the Plant System. Fitted out with office, bedroom, and dining room, it reflected Mrs. Plant's hand in its carved mahogany interior, blue velvet upholstery, and French mirrors.

The magnate's biographer (and minister) wrote: "Its entrance at any station causes sunshine to break on every face, and the old colored men who come, bucket in hand, to wash and polish it where it happens to remain over a night or a day at the station, are fairly beaming when they greet 'Massa Plant' and are always paid back in their own coin with United States currency added."

Plant had the kind of labor relations that his fellow magnates envied: with over twelve thousand employees in extremely contentious times, he never suffered a strike. One reason was that he concentrated his charity on helping veteran employees in need. It was an excellent public-relations gesture: word spread fast. Leaving to others (including his heirs) the endowing of schools, the building of hospitals and churches, he put his giving to work in behalf of the Plant System, and it paid dividends.

Even apart from paid encomiums, he wound up hearing some rather extravagant praise. One after-dinner speaker gushed on about how Plant had "made the desert to bloom like the rose, changed waste places into fertile fields, the swamps into a sanitarium, the sand heap into a Champs Elysées, the Hillsborough into a Seine, and reproduced the palace of Versailles on the banks of Tampa Bay." And, presumably after he rested from those labors on the seventh day, he "brought health and happiness to many homes over which bereavement and sorrow were hovering like the black angel of death."

Plant ate it up. But he was no fool, to be taken in by flowery flattery. He was hardheaded when necessary, and woe betide those who tried to cross him. Feeling that Cedar Key, terminus of the first cross-Florida railroad, was trying to hold him up, he decided to take his line elsewhere and ruin the town. He is reputed to have delivered the curse: "Owls will hoot in your attics and hogs will wallow in your deserted streets!" That's just about what happened when they were denied his link with the outside world.

Places like Tampa benefited from his interest. But in neighboring St. Petersburg the newspaper complained that "The policy of the Plant System has never been helpful to growing industries and new settlements in this section."

So Plant had detractors as well as supporters, enemies as well as friends. Then there was his curious relationship with Flagler.

In the oil business, Flagler would have seen someone like Plant as a rival, taken his measure, found him less well heeled, and presented the ultimatum: join up or be crushed. Why did he not crush him in Florida?

For one thing, they were partners as well as rivals. It was through Plant that Flagler had first invested in Florida. They jointly owned the Jacksonville station where Plant's interstate lines delivered the passengers for Flagler's Florida East Coast Railway. Besides, the state was large. Flagler had enough to keep him occupied in the sections he had chosen, without encroaching on Plant's territory. And there was an element of class solidarity as well. Both poor boys who had grown rich were learning about the loneliness at the top. Wealth made them targets as much as it made them happy. Envy and jealousy were beamed in their direction. Friendships were closed off with those who could not afford their life style. People were always trying to make money from them. Thus separated from most people, they still needed to have a few to relate to. They sparred and contested occasionally, but did not destroy each other.

The temper of the times increased their sense of solidarity. The growing Populist movement trained its fire on the rich. Where the railroads had once been greeted with open arms and given what they wanted, by the 1890s Plant lamented "an unexplained feeling of hostility to corporations—a sort of antagonism to capital—which has worked its way like a devouring worm into the politics of the nation."

He professed mystification at that attitude since, as he saw it, "The interests of the people and the railroads are certainly not conflicting interests. They are common interests and should go hand in hand and heart to heart in the great work of building up this country." That was a philosophy he and Flagler—if not too many Populists—could agree on.

• • •

The two magnates were the most visible figures of the boom by the 1890s, but they were certainly not the only ones cashing in on it. Everyone wanted a piece of the action. Tallahassee, languishing since the secessionists "opened the gates of Hell," hopefully billed itself the center of the Middle Florida boom. One entrepreneur sold lots in "MURAT! The Western Addition to Tallahassee," which was advertised as "The most historic and romantic spot in Florida, having been the home of the celebrated Prince Joachim Napoleon Achille Murat, son of Joachim Murat, King of Naples, and nephew of the Great Napoleon."

Franklin Smith took the money he got from Flagler for the Casa Monica and carried it across the street to build something else. He had originally thought to round out his Islamic collection with a large, onion-domed hotel. But, having failed to prosper in the hotel business, he settled on a shopping arcade instead, where Flagler's guests could spend their money.

The arcade reflected his new enthusiasm for ancient Roman architecture, so the onion domes were left on the drawing board. He had enough money left over to build another reproduction at his summer home in Saratoga Springs, New York: the House of Pansa copied one of the buildings excavated by archaeologists at Pompeii. Opened to the public as a museum, it attracted them by the thousands.

Archaeology was in vogue in Florida too, in the hunt for mammoth and mastodon bones, although the motive was not so idealistic or educational as Smith's· the bones heralded vast deposits of phosphate, a valuable agricultural fertilizer much in demand, particularly in Europe. Albertus Vogt had found it on his property near Dunnellon in 1889. An unreconstructed Confederate veteran, Vogt had gone into the real-estate business, doing well as the railroad opened up land for settlement. He was not too keen on all of his customers, once expressing the wish that he had some lots in hell to sell to damnyankees who came his way.

When he found the phosphate, he knew just what to do. Keeping his mouth shut, he joined with a few partners and quietly bought up thousands of acres containing the deposits. Word got out eventually, of course, but by then they were way ahead of the crowd. And the crowd came: by 1890 a full scale boom was under way. Prospectors and speculators combed the woods for miles around looking for the telltale sign of prehistoric bones. Obliging locals "salted" their fields with bones to extract good prices from the influx of get-rich-quickers. By 1891 twenty phosphate companies had been formed, with a capitalization of over $20,000,000. What they dug up was sent to Tampa on Henry Plant's trains and shipped out of there on his boats. Vogt became rich and Plant became richer.

Citrus had remained a staple product, though years of experience showed it had been somewhat overbilled. Orange fever had cooled somewhat as "the tips of the Frost King's fingers" touched down in 1868, 1870, 1876, and 1880. In that last year, Harriet Beecher Stowe lost a thousand boxes of fruit from her grove at Mandarin.

The main problem was not scarcity, however, but overproduction. The market became glutted as more and more of the postwar groves came to maturity, and prices began to drop—as they had been guaranteed never to do. Grower panic was the result.

Nature helped trim the oversupply in January 1886, when the state had its worst freeze since the disastrous one of 1835. Growers blamed it on the massive cutting of timber in North Florida and Georgia, which had removed a natural windbreak to cold weather. As a postscript to the freeze, the red spider made its appearance and spread rapidly over the entire orange belt.

This natural respite yielded time to plan for dealing with future superabundance—but also pause for worry as to whether that would really be the problem. Diversification of crops and markets was the obvious answer.

Here Mrs. Plant made her greatest contribution to the Florida economy. Noticing that one variety of citrus was typically left to rot on the ground, she asked a grower how much he would sell the fruit to her for. She could have them for free, he said: there was no market for them, and when he had tried to sell them once, he had lost his shirt. Mrs. Plant ordered a bunch sent to New York so she and her friend Mrs. Frank Leslie, the publisher, could popularize them among their fashionable friends.

Thus was born—for all commercial purposes—the grapefruit. It was advertised as a tonic, to purify the blood, help digestion, and cure biliousness. One grower provided a handbill with each box of fruit, outlining its medicinal properties and how to prepare it for the table. The promotion was successful. From a curiosity or monstrosity, grapefruit evolved into a necessity. By 1894 the *Florida Agriculturist* could report that "To those who acquire the taste it becomes to the morning meal almost as indispensable as the cup of coffee."

In the search for expanded markets, citrus were shipped off to France and England, though rough weather damaged and destroyed so much of the cargo that the venture proved less than successful as an answer to overproduction.

However, that would not be a problem for long.

• • •

In 1893 the country was swept by another of the financial panics that have punctuated its economic history. By the time it was over, seventy railroads, five hundred banks, and sixteen thousand businesses had gone under.

Hamilton Disston was one of the victims. Flagler and Plant were among the survivors—the former because of his tremendous oil revenues, the latter because of his general canniness in troubled times. As railroads declared bankruptcy right and left, Plant picked them up for a song—including Disston's St. Cloud and Sugar Belt Railway. Even through the worst of the difficulties the Plant System continued to pay dividends.

As far as St. Augustine was concerned, the most immediate difficulty was competition from Flagler's resorts farther south. In 1893 he decided to extend his railroad to Palm Beach and raced his railway builders against his hotel contractors to see who could finish first. By 1894 the line was completed and the Royal Poinciana, an immense structure dwarfing his other hotels (though it could not hold a candle to the Ponce in artistry), was open, if not entirely finished.

The magnitude of the accomplishment was impressive, considering the quantity of building materials that had had to be brought in by riverboat: 5 million feet of lumber, 360,000 shingles, 4,000 barrels of lime, 2,400 gallons of paint, 1,200 windows, and 1,800 doors. It was good practice for even more amazing feats to come.

Palm Beach had two advantages to Flagler: one natural and one an invidious comparison with the Ancient City. First, since it was farther south, with the Gulf Stream practically lapping at its beaches, the weather was warmer. Winter chills struck less often, and tropical foliage bloomed forth more luxuriantly. Second, since Flagler was starting closer to scratch, he had a freer hand in shaping this resort to his tastes than he'd had in St. Augustine. His enthusiasm for that place had undoubtedly waned. He was tired of running the gauntlet of outstretched hands, and he complained that after all he had done the city officials wouldn't even keep the streets clean between his depot and his hotels. He relished the chance to start anew, learning from past problems.

One thing he did was build "a city for my help"—West Palm Beach. All the necessary support services would be based there, comfortably out of sight of the resorters. Palm Beach would be kept separate, a private enclave for the rich. It was a success from the time the first private railroad car brought in a group of Vanderbilts and their friends. The Palm Beach Inn, later renamed The Breakers, was built to handle the additional demand.

St. Augustine was demoted to a rest stop as high society chugged along to Flagler's new paradise for the winter season.

This was merely a reshuffling of the money within Florida, and so did not reflect on the state's overall prosperity. Two events that followed the Panic of 1893 had a much more serious effect.

The phosphate boom, following the classic pattern, peaked and collapsed. With the market flooded, phosphate prices dropped 75 percent, and many of the boom-time companies went under.

Then, at Christmas 1894, the temperature in North Florida dropped to 19 degrees. Hovering there for a couple of days, it did tremendous damage to the citrus crop, dealing a blow that the growers really didn't need in those hard times.

Fortunately, things warmed up in January—daytime temperatures of 80 dipped only to about 50 at night. The good weather had a positive effect on temperaments that might otherwise have been unduly depressed by the losses they had just suffered. Sap rose in the trees, promising future productivity despite the harm to that year's crop.

Without warning, the temperature plummeted again on February 7, 1895. The rising sap froze and swelled and literally burst the trees. As whole groves popped open, they sounded like battlefields. Years of work were destroyed.

There are stories of families abandoning their dinner tables, places set and meals unfinished, and heading back north without further ado, the sickening crack of orange trees echoing behind them. Some of the remittance men pulled up stakes, counting themselves fortunate if they could trade their holdings for a ticket home to England.

Citrus production dropped from five million boxes to just seventy-five thousand. Ninety percent of the fruiting wood on bearing trees was killed. Losses of $50 million to $100 million were talked of, when everything was taken into account. That the head of the weather bureau lost his job for failing to give warning of the freeze was scant comfort to Floridians who lost their life's work and saw their paradise turned to desolation row.

The damage snowballed, of course. Citrus and phosphate were the lifeblood of the railroads. The cold hand of winter did nothing to increase the state's attractiveness to tourists. And the hard times being felt everywhere also had their reflection in Florida.

This was the most serious crisis Florida faced since the long second boom started gathering steam after the Civil War. Was it the end of the road?

• • •

Eyes focused instinctively on the friendly rival kings of the state's east and west coasts. Would they call it quits? Had they become discouraged, with the rapidly diminishing value of their land holdings, their empty freight cars, and their cavernously unoccupied hotels? Would they seek greener pastures?

Not Henry Plant. His specialty was seeing things through hard times and turning a profit at the end. "Make the best of everything" was his motto. Although his train and express interests stretched from the Atlantic Coast to Texas, and his steamship lines ran from Canada to Cuba, one spot in this vast empire was certainly his favorite. "Florida is one of the President's pets," his associates said. Henry Plant would not desert it in time of need.

"You must publish words of cheer and hope to your people," he told a newspaper editor, "and do all that you can to help them over this trying time. Suggest to them the planting of other crops, the rearing of other fruits. It will not do to be altogether dependent on oranges. The soil is capable of raising many other things besides oranges, and it may be that this calamity will become a blessing in disguise."

Henry Flagler would stay the course as well. He had developed a great sense of noblesse oblige toward his Florida settlers. He might not necessarily welcome them through the front door of his hotels, but in the long run they were more important to the future of the state than all of his wealthy friends combined. It was their produce that would fill his railroad cars during the nine months when the fashionable folk were elsewhere. It was they who settled his towns and cities and made them more than dots on a land-office map. Their children attended the schools, their families worshipped in the churches, whose building lots he had donated. They were the pioneers of his new frontier, day-to-day participants in his dream. He could not let them go under.

Immediate aid was extended—loans, seeds, advice—but a more spectacular gesture would be required to demonstrate that Flagler had not lost faith. Fortunately, one was right at hand. Mrs. Julia Tuttle, a widow from Cleveland, had large landholdings at the mouth of the Miami River in Dade County. She made her home there at Fort Dallas, a relic of the Seminole Wars. For years she had been pestering Flagler to extend his railroad south to her property. For years he had been turning a deaf ear, placing her in the category of all the other people who were trying to sell him something he didn't want.

In the aftermath of the great freeze, Flagler dispatched his chief land agent, J. E. Ingraham, to assess the damage. Ingraham was the most experienced man in the business, having worked for Henry Sanford and Henry Plant, served as president of the South Florida Railway, and been a pioneer explorer of the Everglades before joining Flagler's employ in 1892. He headed south to see if any place had been immune from frost.

Arriving in Mrs. Tuttle's neck of the woods, he was impressed to find things still in bloom, undamaged by the weather. He wrapped some samples in damp cotton and carried them back to Flagler. The oilman was impressed too. He saw a new citrus belt in the making. "How soon can you arrange for me to go to Miami?" he asked. Ingraham's reply shows clearly what a distant outpost Miami was in those days. "If you can give me three days in which to get a messenger through to Mrs. Tuttle, advising her of your coming, so that she may prepare for you and get a carriage and horses to Fort Lauderdale, I will arrange to have the launch meet you at West Palm Beach, take you down the canal to Fort Lauderdale and from there by carriage to Miami."

Flagler made the trip, was greeted by perfect weather, and decided before bedtime to extend his railroad and build another hotel. Mrs. Tuttle and her neighbors the Brickells agreed to divide up their land holdings in a checkerboard pattern, giving Flagler the alternate squares: half of the land served by a railroad was worth more than all of it without one, they figured.

The news that Flagler was once again extending the frontiers of civilization was answered by the influx of hundreds of displaced citrus growers, all too willing, in those difficult days, to become trackmen and road builders and bricklayers and carpenters and hotel clerks and shopkeepers. It beat starving.

Word went out far and wide that the setback was only temporary, that the magnates had not lost faith, that Florida had a future.

• • •

The phosphate industry was reorganized with fewer companies on a firmer basis, and mining began again. Henry Plant's trains hauled the fertilizer to Port Tampa where it was loaded on boats for Europe.

Crops were diversified. The earth produced money from things besides oranges. To broaden the base of Florida's agriculture, experiments were carried out on everything from celery to sapodillas.

Flagler's railroad reached Miami, and the Royal Palm Hotel opened. An old Indian burial mound was removed to make room for its front porch, and skulls were given away as souvenirs. Civilization had arrived.

Ironically, the unhappiest people seemed to be the Brickells and the Tuttles. Mr. Brickell was annoyed that all the development was taking place across the river from his holdings, and he was outraged when Flagler's dredges deposited their spoil in a place that destroyed his view of the water. Mrs. Tuttle, having succeeded at long last in getting the railroad extended to her property, was frustrated when time came to cash in on it: Flagler, with a bit of private-enterprise pump-priming, was building ahead of demand so that Miami would be prepared to take advantage of opportunities as they arose. Mrs. Tuttle, in debt and in trouble, found her alternate squares of land virtually worthless because the oilman's development more than met all existing needs. She appealed for help, but Flagler never sympathized with those who tried to profit from his proximity. "I do not want you to suffer," he wrote her, "but I cannot accept the responsibility of your suffering. For months past, I have advised against your becoming so deeply involved in debt."

Of course, the situation was merely temporary, and in the long run it would work out; but Julia Tuttle did not have long to run. The "Mother of Miami" died in 1898, before she could see just how her city would grow. The value of her holdings was to exceed her wildest dreams—but too late for her to appreciate.

Thanks to emergency actions and timely rebirths, the long-lived second Florida boom managed to avoid a disastrous bust. But it needed another shot in the arm to get moving again, and this came in the form of the Spanish-American War of 1898.

Cuba had been the scene of strife for years, and Florida was drawn in, through geographic proximity and because of its large population of Cuban exiles. Revolutionary leader José Martí was a familiar sight in Tampa, Jacksonville, Key West, and St. Augustine, stirring up support among the cigar makers to free their homeland from Spanish rule. Public sympathy was overwhelmingly pro-Cuban, and public fears were that a new Spanish Armada would respond by attacking Florida. This concern led to a demand for more adequate coastal defenses. One effective lobbyist was John M. Schofield, recently retired commanding general of the United States Army, who was writing his memoirs in a cottage behind the Ponce de Leon Hotel rented from Henry Flagler.

Measures were taken to pump a little money into local coffers. The Ancient City was surveyed for a barracks—never built because of the brevity of the conflict. They did get some heavy guns mounted on a section of railroad track at the beach, to guard the harbor entrance, but these guns were never fired in anger, and a decade later their rusting remains were blown up with dynamite.

Every place clamored for a piece of the action, and each got something.

Jacksonville got Colonel William Jennings Bryan and his Nebraska volunteers, who fought disease but were kept far from any Spaniards, because the Republican administration did not want to share any military glory with the man who had so recently been the Democratic candidate for president.

Miami got enough troops to outnumber its civilians by four or five to one, a randy and rowdy bunch who made it unsafe for women to walk the streets—or even to stay at home. Miamians who had been happy to see them come were overjoyed to see them go, but the soldiers left in their wake going-away presents of typhus, mumps, and measles. After these ran their course, the whole place was quarantined for yellow fever.

It was Tampa that got the lion's share. Just before the fighting broke out, Henry Plant sent one of his aides to survey the Cuban scene and then report to President McKinley at the White House. Appreciating the knowledgeable briefing, McKinley also accepted the recommendation that Tampa would be an ideal port of embarkation.

The war was brief, but included a period of sitzkrieg as well as blitzkrieg. As Plant's ships brought survivors of the blown-up battleship *Maine* back to Tampa, U.S. troops began flooding into the city for what came to be known as the rocking-chair period of the war; its focal point was the front porch of the Tampa Bay Hotel.

"Only God knows why Plant built a hotel here," said one general, "but thank God he did."

The porch was lined with rocking brass who worked up an appetite by walking the long halls to dinner and dancing the night away in the ballroom, to the music of the regimental band. One cynical officer looked on and remarked, "War is Hell!"

The rotunda was a place to watch the peacocks preen. Richard Harding Davis, idol of an age that worshipped war correspondents, was there plying his trade. So were artist Frederic Remington and novelist Stephen Crane (whose *Red Badge of Courage*, about a war he had never seen, proved more enduring than anything he wrote about the subsequent war he did see). More straitlaced guests included hymnist Ira Sankey and Red Crosser Clara Barton. Most celebrated of all was Rough Rider Theodore Roosevelt, who spent some time at the hotel with his ailing wife while his colorful crew of Harvard alumni, social-registerites, and Wild West cowboys camped elsewhere.

Henry Plant came in to oversee the arrangements personally. Though he had made his reputation by handling things better than others, the magnitude of this task taxed even him and led to some heated confrontations. It is said that Teddy Roosevelt told Plant to shape things up or risk seizure by the War Department. "Seize it and be damned," was the reply. Plant stayed in charge and the grumbling went on.

Of the thirty thousand or more troops that passed through the port, about a tenth were black. They didn't cotton to the Jim Crow practices of Tampa merchants, and tore up places where they were discriminated against. Whites responded in kind, and news of the ensuing race riot was kept from the public only by military censorship.

Tampa had never received so much publicity—even though certain stories were blacked out—but it was not enough to turn the town into a tourist mecca. Tampa's development was destined to take other directions.

In hard times people will seek any relief. Believing the war was just the shot in the arm they needed, they found it painful medicine instead. But it didn't last long. Within a year Tampa had gone from boom town to ghost town, as far as the military presence was concerned. The cast of thousands dwindled to a single officer and a clerk tying up loose ends. That size force didn't pump a lot into the economy, but national prosperity was on the mend, and many were relieved that Florida could get back to booming in more traditional ways.

Henry Morrison Flagler made millions in oil and spent them in Florida. No other man had as great an effect on the development of the state.

Julia Tuttle, a widow from Cleveland, settled in South Florida in 1891 and, through her persistence, earned the name "Mother of Miami."

The immense Royal Poinciana Hotel in Palm Beach was the largest Flagler ever built. After a 1901 addition, its bedrooms totaled 1,081.

The Tampa Bay Hotel, Henry Plant's answer to Flagler's Ponce de Leon, rose like a mirage from the sandy streets of an otherwise inelegant Tampa.

The rocking chair period of the Spanish-American War took place on the front porch of the Tampa Bay Hotel. Weightiest of the rockers was the corpulent commander, General William Rufus Shafter (*seated, center*).

DEATH AND TAXES

•

Henry Plant survived his wartime exertions by only a year: he died in New York on June 23, 1899, at the age of seventy-nine.

As he had grown in importance, he had sought a family background to match. He hired a genealogist to trace the Plant family tree and put great stock in the results. It was a common enough vanity for a poor boy turned tycoon, but the full import of it did not become clear until he died and the will was read. Instead of leaving everything to his wife or his son by his first marriage, he sought to establish a Plant dynasty, directing that the major assets of the Plant System be held intact to benefit his four-year-old grandson and namesake when he came of age.

That was a bit much for the other heirs. They went to court and had the will broken, implying that Plant had been slightly touched in his last days. Even after the eyebrow-raising fees the lawyers made off the case, the heirs managed to increase their take by geometric proportions. Mrs. Plant, who had been slated to receive just $30,000 a year, became a multimillionaire instead, able to live as well as she chose and indulge in philanthropy on the side.

Plant—in addition to his extensive holdings elsewhere—

had built up Florida's mightiest and most profitable railroad network, with 1,196 miles of track, valued in 1901 at $7,475,883. Flagler's Florida East Coast Railway, by comparison, had only 466 miles of track, valued at $2,719,144.

The heirs could not wait to liquidate. In 1902 they sold the railroad to the Atlantic Coast Line, which thereby doubled its size and gained a new director in Plant's son Morton.

The Tampa Bay Hotel was another question. The Atlantic Coast Line didn't care to acquire Plant's Folly—white elephants require loving care and large expenditures. And it is rare that heirs share the enthusiasm for their predecessors' proudest possessions. Plant's certainly didn't.

Morton had a different set of interests. From the time he acquired his first boat at age thirteen, he had been a passionate yachtsman, known to one and all as "Commodore." Typically, he was out yachting when he received word of his father's death. His second-favorite pastime was baseball. Besides being part owner of the Philadelphia Phillies, he maintained for his own convenience a minor-league team near his Connecticut home, though it was a consistent money-loser. With such drains on his finances, he was not about to adopt his father's Arabian Nights fantasy as well.

Mrs. Plant thought she had a solution. She announced with great fanfare that she would give her share of the hotel, plus a million-dollar endowment, to establish the largest Jesuit school in the world. The only stipulation was that Morton also donate his 82 percent share of the hotel. Unfortunately, Morton, an Episcopalian, chose not to participate in her charity.

Son and widow wrangled for a while, then sold the hotel to the city of Tampa for $125,000—a mere fraction of its cost. Tampa thus had a municipally owned hotel for a while, but the amount of tender loving care it received inevitably declined after its proud builder went to his grave.

• • •

Henry Flagler survived and continued building his paradise, yet the happiness he derived from it was long diminished by personal problems, mostly of a family nature.

His daughter, Jennie Louise Benedict, died at sea in 1889. She was on her way to St. Augustine to recuperate after losing a child at birth.

Flagler called on Carrère and Hastings to express his grief through the Memorial Presbyterian Church. It was a thing of beauty, reflecting a heartfelt sorrow. The Venetian-style building they designed ranks second only to the Ponce in artistry. Like that hotel, it too pioneered a style that would be adopted in later Florida architecture. Dedicated in 1890, it was truly fit for a doge of the Presbyterian faith.

Flagler's family did not warm up to his second wife, Alicia, though he did not seek out their opinions. Publicly he seemed devoted to her. His yacht, his private railroad car, and the hospital he donated to St. Augustine all bore her name. Next door to the Presbyterian church he had Carrère and Hastings design her a magnificent fifteen-room "cottage," called "Kirkside," replete with carved oak and mahogany, damask wall coverings, marble floors, and bathroom faucets of sterling silver. There Mrs. Flagler displayed her world-class collection of historical miniatures of European royalty.

Now that she had married wealth, she began to yearn for nobility. Convinced that the czar of Russia was madly in love with her, she claimed they communicated by ouija board. She even sent him an expensive diamond ring to show her affection, though her husband had the ring retrieved before it reached its destination. He found her actions strange, to say the least.

As Alicia went through menopause, she had periods of both lucid and bizarre behavior. Flagler confiscated the ouija board and kept her a virtual prisoner at their Mamaroneck estate. At times she was affectionate; at times she armed herself and threatened to kill him. Doctors advised Flagler to keep out of her way. Eventually she was taken to a private hospital, seemed to recover, and came back home.

But she never gave up her fixation on the czar. She confided to friends that she was surrounded by Russian spies. She got another ouija board, lost touch with reality, and stabbed her doctor with a pair of scissors. When she was returned to the lunatic asylum, she insisted she was Princess Ida Alice von Schotten Tech, widow of Henry Flagler and fiancée of the czar.

Flagler never saw her again; in 1899 he had the courts rule her insane and incompetent.

One thing Alicia repeatedly said was that her husband had been unfaithful to her, and this may not have been entirely a delusion. Flagler was named co-respondent in a scandalous divorce case that gained headlines in the yellow press. It was claimed that, while separated from Alicia, he cohabited with another man's wife for six months, and made her a present of a New York townhouse and $400,000 in stocks and bonds. Flagler's lawyer dismissed it as a blackmail attempt, but fellow Wall Streeters took the charges seriously and felt the oilman's public dallying was bad for business.

The problems with Alicia were compounded by an estrangement between Flagler and his only surviving child. Though young Harry Harkness Flagler had briefly been placed in charge of the St. Augustine hotels, he resisted involvement in his father's business, for his interest lay in music. Father and son quarreled bitterly over this and went their separate ways. "Harry's desertion of me has made my burden much heavier, and I constantly wonder why this additional sorrow was necessary," lamented the father.

With so much unhappiness surrounding him, Flagler naturally sought solace. For some years he had been keeping company with young Mary Lily Kenan. Society wags considered her a poor relation of a wealthy North Carolina family and loved to tell Cinderella stories about the oil prince rescuing her from hard work in the attic.

After Alicia's commitment, a third marriage was the natural thing for the aging Flagler, seeking to squeeze some final happiness out of his wealth. Because New York would not grant him a divorce on the grounds of insanity, he moved his legal residence to Florida, whose divorce law was not more liberal, but was easier for him to change. Flagler was a much bigger fish there than in New York, with its great concentration of millionaires. Indeed, people used to joke that the abbreviation "Fla." stood for Flagler, rather than Florida.

On April 9, 1901, a new divorce law was introduced in the state legislature. On April 17 it passed in the Senate, and two days later it was approved by the House. On April 25 the governor signed it into law.

There was no doubt for whom it was written: its provisions fit Flagler to a T. Insanity was made grounds for divorce if it had existed for four years, if a court had adjudged it so and appointed a guardian, and if the wife was well provided for by her husband. They might as well have written the names Alicia and Henry into the act.

This was not lost on the public, and it crystallized anti-Flagler sentiment. He was charged with having bought the legislature, and his charities from that day forth were seen as crude attempts to pay the bill. Flagler, a product of the class and age that preached "The public be damned," was not dissuaded by the storm, and went right ahead and made it worse. On June 3, 1901, he filed for divorce under the new law. The case was heard on August 12, and the next day his request was granted.

A week later he announced his engagement to Mary Lily Kenan. Three days after that they were married. So that she would no longer be a poor relation, he had already given her $1 million worth of Standard Oil stock. Now he gratified her other wish: to live in a marble palace. Carrère and Hastings were brought in to build the finest house they could think of, in the shortest possible time, on Flagler's property at Palm Beach. Called "Whitehall," it was finished in eight months and cost as much as one of his hotels. Louis XIV or Marie Antoinette might have felt at home in its ornate halls, but lesser mortals found it utterly unlivable—like nothing so much as an over-decorated museum, with all the warmth of a mausoleum. Flagler commented, after living there a while, that he would have preferred a shack.

Mrs. Flagler, the stigma of being a kept woman having been removed, now made up for lost time by becoming a society queen in her new home. But the aftereffects of the divorce scandal would not go away, either in the public mind or in the more rarefied atmosphere of Palm Beach, which had not yet become the upper crust's spouse-shedding capital.

Flagler's second wife had been eighteen years younger than he; his third was thirty-seven years younger. Not even the fountain of youth could overcome that difference. While she was in her prime and ready to party, he was getting to be an old man and required his rest. With the prerogative of a king in his castle, he would stretch out on one of the expensive sofas, cover his eyes with a handkerchief, and take a nap—while his embarrassed wife greeted the guests. Fully intending to live to a hundred, he knew he wouldn't get there by dancing the night away.

• • •

Franklin Smith, after his experiments in Florida, had launched himself on the national scene. In a big way.

His mastery of Moorish and Etruscan architecture left him longing to take on the rest of history's styles. Almost twenty-five thousand visitors flocked to his Pompeiian house in Saratoga Springs during its first season, making it a financial success. Not only did they pay admission, but many bought the souvenir plaster mummies that were sold in the gift shop. More important, from Smith's point of view, they praised it as an educational experience. It made a vivid impression. More than half a century later a woman wrote to *The New York Times* recalling her youthful visit there: "When entering the atrium in the House of Pansa, with its sparkling fountain, and the peristylium, with its columns and goddesses, one felt like a Roman matron entering a home. Nothing was omitted."

Smith would have loved to read that letter. It justified his whole approach to cultural education for a deprived America.

The financial success convinced him that his approach was realistic rather than visionary, so he gathered together the thoughts of decades and in April 1890 ran them by his St. Augustine neighbor James Renwick. A passionate yachtsman, wealthy by both inheritance and marriage, Renwick had long been a winter resident of the Ancient City. To the public he was best known as the architect of St. Patrick's Cathedral and the Smithsonian Institution.

As he had previously done with Flagler, Smith spun his web and drew in Renwick, who volunteered the services of his firm to sketch out Smith's ideas so they could be presented to the public. A young architect named Bertram Grosvenor Goodhue, later to attain great distinction, spent months working on the project, resulting in the publication in 1891 of a profusely illustrated *Design & Prospectus for the National Gallery of History & Art.*

It was Franklin Smith's *summa,* and it was mind-boggling. A London newspaper called it "one of the most astonishing productions which has ever been issued from an American printing-office." Its author they dubbed "Reproduction Smith."

He had weighed all his experience, from the Gothic bird cage, Crystal Palace, and clay models through Villa Zorayda, the Casa Monica, and House of Pansa. He concluded that the next logical step was to take a 40-acre site next to the White House and build reproductions of the Taj Mahal, Saint Peter's Basilica, the Parthenon and Pantheon, sphinxes and pyramids, and more. The finest flower of every civilization would be reproduced in concrete in the nation's capital, making a one-stop culture shop for all who loved education and refinement. World travel would be rendered unnecessary, because the world's greatest attractions would be available at home, complete with guidebooks and costumed lecturers of whom Smith wrote: "I pre-suppose this professor to be a rare man; grand in physique; able in knowledge; energetic and benevolent in impulse; of utterance effective with unction not monotonous in the castanet tones of a showman." Nothing was left to chance. Everything from job descriptions to construction techniques to condemnation procedures was covered in the hundred-odd pages.

The London paper was stunned by "the most Titanic enterprise ever attempted by a mighty nation," but they did not doubt what the American people's response "to the wand of such an Enchanter will be."

Franklin Smith had enchanted a few people in his time. He had never taken on a whole nation, but he was willing to try. Establishing himself as "The Office of the Propaganda for the National Gallery," he started distributing the prospectus to legislators, journalists, educators, art lovers, and philanthropists. Purchasers of bulk orders were offered the immortality of being listed as "original propagandists of the National Gallery."

He found an angel in S. Walter Woodward, wealthy department-store owner, and was able to convert an ice-skating rink on New York Avenue into the Halls of the Ancients, a preview of the entire project that greeted visitors with the Pharaoh's Temple of Karnak, then led them through a Pompeiian annex on the way to the egress.

He followed this up with *Designs, Plans and Suggestions for the Aggrandizement of Washington*, suggesting an avenue of sphinxes leading up to the Washington Monument and a new, much grander Executive Mansion to replace the old White House, which he found excessively modest though worthy of preservation as a historic monument. Both this and his earlier prospectus were published as congressional documents by the Government Printing Office in 1900.

In 1904 he launched *Washington* magazine, "In advocacy of a national society for the aggrandizement of Washington."

Propaganda work kept him too busy to resort in St. Augustine, so he opened Villa Zorayda to public gawkers at 50 cents a head. Then, in 1902, he leased it out as "a gentlemen's high-class club for the accommodation of visitors to the city." No sense letting it go to waste while greater tasks occupied the owner. Besides, he needed the money.

A querulous tone entered the writings of his later years, as he complained about printing costs and lack of contributions. The truth was, he was going broke. He had been philanthropic beyond his means. The financial panic that hit the country in 1907 found him bankrupt. His precious properties were put on the block, but their very uniqueness kept them from finding a ready market.

He should have been cherished as a national character. Instead, he spent his last years trying to stave off disaster. After he died in 1911, at the age of eighty-five, his Pompeiian house became a Masonic temple, Villa Zorayda was transformed into a gambling casino, and the Halls of the Ancients were finally torn down for a garage.

Franklin Smith suffered the fate of a man ahead of his time. The sorrow of failure plagued his final days, but, down the road, ideas like his would prove a bonanza for other entrepreneurs.

• • •

Carrère and Hastings, the other architectural colossi of the second Florida boom, fared much better financially. Flagler stopped having them design his hotels, but he gave them other lucrative jobs, such as the Standard Oil Building in New York. His patronage—and their talent—opened many doors for them. A list of their clients reads like a history of the great American fortunes: Vanderbilt, Rockefeller, Guggenheim, Harriman, Carnegie, du Pont, and Astor. They designed many marble mansions and French châteaux for these millionaires, replete with statuary, fountains and reflecting pools, peristyles and pergolas, arches, domes, quoins, columns, balustrades, festoons, and garlands. Their Beaux-Arts training in ornamentation did not go to waste.

In 1910 the *Architectural Record* placed them at the forefront of the profession and credited them with bettering the work of their predecessors, McKim, Mead and White. They received much attention for their Senate and House Office Buildings in Washington in 1906, but their most famous (and longest-running) commission was for the New York Public Library, begun in 1897 and completed in 1911.

Shortly before the library was done, John Carrère planned a tour of Europe with his family. He was going around saying good-bye to his friends when the cab he was riding in collided with a streetcar; Carrère was ejected and thrown 10 feet to the ground. *The New York Times* demanded editorially that "something should be done, quickly, to compel taxicab chauffeurs to pay some regard to the safety of their passengers." Daily reports were given on the architect's condition, some of them hopeful. But he never fully recovered consciousness, and death claimed him on March 3, 1911. The cab driver was arrested for homicide, and Mrs. Carrère collected the largest accident insurance claim that had ever been paid.

The library whose construction he had so diplomatically guided over the years was first opened to the public so the architect's body could lie in state in its rotunda.

His partner, Thomas Hastings, was laid low with typhoid at that time, and was soon additionally bereaved by the loss of the minister father whose wealthy parishioner had launched the architectural firm a quarter century before.

With so many sorrows, at least he didn't have to worry about going broke. Business was prospering, and he had married the daughter of a wealthy client, who was not only rich but beautiful, having been one of the original models for the Gibson Girl.

He could even afford to build his dream house—though by the time he got around to it he found he had already designed it for a client. He went ahead gamely with another version, only to see it burn soon after, then rebuilt it with modifications and told friends that every house should burn at least once so that improvements based on occupancy could be incorporated into it.

After Carrère's death, Hastings chose to devote himself to

monumental architecture, including parks, memorials, and city plans, but not skyscrapers, which he loathed. He tried to get New York to limit those "elongated packing boxes" by law to eight stories, warning that anything higher would paralyze traffic and injure the health of the citizens by blocking out sunshine. He became an evangelist for these views, joking that in his early days he had run away from reporters and now he ran after them.

Both as an architect and as a member of the Fine Arts Commission, he made many contributions to the good looks of Washington, D.C. He worked on the Capitol building itself, as well as the adjacent congressional offices. His personal favorite among his works was the Memorial Amphitheatre at the Tomb of the Unknown Soldier, which pleased him even more than the Ponce de Leon Hotel. Hastings took the original plans of Pierre L'Enfant as a guide for his work in Washington—not those of his old friend Franklin Smith.

• • •

Henry Flagler last called on Carrère and Hastings in 1906 to design his final resting place, a domed mausoleum attached to Memorial Presbyterian Church in St. Augustine. He had no immediate plans for using it, however: he had just launched his most ambitious project and intended to see it through.

He was going to extend his railroad to Key West, 150 miles beyond Miami. Half the distance was over marsh and water, the rest a series of islands in the Florida Keys. Dwarfing his other projects in scale, cost, and difficulty, it attracted international attention.

Not everyone was entranced. One Miami businessman, remembering what happened to St. Augustine when the line was extended to Palm Beach, complained: "Miami was founded on the idea that this was to be the southern terminus of the road, and those of us who have located in Miami did so with that understanding; and now the town is doomed to decay and death, because there is no possibility of its surviving an extension of the road on beyond here to Key West."

It was not a new idea: Key Westers had been pushing it as long as there had been railroads. But it took someone of Flagler's boldness and wealth to undertake the task, and even he approached it gingerly, over a ten-year period.

He had begun buying land along the way in 1895. In 1899 he bought the Key West newspaper—as insurance rather than as an investment; Flagler had a generally low opinion of the press. He once said, "If I had to take my choice between a den of rattlesnakes and a newspaper, I think I would prefer the snakes." But, realizing the power of the press, he bought or started newspapers every place his railroad went.

Even after his men had investigated the prospects for the extension carefully, he waited until it was clear that the Panama Canal was going to be built. That gave Key West a particularly strategic location which, Flagler hoped, would turn it into the "American Gibraltar." Not until 1905 did he announce his plans to the public.

This was the most expensive project he had launched, consuming about 40 percent of his Florida investment, and was the first undertaking he could not finance out of his own pocket. It was a bad time to borrow: the Panic of 1907 seriously deranged the economy, and he had to convince bankers of the J. P. Morgan stripe to lend him money at the same time that they were suggesting he needed a guardian.

He succeeded. One awed moneyman on an inspection trip remarked reverently, "When the pyramids have crumbled into dust this structure will still stand unharmed by time."

The construction tale is an epic. Denizens of the Skid Rows of the nation were solicited when more sober workers declined the risks. On payday, booze boats peddled their wares, until chased off by supervisors. On other days, water boats were the only source of potable refreshment. The government charged the railroad with violating peonage laws by retaining men against their will.

Six hurricanes, two of them back-to-back, slammed against the project, damaging inadequately designed sections and sweeping away large numbers of men. The lucky ones next set foot on land in Europe or South America, where rescuing vessels deposited them. The unlucky were never seen again.

The magnitude of the task captured the public imagination, with harsh judgments against Flagler softened by an appreciation of his heroic undertaking.

Flagler was growing feeble, his sight almost gone, his hearing going. With a final burst of effort, the extension was completed twenty-four hours before his eighty-second birthday. On January 22, 1912, Flagler rode the first official train into Key West and was greeted by a massive celebration hailing the "Eighth Wonder of the World." A thousand schoolchildren serenaded him. Though he could hear their voices, he could not see their faces. But they could see the tears streaming down his face. It was his finest hour.

• • •

A year later Henry Flagler slipped on the marble steps at Whitehall and broke his hip. He complained to his minister, "Do you think that was just fair of God? I was old and blind and deaf, was it fair to make me lame?"

He rallied only slightly, then lingered for months without hope of recovery. Railroad officials received regular coded reports on his condition. An empire hung in the balance.

He finally just wore out. Harry Harkness Flagler, who had not seen his father since 1901, was sent for at the end, but the old man was in a coma and could not recognize him. All that remained were the bitter words in his will, "My son has not shown for me the filial regard that would make me inclined to do more for him." Leaving Harry a small bequest, he provided that if his son contested the will he should be cut off completely. In other versions he had toyed with over the years, he had provided contingencies to distribute the fortune among cousins, in-laws, and employees rather than let his son receive any substantial portion.

Henry Flagler died on May 20, 1913, and the young Mrs. Flagler, his main beneficiary, did not long survive him: after remarrying in December 1916, she died the next summer. Enough eyebrows were raised at the $5 million bequest she made to her husband of so few months standing that her body was exhumed and examined, to make sure there was no foul play.

The bulk of her estate, the great Flagler fortune, was left to her favorite niece. There was a stipulation that the niece give none of it to her father, who had divorced Mrs. Flagler's sister. Money did not buy love in that family either.

Henry Flagler's death coincided with the passing of an era. A month after he was buried, the Sixteenth Amendment to the Constitution was ratified, providing for a federal income tax. Never again would a man like Flagler enjoy such unhindered use of his wealth.

That same year the governor of Florida proposed that the land grants to railroads be eliminated, and the era of Plant and Flagler was completed. The boom they had figured in so prominently died—like its kings—of old age.

DA EAST COAST

(OPPOSITE, TOP): Behind the ornate gates lies Whitehall, the marble mansion at Palm Beach that Henry Flagler built for his third wife.

(OPPOSITE, BOTTOM): An aged Henry Flagler (*clutching his straw hat*) is surrounded by welcoming crowds as the first official train makes its triumphant entry into Key West in 1912.

(RIGHT): Mrs. Potter Palmer, queen of society and booster of Sarasota.

(BELOW): John Ringling, who went from circus clown to one of the richest men in the world.

READY, GET SET...

•

Florida had lived with Flagler for such a long time that the habit of looking to the king to undertake great projects had become deeply ingrained. Who would take his place?

The state did not lack wealthy winter residents. Miami had merchant prince John Wanamaker and steelmaker-turned-philanthropist Andrew Carnegie. Less well known, but a much bigger spender, was James Deering of International Harvester, who wound up pouring about $8 million into his Miami estate, Vizcaya, and employing a tenth of the city's workforce in its construction.

Richer than all of them was John D. Rockefeller. Although he had long resisted his partner's blandishments, the year after Flagler's death he finally established himself in Florida. He wanted to live to the age of a hundred and had his doctors search out the healthiest possible place. When they recommended Ormond Beach, Rockefeller rented a wing of Flagler's old hotel there. A few years later he bought a house across the street—because, local legend insists, Rockefeller thought he was being overcharged at the hotel.

He spent each winter at Ormond Beach (and finally died there, just short of the century mark), playing a gentle game of golf, reciting home-made poems to visiting celebrities like Will Rogers, handing out the shiny dimes that were his trademark, and avoiding anyone who wanted to talk about investments.

The super-rich did Florida little good when they kept such a tight rein on their checkbooks. Flagler's crown remained unbestowed.

Meanwhile, the twentieth century saw women's increasing emancipation, and there were those who thought Florida's next king might be a queen. This view was especially prevalent in the sleepy Gulf Coast fishing village of Sarasota. There was, of course, a candidate at hand for coronation: Mrs. Potter Palmer of Chicago, Newport, Bar Harbor, London, Paris, and—most recently—Sarasota.

One chilly, windy January day in 1910, she was reading the newspaper at Palmer Castle, her million-dollar home on Chicago's Lake Shore Drive, when an ad caught her eye for a citrus grove in sunny Florida. She decided to investigate. Accompanied by a retinue of father, brother, sons, and servants, she headed south.

Sarasotans had a few days' notice to prepare. Their hotel was rundown, and its cesspool wafted unpleasant odors back into the dining room. Since that would not do for the great Mrs. Palmer, a new sanitarium on the waterfront was spiffed up and put at her disposal instead.

People were delighted that she found their town "quaint" rather than dirty and depressing, which might have been equally applicable adjectives. She asked to see everything that was for sale. Her buying spree netted 80,000 acres around Sarasota and another 60,000 near Tampa. Costs ran from $8 to $400 an acre.

She was enchanted. "Here is heaven at last," she said. "It reminds me of the Bay of Naples." Those words were routinely quoted in advertising copy for the area for years to come. You couldn't have a more impressive booster than Mrs. Potter Palmer, the dazzling queen of society.

• • •

Potter Palmer was a Quaker shopkeeper from New York State who settled early in Chicago and watched his fortune grow with the city. An innovator in merchandising and advertising, he saw practices that had begun in his department store copied by merchants as far away as New York and Paris. By the time the Civil War was over, he was rich—and exhausted. Not yet forty, he was worth about $7 million. He sold his store to Marshall Field and Levi Leiter, and invested the money in real estate, planning a new downtown business district. After Chicago burned in 1871, it was rebuilt just along the lines he had envisioned.

By that time Palmer had taken a wife. He had kept his eye on Bertha Honore since she was thirteen, persevering in his quest until she reached twenty-one and accepted him as her husband. He was forty-four.

As a wedding present he gave her the $3.5-million Palmer House hotel, famed for the silver dollars set in the barbershop floor. A critical Rudyard Kipling dismissed the place as a "gilded and mirrored rabbit warren" crammed with "barbarians," but not everyone was so harsh.

Not Ulysses S. Grant, for instance, who visited in 1874 when his son married Mrs. Palmer's sister. He offered Potter Palmer a Cabinet position, which was declined on the grounds that it might look like nepotism.

Mrs. Palmer's fame as Chicago's greatest hostess was not hurt at all by the presidential connection, nor by the jewels that her husband lavished on her and loved to see her wear. No small-minded snob, she was socially concerned as well as society-conscious: a supporter of Jane Addams of Hull House, a backer of Frances E. Willard's Women's Christian Temperance Union, an endorser of the Women's Trade Union League, and an advocate of equal pay for equal work. She was also a tastemaker in cultural affairs, pioneering the introduction of Impressionist art into the United States.

In 1891 she was unanimously elected president of the Board of Lady Managers of the World's Columbian Exposition. She proved as adept at dealing with the world as she had with Chicago. When a visiting Spanish princess declined to accept the hospitality of "an innkeeper's wife," Mrs. Palmer shot back scathingly that her royal highness was just a "bibulous representative of a degenerate monarchy." The only woman to rival Mrs. Palmer's fame at the fair was Little Egypt, the Cleopatra of the Midway.

After that, as Potter Palmer's health began to decline, they spent several years touring the fashionable spas, royally entertaining the horsey set, and standing on equal ground with the resorting nobility.

When he died in 1902, he left his wife $8 million. The lawyer preparing his will reminded him that Mrs. Palmer might remarry. "If she does, he'll need the money" was the reply.

Marshall Field was appalled. "A million dollars is enough for any woman," was his firmly held belief.

• • •

Mrs. Palmer had started out as a society queen quite early in life. Now her old friends were dropping off one by one: a king here, a president there, an artist, a suffragist, a temperance crusader. The world was changing, but, having scaled the heights of the old one, she saw no need for a repeat performance in the twentieth century. She was an institution, her position secure, and she knew it. Now she should take on something else.

Her husband's parting advice was for her to invest in real estate. With her chunk of Florida heaven she did just that. She had ambitious plans and proved to be as astute at business as she had been at preparing guest lists and planning entertainments.

She planned to become the world's largest grapefruit grower (citrus had made a comeback from the 1894–95 freeze, till production finally returned to pre-disaster levels in 1910).

She set up a model cattle ranch, bringing in midwestern technology, including vats to dip the cattle in for ticks. Natives originally feared the dipping would kill the animals, but learned otherwise from her example. She brought in Brahma bulls for breeding with the scrawny, stringy range cattle that had roamed Florida since colonial times. Never had the state seen such high-class animals as her ranch produced. She also fenced her pastures, only to see the barbed wire clipped and reclipped by Floridians to whom the open range was a more sacred cow than private property.

Of course she planned a resort too, complete with racetrack. Wherever she went her friends would follow, and there had to be suitable accommodations and diversions for them.

She set to work with a will, planning roads, irrigation ditches, crops, and landscaping. She talked the railroad into building a spur line to her property, to make it more accessible. She became the best-paying of local employers.

Chicagoans followed her lead by investing in Sarasota. The fishing village of 840 people began to grow. It acquired electricity, waterworks, sewage system, yacht club, bank, and movie theater.

Mrs. Palmer continued to travel, keeping in touch with her Sarasota manager to make sure the work was progressing. The outbreak of World War I in the summer of 1914 found her at her Paris home, which she hastily evacuated, abandoning her Rolls-Royce at the boat dock. A fortune in household *objets d'art* was shipped to London for safekeeping while she returned to America and war work. In 1916 she attended a war-relief benefit in Palm Beach and wowed them with her jewels, which took some doing there.

Sarasota was a place to escape from the cares of a world in turmoil. Father, sister, aunt and uncle, brothers, sons, and grandchildren all built or vacationed nearby. Mrs. Palmer had originally thought to build another castle but settled finally for remodeling an existing house on the property, which she called "The Oaks." As a bow to the informality of this "beach cottage," she cut down on the amount of jewelry she wore when in residence. But she still dressed in Paris gowns for dinner, and paintings by Monet, Degas, and Cassatt hung on the walls.

She took particular delight in the landscaping, a blend of formal and found. A sunken garden was framed by ancient Indian mounds, and statuary bordered paths through the moss-hung live oaks. "I have found my one talent, if I have any, at Sarasota Bay," she said modestly. "It is to watch beautiful things grow and see flowers blossom as I plant them."

Mrs. Palmer's niece Julia Dent Grant was born in the White House while grandfather (and godfather) Ulysses Grant was president. As the only female of her generation in the family, she was virtually adopted as a daughter by her wealthy aunt. Mrs. Palmer sponsored her coming-out party at Newport and took her to the Riviera, where she met Prince Michael Cantacuzène, who became her husband. Living with him in Russia, Julia became a great favorite at the court of the czar. With the Revolution and the execution of the Romanovs, their coterie fled. The Cantacuzènes joined the family circle in Sarasota and had no more worries about facing a firing squad. Their children could enjoy the rustic camp Mrs. Palmer had established for their generation.

But not everything was idyllic. Although people were generally well behaved while Mrs. Palmer was around, they got out of hand in her absence. Her manager at The Oaks had his life threatened several times.

"I have been greatly annoyed," she wrote, "by the annual criminal assaults on my place and on my innocent, unprotected, sleeping Negroes, by cowardly bands of armed men who came at night to shoot them up and drive them away." She backed her complaints up with a threat: "I should feel very badly to help put any man in the chain gang but perhaps it is our duty."

This, plus her sense, common among her class, that everyone was trying to make a profit off of her, were contributing factors to her decision, finally, not to build a resort. She had a city planner estimate costs to develop a hotel and other facilities on her property at Venice, south of Sarasota, but was horrified to see the price tag. It would have cost more than Flagler had poured into Palm Beach. Mrs. Palmer was not that rich, nor was she that seriously bitten by the Florida bug.

Her health was also beginning to fail. For two years she battled with cancer, then, on May 5, 1918, died at The Oaks. Sarasota's flags were flown at half mast to honor the woman whose social cachet had helped launch their city.

She left an estate of $20 million—more than double the fortune inherited from her husband. Although she'd had her disappointments in Florida, she was not among those who were bankrupted by it.

• • •

World War I was still raging in Europe when Mrs. Palmer died —one reason that neither she nor anyone else succeeded to the crown of Henry Flagler. It was not a "splendid little war" that gave the economy a shot in the arm. It was an all-embracing conflict that had a disorienting effect on the traditional economy. Florida hotel owners saw their occupancy rates up, as former habitués of the Riviera were forced to vacation at home. But the phosphate industry went into a depression, because its market was Europe and ships were no longer traveling that way. Some things boomed and others busted, but nothing was normal.

This was a time not for crowning, but, rather, for lining up, for getting in place until the winds of war had blown over and postwar prosperity could work its magic. The line was forming, and those who had the patience to wait were those who would succeed. It was time for the long view, not the quick killing.

Among those who went to Sarasota in Mrs. Palmer's wake was circus king John Ringling. He first hit town in 1911 and liked it enough that the next year he bought the waterfront home of another impresario, Colonel Charles Thompson of Buffalo Bill's Wild West Show. If Mrs. Palmer represented society at its most refined, the circus king, both by inclination and occupation, represented the rowdier kind.

The seven Ringling brothers had been inspired early in life to set up their own circus. There were enough of them to fill most of the positions—John's first role was as a clown. After struggling through the 1880s against tough competitors like P. T. Barnum and Buffalo Bill Cody, they prospered in the Gay Nineties; in 1907 they were able to buy out the opposition Barnum and Bailey Circus at such a good price that a single season earned them their money back.

By that time the Ringlings had moved out of the rings and into the front office. The former clown became the family expert on railroad routes and schedules. This took a lot of traveling, and as he went he looked around for business opportunities far removed from the big top. His investments ran the gamut from steam laundries to oil wells, from movie theaters to streetcar lines. He was particularly fond of short-line railroads. When he built one to Broken Jaw, Montana, the town was renamed in his honor. Another short line he built into oil country stopped at Ringling, Oklahoma. His name was on the map, his picture was in the papers, and he surpassed his brothers in public recognition and living the good life. The family sport became one of the wealthiest men in the world.

Like Mrs. Palmer, he was an art collector—though of a different genre. His personal favorite was a large recumbent nude that hung over his bar. He poured millions into old masters, educating himself about them so he wouldn't be taken in by conniving dealers. He thought almost everyone was conniving when it came time to pay the bills.

Also like Mrs. Palmer, he gathered his family around him in Sarasota. In 1912 he persuaded brother Charles to buy adjoining property. The next year two other brothers and their only sister came as well.

Apart from his residential estate, John Ringling began picking up other pieces of land: 66,000 acres on the Myakka River; the yacht club's downtown waterfront property; and, starting in 1917, the keys that lay between Sarasota and the Gulf of Mexico.

John Ringling was getting in line, and his brother Charles was not far behind.

• • •

Miami did not wither away, as the Cassandras predicted, with the completion of Flagler's Key West extension. Nor had it grown as fast as Julia Tuttle hoped when she went into debt to prime the pump. It attracted a winter crowd, but for the rest of the year "you could swim bare-assed in the bay" without attracting throngs of onlookers.

The spit of barrier land between Biscayne Bay and the Atlantic Ocean had been the site of a failed coconut plantation, then a more profitable avocado grove. With the growing popularity of surf bathing it seemed the land could make more as a resort—if people could get there. All it would take was the longest wooden bridge in the world for cars to drive over. The recent completion of Flagler's extension made this seem like a minor task, and the owners of the property forged right ahead.

By November 1912 the bridge extended well out into Biscayne Bay but stopped short of its destination: the builders had run out of money. Along came Carl Fisher, the man of whom Will Rogers would later say, "Had there been no Carl Fisher, Florida would be known today as the Turpentine State." He was the right man in the right place at the right time with the right amount of money in his pocket. In return for putting up $50,000 to finish the bridge, he received the usual legal papers plus a mile-long piece of the land spit as a bonus. He acquired another 150-acre lot for lending neighboring property owners $150,000 when they were caught short.

That spit of land was Miami Beach, and, having gotten such a large chunk of it, Fisher naturally sought to develop it as something more productive than mangrove lowlands. As Will Rogers put it, once "Carl discovered that sand could hold up a Real Estate sign" he was on his way.

It was a second—or third or fourth?—career for Fisher, who had not yet reached the age of forty.

Carl Graham Fisher was a native Indiana Hoosier from a disintegrated family with an alcoholic father. He dropped out of school in the sixth grade and put his wits to work for him. In that age of speed and ballyhoo, Carl mastered both and turned them to profit.

The fastest things around were trains and bicycles, and he worked on both of them. As a teen-aged news butcher on the railroad, he later claimed, he concealed a picture of a naked woman under his change apron. When things got slow he flashed the picture to build up good will with traveling salesmen and found it helped business no end. That was ballyhoo.

When the bicycle craze of the nineties swept the country, he got in on the ground floor, patching tires. Then he opened a bicycle shop with his brothers. Business was okay, but it needed a little ballyhoo, so Fisher rode a bicycle across a busy street downtown—on a tightrope twelve stories above the ground. That got their attention.

Then came cars. He owned the first one in Indianapolis and turned part of his bike shop into a garage. He dropped a car off the tallest building in town, then cranked it up and drove away. Sales soared.

Those early cars were primitive and called for lots of improvements. Fisher and James Allison's company, Prest-O-Lite, devised headlights that actually let you see where you were going at night. Their product became standard equipment on cars, and in 1911 Union Carbide bought them out. Carl's share was $5,633,556.44.

Some of it he used to improve and promote his Indianapolis Speedway, first opened in 1909. Some more of it went to publicize another scheme: the first coast-to-coast highway. Cars had to have some place to go and something to travel on besides gumbo. Carl organized those with vested interests—auto magnates, tire manufacturers, paving contractors—and got a war chest to encourage places from New York to San Francisco to pitch in and make the nation safe for drivers. It was called the Lincoln Highway, after the president whose hundredth birthday had recently been celebrated with such great fanfare. He was one of Carl Fisher's personal heroes.

Fisher had plenty of money left over to vacation in Miami, and while there he was bitten by the Florida bug. Legend has it that Miami Beach, in all its glitter and tinsel, sprang full-blown from Fisher's brow the first time he set eyes on the mangrove swamp. That's what he would have liked—he was a great one for doing things fast—but he had to go through a period of trial and error first.

As it stood, the land was a great place to hunt raccoons, catch snakes, trap rats, or be eaten alive by mosquitoes. They were its natural inhabitants.

Fisher had a bulkhead built along the bay side of his property, then brought in dredges to pump up sand and marl from the bottom. It made an awful stink as marine organisms slowly rotted in the sun, but when it was done, not only had the mangrove swamp become high land, but the bay was deep enough for motorboat races. Carl Fisher loved races.

A small army planted hibiscus and oleander and Australian pine and grass so the new land wouldn't blow away in the first breeze. Roads were built, as were tennis courts, the area's first golf course, and grandstands from which to watch the upcoming speedboat races.

Building lots were put up for sale, but there was no rush to snap them up. Time for a little more ballyhoo. Fisher's hometown bard, Hoosier poet James Whitcomb Riley, was brought over to plant a tree and recite some homespun doggerel. A polo field was added to the sporting attractions. The modest bathing pavilion grew into the Roman Pools, with a Dutch windmill to bring in the water. The pools gave Fisher another idea: "We'll get the prettiest girls we can find and put them into the goddamndest tightest and shortest bathing suits and no stockings or swim shoes either. We'll have their pictures taken and send them all over the goddamn country." Thus were born the bathing beauties that became Miami Beach's trademark. The original versions would raise eyebrows today only for their incredible dowdiness.

He had one more trick up his sleeve. The Lincoln Highway had been such a success, he decided to do another one. This time it would be the Dixie Highway, running from Michigan all the way down to his doorstep in Miami. If that didn't bring them in, nothing would.

Nothing would. With the world at war and America belatedly entering in a combat role, it was not the time to launch a new development.

Fisher had a lot of money sunk into Miami Beach and would have to bide his time until conditions changed before getting anything back. He couldn't just walk away from it. As he told a friend, "When you've got a bull by the tail, you can't let go."

Carl Fisher and his bull were lining up.

• • •

Fisher was not the only speed demon around Miami those days. Another ex–bicycle mechanic, named Glenn Curtiss, was also very much in evidence.

Curtiss had grown up in the same part of New York State

that produced Henry Flagler. While fixing and racing bicycles, he also tinkered with internal combustion engines on the side. He attached one to a bicycle and whizzed along so fast he decided to do it professionally.

A popular racing spot in those days was the beach at Ormond, Florida. Henry Flagler thought automobilists were a bunch of cranks, but he bowed to the inevitable and gave them special rates to bring their machines in on his railroad so they could race them down the broad sandy beach—which was better than most of the existing roads. Louis Chevrolet, Ransom Olds, Henry Ford, Barney Oldfield, and Willie Vanderbilt were among those who came.

Glenn Curtiss joined them in 1904 and set a speed record that lasted for years. In 1907 he was back, with a souped-up motorcycle that the judges clocked at 136.3 miles an hour. Newspapers hailed him as "the fastest man in the world."

Dr. Alexander Graham Bell, an early aviation enthusiast, joined forces with Curtiss and others to form the Aerial Experiment Association. The Fastest Man in the World put his engine into airplanes and set some more records. He made the first public flight of over a mile, set an international speed record, and electrified the world with his daring flight all the way from Albany to New York City in 1910. Along the way he got involved in patent litigation with the Wright brothers that dragged the aviation pioneers through the courts and through the mud for years.

The way to make money in those early years was to win prizes and put on exhibitions. When Miami wanted to celebrate its fifteenth birthday in style, officials paid a member of the Wright flying team to put on an aerial exhibition over the city. Then they decided an aviation school would lend the locality further distinction. The Wrights weren't interested, but Glenn Curtiss was.

He had devised a hydroplane that would take off and land on the water. Biscayne Bay would be an ideal place not only to test it, he figured, but also to demonstrate its possibilities to "men of prominence who were accustomed to go to Florida during the winter season." When the city came up with $1,000 and the gift of a field on Miami Beach, Curtiss opened Florida's first flying school, in 1912. He did not supervise it personally, but he did spend some time at Flagler's Royal Palm Hotel in 1916. By then the avocado trees were not the only occupants of Miami Beach, and the new ones protested to Curtiss about the throbbing and buzzing of his low-flying planes. When one of his daring young men went courting in a flying machine and dropped a love letter attached to a grapefruit that made an awful mess on landing, Curtiss agreed to look for another site. Inland from Miami he found a vast cattle-grazing field, suitably remote and unpopulated, and asked to buy it. The owner, James Bright, was only too glad to donate a section to the famous aviator.

Glenn Curtiss thought he was just building an airfield, but actually he was lining up.

• • •

Then there was the dreamer.

George Merrick was a local boy who grew up with Miami. There wasn't much of it when he arrived in 1898, at the age of twelve. His father, Reverend Solomon Merrick, was a New England minister whose wife could no longer stand the harsh winters. With $1,100 in savings he bought a 160-acre farm in the sticks beyond Flagler's new city and grew vegetables that George peddled from the back of a mule wagon. The money they made was put into orange seedlings, because the dream of golden apples still lived that far south in Florida.

The Merricks prospered enough to buy additional acreage and build a house of the distinctive native rock. Reverend Merrick was an admirer of Grover Cleveland, whose summer home in Massachusetts was called Grey Gables. Borrowing from that and adding a local touch, the minister called his place Coral Gables.

George went off to college, first at Rollins, then at Columbia. He did well, though his preparation had been a bit sketchy (he never received a high-school diploma), but his college career was cut short when his father fell ill and George returned home to manage the family property. Solomon Merrick died in 1911.

In 1916 George took a bride, Eunice Peacock, whose parents had operated the first hotel in the area. Coral Gables Plantation prospered and grew, becoming a showplace. But George was not content to leave it at that. He was stirred by visions of the City Beautiful, a movement that swept the country after the 1893 Columbian Exposition. The area was so beautiful, George reasoned, why not build an ideal community there? Everything would be done with a touch of art: ugliness would be banished by good planning and stiff architectural controls. It would be a suburb free from the urban blight that, even at that early date, plagued Miami.

When he took his idea to the bankers, however, they dismissed him as a dreamer. It would never work. Coral Gables was miles from the water. Nobody would buy there. George Merrick should stick to his fruit growing and poetry and stay clear of the development business.

Instead, he went to work in a real-estate office and began acquiring land, moving Coral Gables, bit by bit, closer to the water.

George Merrick was getting in line.

Miami bathing beauties of 1920 in their daring outfits.

(ABOVE): Addison Mizner, architect and society wit, who found his niche in Palm Beach.

(RIGHT): Carl Fisher, speed king and master of ballyhoo, in his favorite floppy hat.

•

Two men had come to Palm Beach to die. It got boring. As they sat rocking on the porch of the Royal Poinciana Hotel, it struck them that reports of their impending demise had been greatly exaggerated.

"What are you going to do about it?" asked one.

"What would you do about it," said the other, turning the question around, "if you could do anything you wanted?"

"I'd build something that wasn't made of wood," was the answer. "And I wouldn't paint it yellow."

Henry Flagler's favorite color was a lemon variant known officially as "Florida East Coast Yellow." The man who didn't like it was Addison Mizner. His hefty bulk, approaching 300 pounds, had arrived at Palm Beach on a stretcher in 1918. He was suffering from a general breakdown as well as an impressive variety of particular ailments, and had borrowed the money to get there by promising his friends that he wouldn't be around to borrow much longer.

The man who rocked next to him had arrived similarly debilitated but not equally in debt. His name was Paris Singer. His father had procreated an impressive twenty-four children and produced an even more impressive fortune in the sewing-machine business. Paris had devoted much of his life to spending that fortune. He loved art and artists—particularly Isadora Duncan, who had recently jilted him.

In his off hours he donated hospitals. He had given one to England and one to France; now it was America's turn. Since a war was going on, the wounded needed a place to recuperate. Why not Palm Beach? Singer would donate the facilities.

Mizner would design them. He was an architect, of sorts. He had no license, but he did have a great sense of beauty, color, composition, landscaping—all the big things. And he had a meticulous knowledge of all the fine crafts involved. It was the area in between—embracing all the subjects that architecture schools taught—where he was weak. He lacked even some of the most basic skills. Addition and subtraction were not his strong points, and he boasted that he couldn't spell in any language.

But he knew just what he needed to know to bring about a revolution in Florida architecture.

Paris Singer launched him. As the hospital walls rose, Palm Beachers were not at all sure they approved. There was even talk of getting an injunction, though nothing came of it. When the building took shape it appeared to grow from a Spanish mission on Lake Worth to a Mediterranean tower as it moved inland. It was definitely neither wooden nor yellow. Palm Beachers were intrigued. It reminded them of the Riviera, from which they had been barred by wartime travel restrictions. They could examine its many intricate and ingenious facets up close—without ever having to see a wounded soldier, for it never opened as a hospital: the war ended. Why waste such a good building? It opened, instead, as the Everglades Club, with Paris Singer deciding, year by year, who could hold membership. That made him a social arbiter—one of the busiest jobs in town. He forgot all about dying.

Mizner didn't have time to die either. Mrs. Edward T. Stotesbury, queen of resort society (and one-time mother-in-law of Douglas MacArthur), wanted him to design a cottage for her in the same style. It was a modest affair, just thirty-seven rooms. Fewer than the number of baths in the family's 145-room Philadelphia home.

Mrs. Stotesbury was a tastemaker. What she had, others copied. Commissions poured in. "Playa Riente," which Mizner designed for the new-rich Joshua Cosdens, was so huge that Mrs. Stotesbury called the architect back to do an addition on her "El Mirasol" so it wouldn't be overshadowed. That launched a kind of warfare: rival hostesses would fight it out, wielding Mizner architecture as a weapon. Each house had to cost more and have a new set of special effects or the owner would be seen as a piker or a has-been.

Mizner loved it, encouraged it. He was right in his element, and he knew just how to treat his patrons.

"If an architect could chloroform his client," he once said, "the house would be more attractive and coherent." Then he added, smiling, "Possibly I have used a little of that chloroform on my clients."

He built during the off season, when his patrons were elsewhere. Returning the next winter, they were presented with *faits accomplis.* If they didn't like the result, he cursed them. His insults were treasured. As Paris Singer noted, "His mastery of Tavern English is a joy to everybody within hearing."

Addison Mizner was a whole show. Palm Beach was his stage. He not only designed the set, but wrote the script and played the lead during its flashiest era.

• • •

Mizner's road to Flagler's paradise had certainly been roundabout. He had hand-colored stereoptican slides in Samoa, boxed professionally in Australia, panned for gold in the Klondike, been decorated by the deposed Queen Liliuokalani in Hawaii, and courted an heiress who jumped to her death from a seventh-story window of the Waldorf-Astoria. A con man with gilded credentials, he dealt in art, architecture, antiques, sarcasm, and society.

His great-great-uncle was the artist Sir Joshua Reynolds—a kinship that showed, he said, in the fact that "I josh and I paint." Two of his uncles were generals, another was governor of Washington, and his father barely missed a bid to become governor of California.

The Mizners were recognized as part of the pioneer American aristocracy in California, at least until they started to go astray, in Addison's generation. Mama Mizner, a young belle who became a *grande dame*, once called her brood together—all ton and a half of them—and complained: "Lord, Lord, when you were all young I had some ambition for you; I thought at one time you would be presidents of the United States, bishops, and men of ability and respect; but, now the only ambition I have for you is to keep you out of state prison."

The children must have picked up their wit from her. When one wired, "Please send me five hundred at once," she turned the message over and wrote, "Sorry did not receive your telegram."

Lansing Bond Mizner, the father of the clan, perspicaciously supported Benjamin Harrison for president in 1888 and was rewarded the next year with an appointment as minister plenipotentiary to five Central American countries. The teen-aged Addison went along, thus developing a taste for Spanish colonial architecture, filling his sketchbook with details that would later reappear in Palm Beach. A stint at the University of Salamanca in Spain further educated him along those lines.

When he returned to San Francisco he apprenticed himself to an impecunious architect, read his library, and became a partner in lieu of pay. That could not last forever, though; before long he left for a decade of around-the-world adventuring in search of wealth. He wound up in New York, where his wit made him a society pet. He met—and worshipped—Stanford White, who threw a few small jobs his way. By the second decade of the twentieth century Mizner was practicing architecture—

without a license but with a good address on Park Avenue, a few wealthy clients, and an outside income from his scavenging work, which took on international proportions.

"Thou shalt not covet was the command I broke most often and generally I broke it hardest in the great churches and monasteries," he once said, boasting, "I have looted cathedrals, churches and palaces, and brought a shipload or two of everything from stone doorways to fine laces from both Central America and Europe."

Those he could bear to part with found a ready market, and the best he kept for himself. The Addison Mizner Crucifix Collection, now in a Palm Beach museum, is quite impressive, if your tastes run in that direction. He didn't steal them, exactly: he bought them from impoverished clerics and carted them off with the aid of highly placed friends, including the king of Spain. "That little son of a bitch will do anything for me," Mizner bragged affectionately.

Then came World War I, injury in a robbery, the death of his beloved mother, financial reverses, physical collapse, and Mizner was bundled off to Palm Beach.

He had been something of a Renaissance man, but his efforts were so scattered and diffused that he really hadn't left his mark. The brush with death narrowed his focus—to enough things to keep only about half a dozen men occupied—and permitted his genius to blossom forth in the sunshine. All that had gone before represented his apprenticeship, and in Palm Beach he became a master.

He recognized, as had Franklin Smith and Carrère and Hastings before him, the appropriateness of Spanish architecture for the subtropical climate. But he was not a copyist. He saw the duty of architects as "absorbing the best of the old world and letting it run out of their pencils." He had no hesitancy about turning Spanish architecture inside out to suit the conditions he met at Palm Beach. Fortified structures gave way to open ones, small windows to large, and severe landscapes were made lush with tropical foliage, both in the ground and in pots. Then, having created such gardens, he loaded his houses with patios, cloisters, and loggias to take advantage of the view.

It later became fashionable to deride Mizner as a practitioner of the "Bastard-Spanish-Moorish-Romanesque-Gothic-Renaissance-Bull-Market-Damn-the-Expense-Style." There is some truth in the latter part of the formulation. Mizner said that the first question to ask in designing a house was "Is it to be a Ford or a Buick or a Rolls-Royce?" He left no doubt which model he preferred. Palm Beach was ideal because "these people can't stand the sight of anything that doesn't cost a lot of money."

But the evaluation is wrong in assuming Mizner's work is an unknowing mishmash. Both well informed and highly conscious, he designed his buildings with the long view. They were to resemble the product of ages, during the course of which styles changed. He made stories to go with his buildings. Indeed, had his art taken a different form, he might have been an excellent costume-novelist.

"I sometimes start a house with a Romanesque corner," he said, "pretend that it has fallen into disrepair and been added to in the Gothic spirit, when suddenly the great wealth of the New World has poured in and the owner had added a very rich Renaissance addition."

In the ordinary course of events he might have gone to Spain and looted a castle or cathedral for materials to build the Everglades Club. But wartime restrictions stymied that—ships were not risking destruction by U-boat to transport antiquities—so he had no choice but to make them himself. In so doing he launched a new and profitable industry. He was well-suited for the task, being not only a connoisseur, knowledgeable in values, but also a skilled craftsman, learned in the tricks of the trade. He taught his laborers how to shape roofing tiles by molding clay over their thighs, and managed to improvise other materials as well. After creating them, he had to train his builders in what to do with them. Hollow clay tile was the essential sub-stucco base of a Mizner building. Somebody asked, the first time they saw one, if it was a skunk trap. Workers soon learned better.

The oversized architect scrambled around the scaffolding giving lessons. He claimed that of all the honors and decorations he received, he was proudest of his honorary membership in the local Union of Painters, Decorators and Paperhangers.

When the Everglades Club was finished, and Singer had no more use for the tile workshop, Mizner took it over, expanded its line of products, and rechristened it Mizner Industries, Inc. In addition to roof and floor tiles it made pottery, period furniture, leaded- and stained-glass windows, wrought iron, ornamental stonework, and other essential items for the new-style buildings. His company was particularly noted for its skill in reproducing antiques. Given half of a sixteenth-century door, it was said, "Mizner Industries will make the other half with age, worm holes, and all the scars of time." Customers found it "practically impossible to pick the original from the reproductions."

Mizner's techniques for taking the curse of newness off things have become legendary. The dinge caused in the Middle Ages by charcoal braziers and pre-electric lighting systems was reproduced by spraying walls with condensed milk, then rubbing them down with steel wool—or, in a quicker version, just burning some tarpaper and letting the smoke do the work. Men in hobnail boots were sent to march up and down not-quite-dried concrete stairways to imitate the wear and tear of centuries. Reproduction furniture was aged by a combination of quicklime, sledgehammers, chains, ice picks, broken beer bottles, and air rifles. Such treatment, of course, carried a higher price tag than a spanking-new piece with no patina.

• • •

In having the money to build at all during those years, Palm Beach was atypical. The rest of Florida had to wait for conditions to get back to normal.

The man who was elected president in 1920 pledging a

"Return to Normalcy" gave the state a boost by heading there during the cold winter months between his election and inauguration. It was at St. Augustine's Ponce de Leon Hotel that Warren G. Harding selected the most corrupt Cabinet in American history, though that would not become obvious until later. At the time, he was riding the crest of his popularity, and all of Florida hoped that some of it would rub off.

Carl Fisher didn't just hope. He sent his winsome secretary off to give the full Miami Beach pitch to Harding, and the president-elect agreed to visit.

He stayed at Fisher's hotel, swam at the Roman Pools, fished, golfed (with an elephant named Carl II for caddie), and obligingly posed for pictures that were reprinted everywhere. Miami Beach was made.

Out of sight of the cameras, Harding played poker and sampled Scotch from Fisher's private stock. Prohibition had been in effect for a year, but Fisher had prepared for it by buying the Indianapolis University Club's cellars. Cases of Scotch were buried around his Miami Beach home, and his yachts were fitted with secret compartments to bring in refills from the Bahamas when necessary. Instinctively resistant to the Noble Experiment, Carl began drinking more than ever. He was not alone in that: the dry years were probably the booziest in American history.

The boost from Harding helped put Fisher over the top. For several years it had been touch and go—a lot of money had gone into Miami Beach but not much had come out.

In 1916 Fisher built the thirty-two-room Lincoln Hotel, a modest beginning for what would later become a chain. In 1917 he began creating additional land by pumping islands up out of the bay. At the same time that he was adding to his real estate, it was hard to capitalize on what he had. When the United States entered the war, in 1917, he patriotically turned his holdings into a vegetable farm for the duration. In 1918 he leased his polo field to the Signal Corps for a dollar a year for the purpose of conducting aviation experiments. The war ended before they could do any damage to the turf.

Five weeks after the armistice, Fisher brought in the polo ponies and was again in the business of promoting a resort. His period of trial and error came to an end when he decided he had been aiming at the wrong audience. He had tried to lure "the very best people in the country" to a place of "subtle refinement and homelike restfulness where high strung nerves could relax." But those people were already in Palm Beach, and looked straight down their noses at Fisher. Not all the polo ponies in the world would lure them south.

Such a place would also have been out of character for him. No one ever relaxed around Carl Fisher. A dynamo, a speed king, with his floppy hats and an allergy to neckties, he would never have fit in at Flagler's resort, where people religiously changed their clothes five times a day and Mrs. Stotesbury kept a staff artist to sketch her gowns for easy reference. Fisher was a wild stallion, not a clothes horse.

Nor was his language suitably refined and tempered for the drawing room. Someone once suggested he put up a church. "It's a helluva good idea," he replied. "I'll build you the best Goddam church there is." That was Carl Fisher.

His friends in the automotive aristocracy had money that was a generation newer than Palm Beach's, but no less green or plentiful. They were the natural people to get. "I was on the wrong track," he realized. "I had been trying to reach the dead ones. I had been going after the old folks. I saw that what I needed to do was go after the live wires. And the live wires don't want to rest."

Fisher had just the place for them. He made it look different with flamingos and peacocks and elephants and exotic plants. He put it in motion with streetcars, yachts, speedboats, and gondolas. He provided accommodations by enlarging the Lincoln Hotel, then launching the even larger Flamingo Hotel, with its eleven-story tower. Then he enlarged that and started the Nautilus. Then the King Cole and the Boulevard.

He expanded his acreage by pumping up more islands,

which he named for friends such as James Allison, his old Prest-O-Lite partner, and John La Gorce of *National Geographic*, who had given Miami Beach a great boost with a lead article on its attractions. On one of his islands he built a memorial to Henry Flagler. The oilman might not have been a live wire in Fisher's book, but even so, "I think that Florida owes Mr. Flagler more than any other man who has ever set foot in Florida."

There was no doubt that the speed king was following in those footsteps. He had put his all into Florida; the improvements he made had stretched his credit to the limit by the time Harding came. Then he began to get it back by selling lots. In 1920 almost $2 million came in. By 1923 that was tripled, and in 1924 it quadrupled. Then it really took off.

New Yorkers, in the cold winter months, were treated to a little of Fisher's ballyhoo. An illuminated sign at the corner of Fifth Avenue and Forty-second Street flashed out the message: "IT'S JUNE IN MIAMI."

Goddam right!

• • •

Glenn Curtiss was not reduced to victory-gardening during the war. He produced airplanes. Curtiss Jennies and flying boats were standard models, and his factories worked overtime getting them out. When the war was over, Curtiss was worth $32 million.

He went into partnership with the man who had given him the airfield space near Miami. Their Curtiss-Bright ranch boasted the area's largest dairy and poultry yards. They bought up more land, well over 100,000 acres. They bought it cheap.

Then it turned out to be worth something. The section nearest Miami was developed as the town of Hialeah in 1921. Hialeah was a Seminole word which meant "best pearl in the heap" by the time the advertising men got through with it. Lots were snapped up—$1 million worth in ten days. Curtiss built himself a home there. Showing he had a bit of the Franklin Smith touch, he designed it in the style of one of the Indian pueblos he had admired in the Southwest.

He and Bright donated land for churches and schools, government offices and a golf course. Then came the other amenities: a movie studio, horse and dog tracks, jai-alai fronton, slot machines. It became a mecca for gamblers and bootleggers. Politicians hired rival police forces who sometimes hijacked shipments of liquor and sold it themselves. Bodyguards were much in evidence. It was a hot little town.

It wasn't exactly what Glenn Curtiss had had in mind when he started subdividing the ranch. He neither drank nor smoked himself. Hunting, tinkering, and thinking were his pastimes. He imported foxes and turned them loose, to hunt later. He pioneered the sport of archery golf, where bows and arrows replaced putters and balls. Publicity shots showed him challenging a Seminole Indian to a game.

Wherever he went he built workshops. If there wasn't one nearby, he'd just scratch down his ideas on whatever tablecloth was handy. As for thinking, well, it was hard to do that with rival gangs rubbing one another out in the background.

Fortunately, he wasn't confined to Hialeah, for he had a lot more land. He developed another chunk as a quieter residential area called Country Club Estates, breaking sharply from the grid pattern of neighboring settlements by featuring broad, winding streets. Curtiss sank $150,000 into a larger pueblo with both a swimming pool and an artificial lake on the grounds. Another $80,000 went into furnishing the place. He liked it so much he decided the pueblo style should be standard for the new development. If it was a little out of place geographically, it was no more so than the Chinese or Tudor or Norman buildings going up elsewhere in Florida. But it never became as popular as Addison Mizner's Mediterranean Revival, which swept the state like wildfire.

People started to say that Glenn Curtiss was making more in Florida real estate than he had in aviation. That was not true, although business was good enough to support a squad of 250 salesmen, and Curtiss established eighteen corporations in connection with his Florida ventures, including a bank to lend money to people who bought his lots and wanted to build homes.

By giving Miami its municipal water supply and an airport, he made himself a public benefactor. He'd come a long way from that bicycle shop in Hammondsport, New York.

● ● ●

George Merrick kept adding to the family homestead. It grew from 160 acres to 300 to 500 to 1,000 to 1,600 before he ever sold a foot of it.

In 1920 he began gathering a brain trust around him. He was not about to go off half-cocked. Coral Gables would be the best-planned community his money could buy, worthy of the title "America's Finest Suburb."

He brought in Frank Button, the landscape architect who had designed Chicago's Lincoln Park. As architectural consultant he got Phineas Paist, who had worked on James Deering's lavish estate, Vizcaya, one of the first complete examples of the Mediterranean Revival style in the state. Merrick's uncle, Denman Fink, a talented artist, was hired to render the dreams in a form that people could see and appreciate.

The original idea had been to build all the houses from native rock. When this did not prove feasible, Merrick's planners opted for stucco with little accents of what they mislabeled coral. A promotional bulletin later conceded it was "not the coral of which reefs and atolls are made, but a porous lime formation which resembles it and goes by that name." Coral Gables itself was a misnomer, though certainly more euphonious than Oölite Gables, which might have been more accurate.

Other suburban developers had been guilty, in Merrick's view, of "the most distressing crimes against good taste." He would avoid such crimes by doing his planning before he sold his lots, and guaranteeing adherence to the plan by having all construction approved by an architectural review board. "We had more difficulty at first in selling the idea of architectural harmony than in selling the land," he recalled later. "People resented it as a sort of censorship of their good taste." But since it was crucial to his plans, he stuck to his guns and made it work.

Like Addison Mizner, he sought to take the curse of newness off his buildings. The ruins of Spain, Morocco, and Cuba yielded up their tiles so that the roofs of Coral Gables might have the look of age. Stucco walls were stained to give a weathered appearance and in places were chipped away to reveal inset patches of brick, placed there purposely to give the illusion that time had taken its toll. The newest-looking building in Coral Gables was actually the oldest, the Merrick homestead.

Necessities that usually cast a pall of ugliness upon a community were turned into attractions instead. A rock quarry became "The World's Most Beautiful Swimming Pool." A drainage ditch, required to remove water from low-lying areas, became "Forty Miles of Inland Waterway," complete with gondolas. The railroad right-of-way, usually an eyesore, was planned instead as a 300-foot park, lushly landscaped and focusing on a magnificent station that was to be one of the architectural landmarks of the area.

While creating his City Beautiful, Merrick was not unmindful of its business aspects. He excelled at them as well. The bankers were slow to come on board, but he discovered an alternate source of financing in the cash-heavy insurance companies. They found him a solid and articulate fellow, a successful grower, a respected public official. Being out-of-towners, they didn't have the local bankers' fixation on waterfront property.

Just as he had gone for men of talent in the artistic sphere, so did Merrick seek out the best in the area of selling. E. E. "Doc" Dammers was already a legend by the time he took charge of the Coral Gables real-estate operation: he had sold the first lots for Carl Fisher over at the Beach, and people were fond of saying that he was talented enough to make his fortune selling ice cream to Eskimos. When Coral Gables was finally incorporated as a municipality, Dammers became the first mayor.

Merrick was the generalissimo—or philosopher-king. He got the best advice he could, secluded himself to mull the options, and emerged in public to announce the decisions.

On November 27, 1921, the first lot was sold in Coral Gables. In 1922 the first roads were built and the first store went up. Doc Dammers started out giving his pitch from the back of a wagon. Then busses were acquired, a whole fleet of them. Sales for 1924 totaled $12,613,854. George Merrick, who owned it all without partners or shareholders, was a multimillionaire—at least on paper. But what he made, he put back in. There was a lot of work yet to do to transform his dream into reality. The time for profit taking would come later, maybe in 1927 or 1928. In the meantime, Coral Gables forged ahead in the vanguard of what the nation recognized as a new Florida boom.

Merrick was no slouch when it came to ballyhoo. A textbook could be written from the methods he used. In January 1925 he announced his greatest triumph to the world: henceforth William Jennings Byran would speak twice daily at the Venetian Pool to the crowds brought in by the Coral Gables bus fleet. Those who might have passed up the alligator wrestlers and shimmy girls could hardly miss the mellifluous and leather-lunged king of the sawdust trail, who had thrice been a candidate for president of the United States. Merrick was said to be paying his orator $100,000 a year—half in cash and half in land.

Bryan's foes took malicious pleasure in the spectacle of the Great Commoner becoming (as H. L. Mencken put it) "a crimp for real-estate speculators—the heroic foe of the unearned increment hauling it in with both hands."

He was riled by press reports of his wealth. "I am not a millionaire; I am far from it, and never shall be," he protested, "but I have been fortunate in the matter of finances." That "but" continued to make him the butt of ridicule in unsympathetic circles.

There were not a lot of Bryan baiters in Florida. The state had backed him on all three runs for the White House, and his cousin, William S. Jennings, had been governor of Florida.

Bryan himself started buying up Florida property in 1912 and built a waterfront home, Villa Serena, in Miami, which he first occupied while serving as Woodrow Wilson's secretary of state. Instantly hailed as the city's most distinguished resident, he soon had problems with unwanted visitors, who turned him into a tourist attraction.

His tenure in Wilson's Cabinet was brief, for the Prince of Peace and the Man Who Kept Us Out Of War did not see eye to eye on how to respond to Germany's sinking of the *Lusitania.* Soon the great orator was back on the lecture circuit.

Since the Miami weather soothed Mrs. Bryan's crippling arthritis, the family spent more and more time there. In 1921 they made it their legal residence. Bryan joined the local Elks and Masons and Knights of Pythias, raised money to build a YMCA, and conducted a very popular Tourists' Bible Class at Royal Palm Park. The two to twelve thousand people who attended were only the first level of those reached by Bryan's message. His talks were also broadcast on radio and syndicated through newspapers, giving him an audience of over twenty million people—and a pretty good income as well.

It was only natural that he should be talked up as a possible senator from Florida. The state had a lot to gain, noted one boosting newspaper, because "he would directly be worth millions to it in advertising." Bryan was interested, but chickened out when the incumbent declined to step aside and made menacing campaign growls. "If, in a Democratic state, and after my experience in public life, I was defeated for a nomination, my enemies throughout the country would make effective use of it," he explained in announcing his withdrawal.

But he was laying the groundwork for a future try. He launched a vigorous campaign to be elected delegate to the 1924 Democratic National Convention, speaking in every one of Florida's counties and running well ahead of the rest of the slate. On the basis of that success, he decided to go ahead with a Senate bid in 1926.

At the 1924 convention, he further endeared himself to the homefolks by suggesting that A. A. Murphree, president of the University of Florida, would be an ideal candidate for the White House. Although other delegates ridiculed the notion, they did nominate the Commoner's younger brother, Governor Charles W. Bryan of Nebraska, for vice president, on a ticket that went down to crashing defeat in November.

Bryan combined his political and religious interests when he convinced the Florida legislature to pass laws requiring Bible reading in the schools and banning the teaching of Darwin's theory of evolution. But his image in the state was neither sharp politician nor angry god. Rather, he was seen as a public benefactor and booster. Florida loved him as only promoters are loved during a boom. And Bryan loved Florida—if not wisely, then certainly too well.

He was ever ready with something good to say about his adopted home. All you needed to do to make money in Florida real estate, he enthused, was to come into the state, take off your hat, throw it down, and buy the property where it landed.

"Miami," he said, "is the only city in the world where you can tell a lie at breakfast that will come true by evening."

No wonder they called it the Magic City.

President-elect Warren G. Harding plays a game of golf and helps to put Miami Beach on the map in 1921.

One of Carl Fisher's baby elephants caddies for Robert ("Believe It or Not!") Ripley.

Dreamer George Merrick (*right front, in white pants*) confers with his marketing wizard, E. E. "Doc" Dammers (*wearing straw hat*), at a Coral Gables land sales office in the 1920s.

Aviation pioneer Glenn Curtiss built this house at Hialeah in the style of a Southwestern Indian pueblo.

Three-time presidential candidate William Jennings Bryan didn't require a microphone when he spoke from this raft in "The World's Most Beautiful Swimming Pool" to crowds brought in by the Coral Gables bus fleet.

GOING!!

•

John Ringling was an old friend of Warren G. Harding. They both enjoyed the pleasures of the good life. Ringling was impressed with the boost Harding gave to Miami Beach. The circus king owned a lot more land than Carl Fisher, having bought up the keys between Sarasota Bay and the Gulf of Mexico, which he believed had great potential.

"Reminds me a lot of the Mediterranean," he said, "only it's a damn sight better looking."

With the postwar prosperity, he had money to invest in developing. But all eyes were focused on the wrong coast of Florida; something was needed to turn their attention to Sarasota. Ringling knew just the thing. In April 1923 he stopped by the White House to give the president some free passes to the circus and an invitation for the following winter.

"I'd like for you to see the West Coast of Florida next time you're down there," he said. "I've got a nice layout where you could rest and do a little fishing and relax—away from all that Miami hullabaloo."

When Harding agreed, Ringling could scarcely contain his enthusiasm. "This'll be the biggest thing that ever hit this town," he gloated to his associates. "Ought to make the natives' eyes pop—and raise the price of land fifty percent."

He wasn't just thinking of a quick visit, for he had something more permanent in mind—a Winter White House—and he had just the place. Edzell Castle, on Bird Key, was remote and easy to guard, sumptuous and suitable for the chief executive. It even looked a little like the White House.

He put his men to work. "I want everything in shape," he ordered. "It'll mean a hell of a lot to have him down there and I don't want any slip-ups."

On his annual European tour, he bought silver and art works for the castle, and a bullet-proof limousine that had been custom-made for the czar of Russia. He purchased a 125-foot yacht, because there was no bridge to Bird Key and the president had to have some dignified means of transportation. He prepared a warm reception for the accompanying reporters, thinking of the Sarasota datelines that would be appearing in their papers.

Then, on August 2, 1923, Harding died.

Ringling was out $50,000 or $100,000 (he threw those figures around lightly), and the best he could do was announce to the press that Harding had been planning to visit. This got a little attention during the mourning period, but was hardly the shot in the arm he had been counting on.

However, interest in Florida was heating up to the point where one man, even a president, could not make or break it. So Ringling continued with his development plans.

He put $750,000 into a causeway to make his "Ringling Isles" accessible from the mainland. "I plan on cuttin' it up into lots," he told his friends, "and making a residential section—exclusive as hell, you see?"

A yacht canal was dug, tropical foliage planted, and fountains and statues were brought from Europe to line the streets. He started a hotel and, wanting it to be a class act, paid $5,000 a year for the right to call it the Ritz-Carlton.

When the causeway was completed, he brought in the Czechoslovakian band from his circus and invited everyone over to a daylong spectacle, party, and sales pitch. Over $1 million worth of lots were signed for. Sarasota was definitely booming.

Death had reduced the Ringling brothers to two—John and Charles—and a lively rivalry grew up between them: John had a larger private railroad car, but Charles outdid him in the yacht department. While John was planning the Ringling Isles and Ritz-Carlton, Charles was turning a downtown golf course into high-rise office buildings and the three-hundred-room Sarasota Terrace Hotel. John was president of the Bank of Sarasota, and Charles had his Ringling Bank and Trust Company.

They were next-door neighbors. As things boomed, their old homes did not seem ostentatious enough. Hearing that John had some grandiose plans, Charles rushed ahead and built a Georgian marble palace for $880,000. It was nice enough, for the price, but couldn't compare with what his brother did.

John and his wife, Mable, shared the Venetian fantasies common to the age. They went to an architect and asked him to design something along the lines of the Doge's Palace topped with the tower from Madison Square Garden. This plan was modified, but not much. Costing over $1 million, it was certainly one of the most egregious houses of that, or any, era. Only a man thoroughly steeped in the circus aesthetic could have called it home. In keeping with the Venetian theme, they parked a gondola on the waterfront, until a storm smashed it to bits. The place was christened Ca'd'Zan—translating to "House of John." No residence on that scale could possibly go nameless.

Sarasota burst its old-time seams and by legislative act was expanded from 2 to 69 square miles. New subdivisions blossomed, with such alluring names as Sapphire Shores and the Garden of Allah.

Creating and marketing these places was a diverse crew. John had convinced his friend John J. McGraw to bring his New York Giants to Sarasota for spring training in 1924. The famed manager built himself a $75,000 home, then recouped his money by launching Pennant Park subdivision, where $100,000 worth of lots were snapped up by those who wanted to get in "before the ninth inning."

Colonel Jacob Ruppert, owner of the New York Yankees (and erstwhile baron of Knickerbocker Beer) bought into Ringling Isles, then developed his own Ruppert Beach and Ruppert Islands, near St. Petersburg.

Ty Cobb's younger brother appeared in Sarasota in 1924 to sell real estate; later he headed a baseball committee under the auspices of the Chamber of Commerce which persuaded the Boston Red Sox to choose the city as its spring training site.

Mrs. Potter Palmer was dead, but her estate was still a major landowner in the area. Drainage was begun on thousands of acres of lowland for division into 10-acre farming tracts, under the direction of Prince Michael Cantacuzène. Mrs. Palmer's niece Julia, who had fallen in love with Sarasota at first sight "because of its sunny, turquoise sky and sea, and smiling landscapes," wrote articles booming Florida, as well as memoirs of the czarist court, all of which she signed fully as "Princess Cantacuzène, Countess Spéransky, née Grant." She became active in a variety of hereditary societies, including the Republican Party.

Mrs. Palmer had been too canny to sink her millions into the development of Venice, Florida, as a resort. In the heady days of the boom, that project was taken on by a labor union. The Brotherhood of Locomotive Engineers put over $16 million into transforming what was no more than a stop on the railroad line into a city with three large hotels, a bank, a theater, and a business district. The union bought over 30,000 acres of land, and the population grew to four thousand people.

With things starting to look good all over Florida, there were many who claimed credit for starting the boom. The Sarasota Chamber of Commerce saw it as a natural outgrowth of their 1923 advertising, noting that "after the campaign started, land that had gone begging at from $25 to $100 an acre took on a new lustre and was readily snapped up at from $3,000 to $5,000 an acre. Fortunes were made overnight. Widows and orphans, land poor, began to buy self-playing pianos and automobiles with jeweled mud guards." With that example before them, other communities naturally decided to get in on the act. "By the spring of 1925, the whole state was thriving—thanks to Sarasota."

• • •

What did start the boom, local puffery aside?

Postwar prosperity was at the base of it. Never before had so many people had so much money. When they thought of spending it, they thought of Florida, for the decades of publicity from Flagler on, stressing that it was a resort for the rich, left the state with great snob appeal.

Florida was no longer an unknown frontier. Medical experiments growing out of the Spanish-American War and the construction of the Panama Canal had isolated the villain of yellow fever: a mosquito, rather than noxious vapors, rotten fish, untended garbage, or dirty bed linen, as previously thought. Sanitation measures put an end to the dread epidemics that had plagued Florida right up to the twentieth century—often following embarrassingly soon after the opening of Flagler's great hotels. With that menace removed, the state was a less dangerous and more attractive place to visit.

It was not just that more people were rich enough to afford Florida. At the same time, Henry Ford's Tin Lizzies put the trip within a much more modest price range. "Tin Can Tourists" flooded the state. The standing joke was that they came with one shirt and a twenty-dollar bill and didn't change either all winter. Though their expenditures may not have pumped a lot into the economy, they were great at talking up the virtues and attractions of Florida when they got home, luring others in their wake.

Their flivvers needed roads and bridges to travel on, and these things assumed an importance equivalent to the laying of railroad tracks in the era of Plant and Flagler.

Carl Fisher was a pioneer with his Dixie Highway, but he was not the only one. Great Lakes shipping magnate W. J. Conners (immortalized as Jiggs in the comic strip *Bringing Up Father*) built a toll road from Palm Beach to Lake Okeechobee to open up his vast holdings in that area. Even more ambitious was the Tamiami Trail, from Tampa to Miami, eventually completed with the help of Barron G. Collier, the wealthy mogul of streetcar advertising, whose million-acre chunk of the Everglades along the route of the trail was reorganized as Collier County.

Madison Avenue was coming of age, making new advances in the scientific hard sell. One of Florida's leading developers wrote that the boom "would have been impossible without the liberal use of these new methods of bringing the buyer and the goods he desires together."

Sigmund Freud's theories were going public, sweeping through intellectual circles in the postwar years. Carl Fisher's bathing beauties were an early example of linking them up with the art of salesmanship. Sex sold things.

Fisher's ballyhoo was emulated by others. No development was complete without a golf course and a country club. Bobby Jones, Gene Sarazen, and Walter Hagen played at the former, using phosphorescent golf balls for nighttime exhibitions. Paul Whiteman, Jan Garber, and Isham Jones led their bands at the latter. It was the Jazz Age, and Florida had jazz.

It was also the Bootleg Age, and Florida had Bimini and Havana right off shore, with their ample, legal stocks of high-quality alcohol. But visitors didn't even have to go that far. Prohibition was a joke in Florida, its enforcement routinely ignored as being bad for business. When a Florida representative solemnly proclaimed his state "as dry as the Sahara," he was laughed off the floor of Congress. Everybody knew.

It was the golden age of sports, and Florida had the heroes. Babe Ruth appeared at hotel openings. Gertrude Ederle swam at the Alcazar pool. Red Grange played the Coral Gables football team. Big Bill Tilden starred on stage as well as the tennis court. Gene Tunney was sales manager for a South Florida development. Half the starting lineup of the Pittsburgh Pirates pitched Miami real estate in the off season.

There was hardly a celebrity of the day who didn't make an appearance—usually as a guest or on the payroll of some developer. Gilda Gray shimmied, Rudolph Valentino sheiked, Texas Guinan suckered, and Jack Dempsey shocked his hosts by saying something nice about the state's archrival, California.

Every last bit of publicity was squeezed out. When a wealthy polo player dropped dead on dismounting, a press agent was handy to remind reporters to give it a Miami Beach dateline. Florida was in the news.

What's in a name? Gold, as far as the promoters were concerned. Embarrassing appellations were changed, bland ones upgraded, and the sky was the limit as far as new developments were concerned. Bull Island became Belle Island. Mosquito Inlet was rechristened Ponce de Leon Inlet. Pine Key was improved to Monte Cristo Isle.

History, mythology, and fantasy were plundered for suitable names. Venice, Naples, and Lido Beach were hyped. You could buy a lot at Mecca Gardens in Fort Myers, or go across the state to Olympia, where the streets were named for Greek gods. You could fly your magic carpet to Aladdin City—since the roads were not in yet—or feed your greed at Gold Mine Heights in the nonmetallic flatlands of St. Augustine. Those with a yen for stardom could buy at Picture City. One chronicler recalled, "they were going to make most of the movie films for the whole country there, as soon as the Humboldt Current succeeded in freezing the studios out of California."

Any place that met with success would find its name expropriated, with "Shores," "Ocean," "Hills," or "Gardens" tacked on. Things so often meant their opposites that it became a joke: "By-the-Sea" meant far inland; "Heights" was a dead giveaway that swampland was being peddled. One particularly remote location transcended reality with the name "Manhattan Estates"; it was a suburb of an abandoned turpentine camp.

Developers were not averse to immortalizing themselves or their families, sometimes fancying things up a bit. Owen Burns christened his Sarasota hotel the El Vernona; Vernona was Mrs. Burns's first name. When John Ringling bought the place, he promptly gave it his own name—and added a 7-foot doorman from the circus, so no one would miss the point.

Pennsylvania oilman Aymer Vinoy Laughner named his multimillion-dollar hostelry the Vinoy Park. Handsome Jack Taylor built the Rolyat—which is Taylor spelled backward. Fort Lauderdale's Croissantania Hotel was the project of G. Frank Croissant, not a subtle reference to a continental breakfast. A spot on the map called El Jobean was actually a scrambled version of the name of developer Joel Bean, with a little Spanish fantasy thrown in.

During the boom the state did its part to be as obliging as possible. Income and inheritance taxes were barred by constitutional amendment, and corporation laws rewritten to compare favorably with those of Delaware.

Florida boasted the nation's highest speed limit: 45 miles per hour. In no other state could you legally clip along faster than 35. And no driver's license was required in the Sunshine State.

There were, of course, the hazards of roaming razorbacks and free-grazing cattle, and newspapers complained that parts of the Dixie Highway were paved with nothing more than good intentions.

Even paradise had a few minor problems.

The confluence of all these factors—prosperity, promotion and the like—laid the basis for the boom and made it possible. But what really got it under way and fueled it was greed, pure and simple. Easy money was the irresistible lure.

It started modestly enough.

People would take a Florida vacation. Before returning home, they would buy a small building lot. The next winter they would sell the lot and make enough to pay for their vacation. They told their friends. A few more tried it. The circle of cognoscenti increased by geometric proportions.

Then the press got wind of it. Easy money is always news. It sells papers. Out of Florida came a flood of stories.

One man set up a deal and pocketed $10,000 with no more strenuous exertion than turning his head from one side of a chair to the other. Two bottles of bathtub gin were parlayed by another man into $75,000 worth of real estate. A Fort Lauderdale high-school student made $20,000 in an afternoon. Good, but not as much as the eleven-year-old Fort Myers boy who wound up with $100,000. A barber turned $80 worth of tips into a fast million. A retired railroad employee who had bought 960 acres for a dollar apiece disposed of them for $4 million. N. B. T. Roney, a Miami Beach developer, was widely reported to have made $6 million between 9:00 A.M. and 3:00 P.M. of a single day by selling lots in a newly opened subdivision.

Of course, developers were supposed to make money—that was not news. But when they paid huge premiums to buy back land they had previously sold, that got some attention.

Joseph Young of Hollywood By-the-Sea did just that. A lot he had sold for $1,600, he bought back for ten times that amount. He paid twenty times the $1,800 selling price to reacquire another. To get back one he had sold for a paltry $800 he paid a handsome $65,000.

Young could afford it. He had brought in General George Washington Goethals, legendary builder of the Panama Canal, to plan a $15-million harbor for his project. Hollywood was to be laced with canals, so that Venetian fantasies could be lived out on a day-to-day basis. He planned a 100-mile-wide greenbelt, extending back into the Everglades, to be sold as farming tracts. His own crew of agricultural experts would test the soil and guarantee infallible crops.

If people didn't like the land they bought from him, Young had a standing offer to buy it back at 6 percent interest. Carl Fisher would do the same thing at Miami Beach.

How could you lose? It was foolproof.

The slogans said it all:

"One Good Investment Beats a Lifetime of Toil."

And:

"The only man that doesn't make money in Florida real estate is the man that doesn't own any."

• • •

D. P. Davis was the quintessential boomer. Floridians took special pride in "Doc" Davis because he rose higher and faster, and became richer, than any other native son during the Roaring Twenties.

Davis's life had been intertwined with Florida's booms and busts. He was born in Green Cove Springs, a steamboat-era resort, in 1885—the same year Henry Flagler launched the Ponce de Leon Hotel and his railroad-served Riviera, which stole the tourists from the St. Johns River route and sent settlements there into decline.

Davis's father had bet on golden apples and was wiped out by the freeze of 1894–95. The family moved to Tampa. Young Doc hawked newspapers there during the Spanish-American War and learned his first lessons in salesmanship.

"In those days a boy who hustled could earn from two to three dollars a week selling papers in the afternoon," he later recalled. "I found that I could double these wages getting up at daybreak and delivering the morning papers before breakfast."

His father was a ferryboatman with four children to look after, so when Doc went off to college he was on his own. The University of Florida had just located in an outlying district of

Gainesville. Davis bought a stretch of the piney woods that separated the campus from downtown, subdivided it, sold the lots, and paid his way through school. When he returned to Tampa, he continued his apprenticeship as a salesman for the Tampa Bay Land Company.

Tracking down the specifics of Davis's career is a little like trying to nail jello to a tree. Once he became successful he had a crew of press agents to foster the Davis legend, wherein all the steps along the way pointed to the fantastic conclusion. But his rise to riches was not uninterrupted. Though he prospered in some of his ventures, he always managed to wind up broke. In 1915, at the age of thirty, Davis was back in Tampa. Some say he had been working on the recently completed Panama Canal, but in any case he was penniless, and had to borrow the railway fare to Jacksonville, where he had a job offer. He also got married there, and the next year became a father.

When World War I started, Davis took over the commissary at one of the Jacksonville military bases. Figuring that the recruits wouldn't like the mess-hall grub, he stocked up on hot dogs and did a land-office business. Then the war ended, and it was back from boom to bust.

He headed south to Miami, found some lots that had been languishing on the market during the wartime slump, applied a little go-getter advertising, and made a profit of $40,000 in ten days. That attracted some attention. A rich man offered a partnership: he would provide the money and Davis would do the work. More than half a dozen subdivisions resulted.

In 1919, at the time Davis started, Carl Fisher was the major figure in the Miami real-estate world. Coral Gables had not yet gone on the market; it was still a dream in George Merrick's mind. Then, as the years went by, the area became glutted with operators. There were no more deals to be had in Miami—even the garbage dump had been sold—so Davis headed back to Tampa. The year was 1924.

Newspapers hailed him on his return as a conquering hero;

they said he was worth $7 million or $8 million. He was also a widower: Mrs. Davis had died in 1922, shortly after giving birth to their second son, D. P. Davis, Jr.

As a boy, Davis senior had searched for pirate gold on some muddy islands in the bay at Tampa; now he sought to turn the islands themselves into gold. Having seen Carl Fisher do it in Miami, Davis meant to top the master and become Florida's premier "Maker of Islands."

Big and Little Grassy Keys and their appendages were not exactly islands, for a good stiff high tide could put them under. Boy Scouts camped on them, in appropriate weather, and swatted mosquitoes. They had a little greenery and a lot of mud.

But they were a great basis for islands, and Davis knew just what to do. There were a few hurdles to overcome before he could begin, but he took them like a seasoned jumper. He acquired the privately owned section and engineered a referendum to permit the city's share to come his way—then fended off a lawsuit by wealthy bay-front residents who did not want a new development popping up in their line of view. Once he had built a bulkhead, he brought in the world's largest private fleet of dredges. The mudflats were turned into 875 acres of high ground.

As important as the landfill operation was the advertising machinery put in motion, for that was where Doc Davis really excelled. Davis Islands promised "picturesque gondolas and other sorts of craft moored to fantastically colored poles—right at one's door-step—ready for the moonlight sail to the accompaniment of music which steals across the bay."

The Boy Scouts lost their camping ground, but got a well-publicized $10,000 contribution from Davis. He got more publicity by hiring a champion woman swimmer to stroke her way around the islands, and by paying a famous golfer $1,000 for hitting a ball from downtown to the new development. Doc Davis was a believer in location, location, location. He wanted to emphasize that this paradise was rising up just half a mile from City Hall, just 1,500 feet from one of the most expensive residential districts in west coast Florida's largest city.

Davis Islands featured everything from the world's largest lighted fountain to the nation's second-largest coliseum and a country club with a sliding roof for starlight dancing and dining. Doc announced a series of apartment buildings based on the famous palaces of Italy. Franklin Smith would have loved it.

While all these things were being built, people could feast their eyes on artists' renditions and enjoy the hoopla of Davis's promotional speedboat races; he had a fleet of yachts and seaplanes that ferried lot buyers over before the hundred-thousand-dollar bridge to the mainland was completed.

When Davis Islands property was going on sale, in October 1924, people lined up forty hours in advance to plunk down their money. One man chained himself to the door to be first in line. Opening-day sales topped $1.5 million and kept right on going at a furious clip while the putative paradise was still largely under water. People had faith in D. P. Davis.

After six months he abruptly stopped selling his land, so that those who were still clamoring to buy had to go to owners who had gotten in earlier and pay them a higher price. This went on for a while, with the Davis organization taking full-page ads to publicize the 500 percent profits being made. Then Davis put his own lots back on the market—at a much higher price. That maneuver made him a superstar, and a lot richer as well. At the end of a year, Davis Islands had been completely sold out, for $18,138,000. Another $8,250,000 had to be returned to would-be buyers because there was no more land to sell.

Meanwhile, a grand announcement of the next Davis project had just been made, and it would overshadow the previous one. Sixty million dollars would be spent transforming the marshy northern end of Anastasia Island ("only 2200 feet from downtown St. Augustine") into five separate islands, with 20 miles of waterfront protected by ornamental sea walls.

It would be the largest dredging operation ever launched,

in which three shifts a day would work nonstop to suck up 1 million cubic yards a month for over a year. The bottom of Matanzas Bay would be deposited atop the mudflats to create 1,500 acres of high ground. There would be a $1.5-million hotel, a $250,000 country club, a $200,000 yacht club, a $200,000 Roman pool and casino, two eighteen-hole golf courses, 50 miles of streets, 100 miles of sidewalks, and elaborate landscaping. Every lot would touch on either a golf course or the water. A million-dollar bridge ("The Most Beautiful Bridge in Dixie") was already under way to link the Ancient City with its newest suburb.

Three thousand Davis employees were expected to come to St. Augustine to work on the project, pumping additional millions into the local economy, and the developer pledged $200,000 to publicize the area.

The "Welcome-to-Davis" issue of the *St. Augustine Record* was the largest they had ever published. The Board of Realtors pooled its resources for a floral spread more ornate than anything seen since the death of Henry Flagler—which was appropriate, since Davis was planning to spend more in St. Augustine than Flagler had spent in all of Florida. Full-page ads greeted the new colossus who had "builded beauty spots out of wildernesses and lifted fairy gardens and ideal home sites from the depths of the sea itself." Others shouted, "A Thousand Times Welcome to Mr. D. P. Davis." The Ancient City prostrated itself at his feet.

As a member of the governor's military staff, he was referred to as "Lt. Col. Dave P. Davis"—he who had sold hot dogs during the Great War. Davis himself used the title sparingly, not with the regularity of his predecessor General Sanford.

According to his publicity releases, Davis was a modest man. This meant he preferred the simple appellation "genius," and the press was only too happy to oblige. To his flocks he was thrice a genius: as visionary, doer, and leader. He counted his wealth at $30 million, and plunged every bit of it back into his Florida developments. He believed in what he peddled.

The twenty-one offices of D. P. Davis Properties throughout Florida beat the drums for the new project. Advertisements conjured up "lingering and refreshing memories of days long past—of favorite teachers pointing out the location of St. Augustine on the map—the very spot where today D. P. Davis is creating Davis Shores, destined to be America's foremost watering place." The modest genius and his crew sold $19 million worth of lots in a single day.

• • •

Signs of the boom were everywhere: majestic entrance gates, white-way lighting, and tropically landscaped roads leading off to nowhere. The famous Douglas Gate at Coral Gables cost $1 million, though others were more modest: plaster on chicken wire, designed to last until the developer had sold the final lot. Bus fleets, free barbecues, subdivision orators "with leather throats and angels' tongues who often enough spoke ten hours a day for weeks at a time, with tears trembling in their voices to the end"—those were the signs of civilization that punctuated the Dixie Highway at regular intervals on its journey south from the state line.

Miami, birthplace of the boom, was at fever pitch. Julia Tuttle should have been there. Her heirs sold the old homesite for $500,000, and the Julia Tuttle Apartments for $700,000; they were the merest fraction of her checkerboard holdings.

Churches found the building lots Henry Flagler had given them so increased in value that they tore down their houses of worship and replaced them with high-rise buildings combining commercial and religious uses.

The skyscraper age reached Florida. Every city boasted of its skyline, actual or proposed. Artists with vision designed ads in which every subdivided cow pasture looked like Manhattan Island.

The citrus belt was denuded. As their real-estate value outpaced the worth of their golden apples, many of the state's oldest and largest bearing groves were leveled. The remaining growers applauded, sure that the contracted supply would hike up the price of their oranges.

Florida's population passed a million, that of Miami alone zooming beyond a hundred thousand. Learned guesses were given on just how many people could be stuffed into Florida. Conservatives said five or ten million, others pegged it at twenty million, but optimists figured eighty million and proclaimed themselves realists as they quoted Thomas Edison's remark that "There is only one Fort Myers and ninety million people are going to find it out." A baseball statistician topped them all by setting the number at three hundred million. Whatever the figure, the mass migration beat everything since the California gold rush. Other states feared depopulation, while Florida swelled from the influx.

The land was ready for them, all neatly divided up on plat maps into 50-foot lots, but of actual housing an acute shortage developed. Porches and hallways proved eminently rentable. Carl Fisher set up a hundred tents to accommodate his workmen. The Chamber of Commerce brought in portable houses to rent at $60 a month. The telephone company built a $200,000 dormitory to house its operators, who had increased fivefold in a year. Mississippi River steamboats and other floating hostelries appeared in Jacksonville, Tampa, and Fort Lauderdale. One manufacturer of canvas houses reported they were "going like hot cakes" in Miami.

George Merrick planned to take up some of the slack in a grand manner. On August 1, 1925, he placed the largest order for homes ever signed—$75 million for a thousand buildings. He had a dozen architects design models in French, Dutch, Venetian, and Chinese styles, all to be built in their own architecturally harmonious neighborhoods and sell for $20,000 to $100,000 each.

Glenn Curtiss was planning a new city for his pastureland. He first thought to make it a medieval English village, of the

Robin Hood era, with thatched roofs and half timbers. Then, thumbing through a copy of *The Arabian Nights*, he was inspired by a different theme and decided to build the "Baghdad of Dade County" instead. The architect of his mother's Christian Science church in New York was brought in to design buildings that bristled with domes, minarets, and middle-eastern fortifications.

The man who had laid out the streets of Coral Gables was brought in to plan the locations of Sesame Street, Ali Baba Avenue, and, incongruously, Curtiss Drive. The aviator wanted one street named for Scheherazade, but his publicity crew convinced him it was too hard to spell or pronounce, so it was cut back to Sherazad. Curtiss was open to such contractions. The Seminoles had called his land Opatishawockalocka—a mouthful he shortened to Opa-locka.

That summer of 1925, Coral Gables lost its orator: William Jennings Bryan died before he ever got a chance to run for the Senate from Florida (though his daughter would, a few years later, become the State's first Congresswoman). He had just prosecuted John Scopes for teaching evolution in Tennessee, an act that did more to damage the Commoner's reputation than all his Florida real-estate ventures. "He came into life a hero, a Galahad, in bright and shining armor," wrote Mencken. "He was passing out a poor mountebank." Not poor in a worldly sense, however: the 1927 appraisal of his estate was $1,111,948.50, so he was a millionaire at the very end. Thousands gathered in the rain for a memorial service in Royal Palm Park.

In slower times, his loss would have been a blow, but there was nothing slow about 1925. For the first time Florida had a summer season. Hotels that had previously been quiet as a tomb after Easter were busier than ever that August.

Coral Gables made do without its star attraction, as its publicity men worked double shifts cranking out stories from every possible angle to fill the columns of the nation's newspapers. The development's advertising department worked round the clock and had a budget of millions. They could afford it. Three thousand salesmen peddled nearly $100 million worth of Coral Gables property that year.

Merrick increased his holdings from 1,600 to 3,000 to 10,000 acres. He sent his architects off to New York, Chicago, and Atlanta, to do quick façade remodelings of the company's offices there in a style that would give passers-by a little taste of Coral Gables.

He paid novelist Rex Beach $18,000 to write a slim, syrupy volume, *The Miracle of Coral Gables.* Although not much as literature, it was a gem of the bookmaker's art, and copies were sent free to everyone who answered a newspaper advertisement. Meanwhile, Merrick announced that he would give 160 acres of land and $5 million to help establish the University of Miami, a gesture designed to make the Magic City the Athens of the western world.

Not everyone spent as long as Merrick or Carl Fisher in organizing and planning a utopia. The stories of fabulous wealth inevitably lured the easy-money crowd to Florida, those who dealt not in dreams or visions or man-made islands, but in pieces of paper: binders on property that were good for thirty days and could be had for 5 percent of the selling price.

A $500 binder, which would hold down a $10,000 piece of property, could be sold the same day for a profit, and would probably be resold dozens of times before the thirty days were up. By then the $10,000 price might have been kited to $50,000, while everyone along the line took a share of the profits. The original $500 plus profit could be put into other binders, the process repeated, and within a short period of time an impressive paper fortune would result.

The prestidigitators who made their money this way were called "binder boys." ("Binder" they pronounced to rhyme with "cinder," showing that wherever they came from, it wasn't Florida.)

The typical binder boy would hop off the train with three questions on his lips:

"Is this Miami?"

"Where can I rent an office?"

"What is the price of acreage?"

And they were in business.

Their invariable uniform consisted of golf knickers, which conveyed the life style they were purveying, and which didn't have to be pressed.

Realtors did a great business at 10 percent commission. After selling a property, they would encourage the buyer to put it right back on the market at a higher price. They might sell the same thing ten times a month, picking up progressively higher commissions each time.

Their ranks swelled. Miami was issuing sixty new licenses a day. In St. Petersburg, which had entered the decade with a population of 14,237, there were six thousand real-estate salesmen in 1925. Brokers could pick and choose. One hired only ministers to work for him, finding they had a particularly convincing sales manner.

With all this boosting, prices rose to fantastic levels. On Miami's Flagler Street, $50,000 a front foot was paid in August 1925, then topped by $70,000 a front foot the next month—more than prime property in Manhattan. Both figures were for real-estate offices. Such prices were publicized as much as the earlier tales of great fortunes made by barbers, widows, and children.

Of course, prices paid had nothing to do with the income that could be derived from development. One man said he would have to build a two-hundred-story office building and lease all the rooms in perpetuity at the existing high rates to justify what he had paid for the land. Instead, he turned around and quickly resold the lot at a large profit. Turnover was the name of the game.

"For Sale" signs became redundant; almost everything could be had. Instead, in the summer of 1925, "Not For Sale" signs made their appearance on property owned by those who had decided to sit out the boom. They were few in number.

When September came, schoolteachers didn't report back

to work, because they could make more in real estate. Police forces were decimated for the same reason (in Miami the Ku Klux Klan patriotically offered to take over their duties, claiming they had run the crooks out of St. Petersburg already). Even funeral directors found they could make more being unctuous in another line of work.

Writer Ben Hecht, who was there as publicity man for one of the developments, later remembered: "Everybody was trying to get rich in a few days. Nobody went swimming. Nobody sat under the palm trees. Nobody played horseshoes. Seduction was at a standstill. Everybody was stubbing his toe on real-estate nuggets."

All indicators were up, up, up.

Miami bank deposits had amounted to $37 million in November 1924; a year later they stood at $210 million. Building permits for $17 million were issued in 1924; that figure was doubled in the first eight months of 1925, a year that saw 481 hotels and apartment houses under construction.

Miami newspapers set world records for advertising linage. They had to turn down as many as fifteen pages of ads a day because of the limited capacity of their printing presses. Even so, their size was impressive. One woman said she'd like to take the Sunday paper "but I'm afraid it would fall on me." The high point was reached when a special 504-page issue came out in July.

There were more Rolls-Royces in Florida than any other state. As 1926 dawned, Miami claimed to be the richest city in the world.

"The sun of Florida's destiny has arisen," proclaimed Governor John W. Martin, "and only the malicious and the short-sighted contend or believe that it will ever set."

• • •

Addison Mizner was doing better than ever. Straight-faced critics were comparing his version of Palm Beach with Athens during the Age of Pericles. He was not only society's pet and darling, but also its trend setter. When he wore his shirttails out to cool his great girth in the warm weather, for instance, the sports shirt was born. Clients pointed with pride to items that Mizner had forgotten to include in their houses—like doors or stairways or bathrooms. It became such a status symbol to own a Mizner slip that people were known to invent them if they didn't exist. He was the stuff of which tall tales were made—a veritable Paul Bunyan of the Palm Beach gossip circuit.

Business was brisk: he said he had a hundred projects going at once in 1925, and he was in such demand that he could satisfy a client merely by sketching a design in the sand or on the back of an envelope—though he then had the good sense to turn it over to his stable of associates to fill in the fine points. He claimed to have millions in government bonds salted away.

He didn't need to do more, to become a developer and get involved in the frenzied part of the boom. But he did. All that easy money was too exciting to pass up. Besides, Wilson was egging him on. Wilson was Addison's younger brother—the spoiled baby and most thorough scapegrace of the Mizner clan.

"Among our friends Wilson and I were known as the 'night' and 'day' editions of the Mizners," wrote the architect, but he was exaggerating the differences between them. A close-knit pair, they merely covered separate territories: Addison was an artist in construction, Wilson in conversation. They were both living legends.

Author Anita Loos loved Wilson. He was no gentleman and she was no blonde. She found herself curiously drawn to his "bare-faced rascality" and "ignoble operations." His admirers considered him the Abe Lincoln of the underworld, and he won the esteem of its chroniclers, from O. Henry to Damon Runyon.

An honest con man, he believed that suckers wanted to be taken, and that therefore he was doing them a favor. To accept compensation for it was only natural. "The con games I've invented all took more work than any legal effort," he said.

He was, simultaneously and by turns, prospector, playwright, patent-medicine salesman, prize-fight promoter, poker player, opium smoker, cocaine snorter, and gigolo. He was also America's most celebrated aphorist, a man whose comments have never ceased to be quoted.

"Be nice to people on your way up," he advised, "because you'll meet them on your way down." (For brawlers he had a more practical suggestion: "Always hit a man with a bottle—a ketchup bottle preferred, for when that breaks, he thinks he's bleeding to death.") According to his most famous literary pronouncement, "If you steal from one author, it's plagiarism. If you steal from many it's research."

Insults like "You're a mouse studying to be a rat" were his forte. Palm Beach's favorite came when Wilson saw a mansion designed by one of his brother's competitors. "My God," he said, "Harry Thaw shot the wrong architect."

"Always treat a lady like a whore and a whore like a lady" is probably his most widely repeated saying—though if he truly coined "Never give a sucker an even break," as some insist, that would have to be considered his classic.

Once, when asked the secret of his success, Wilson replied, "Impudence." That got him far, but his run of luck seemed to vanish just as the twenties began to roar. He was convicted of gambling, beaten to within an inch of his life, broke, and struggling with morphine addiction. The good times had rolled by. Addison brought his brother to Palm Beach in 1921 to try and rehabilitate him—not without misgivings about what it might do to his social standing.

After manfully kicking the morphine habit, Wilson started taking laudanum instead. In his wake, all variety of dips and frauds and cons—the friends of his earlier life—made their appearance on the scene. They were the kind of people Wilson described as being "wanted everywhere and welcome nowhere." Many a Palm Beach matron found it wise to stash her ice and wear her paste—in the lingo of the day.

Wilson was put in charge of the tile factory, and spent his nights gambling. The greatest gamble, though, was not at the card tables or roulette wheel, but in real estate. Such an experienced con man could hardly pass up a golden opportunity like that. He and Addison combined their skills to create the mythic realm of Boca Raton and sell it to a willing public.

Boca Raton was to Addison Mizner what Palm Beach had been to Henry Flagler: a place to start fresh after making impressive additions to someone else's city.

Mizner's defection from Palm Beach, the resort where he had been responsible for $50 million worth of buildings and a whole visual revolution, was compounded by the simultaneous defection of his old crony Paris Singer. Poor Palm Beach! After three decades at the top, was it to be cast on the ash heap of history? It was threatened with a squeeze play from the Mizners on the south (who aimed to turn it into a servant's quarters for Boca Raton) and the sewing-machine heir on the north (whose Singer Island was supposed to make Palm Beach look like a slum).

After several years of social arbitrating, Paris Singer sold the Everglades Club to raise capital for his new, ritzier development. He had Mizner design not only a hotel, but also a bizarre "aerial ferry" that bore a resemblance to the engineering work of Rube Goldberg.

Meanwhile, Palm Beach was also devastated from within, when its popular Breakers hotel went up in $2 million worth of smoke, caused by a short circuit in an electrical hair curler.

Flagler's old mansion, Whitehall, was quickly pressed into service, with a twelve-story, four-hundred-room hotel addition. The Breakers was rebuilt, more lavishly than before, in Italian palazzo style. (It was not Mizner, but at least it was not wooden and not yellow.) That took time, however, and the fire cast an immediate pall over the resort. Inevitably, some people looked elsewhere.

They didn't have to look far: Every swamp and cow pasture in Florida was being touted as the coming Nice or Venice or Monte Carlo. Amid the cacophony, Wilson bragged, he "stood toe to toe with the loudest liars available and outpredicted them." He was the director of special effects, and did not plan to be outdone by the ballyhoo of others. When buried treasure started popping up at different developments, Wilson produced a handful of gold doubloons, which he attributed to the pirate Blackbeard. He would do as much as anyone else, and more than most.

Boca Raton based its appeal on being more exclusive than any other place. The idea was to "get the big snobs and the little snobs will follow." Purchasers would have to be screened by a social committee (headed by Wilson, who ordered his staff, "Don't ever let me hear of your turning down any money"—but the screenees didn't know that at the time). Boca Raton had its own crew of celebrities to lend their glitter: Irving Berlin, Elizabeth Arden, General T. Coleman du Pont, and Marie Dressler (on the screen she was Tugboat Annie, but in Mizner's paradise she was the "Duchess of Boca Raton"). There was even a Rumanian princess on the sales staff.

The greatest draw of all was Addison Mizner himself—"one of America's greatest architects," as the publicists said in hushed and reverential tones. He designed the ornate Cloister Inn, and an administration building modeled on El Greco's home in Spain. He had his own dream house on the drawing boards, a Spanish castle on an island, complete with drawbridge and watchtower—from which he threatened to have a servant throw things at unwanted visitors. He had to approve all construction he didn't design himself. There were to be no shacks. Ocean-front homes had to cost at least $40,000, though less expensive ones could be built inland.

Boca Raton was reached by the world's broadest highway, a magnificent twenty-laner with indirect lighting called El Camino Real. It was beautifully landscaped, of course, and bisected by a canal on which the obligatory gondoliers made their appearance (the boom did wonders for the gondola industry). The effect was impressive enough to overcome the fact that it was less than half a mile long. But boom-time grand entrances weren't really expected to go anywhere: they were merely a promise of better things to come.

Opening-day sales were in the millions, and Mizner Development Corporation stock soared from $100 a share to $1,000. Money was literally being thrown at them, as checks had to be gathered up in wastebaskets to await processing. Wilson's description of Boca Raton as "a platinum sucker trap" was proving apt.

It was a con man's dream.

Ca'd'Zan, circus king John Ringling's waterfront home in Sarasota, is now a museum.

This monumental hotel, with steps down to the gondola landing, was to help make Davis Shores "America's Foremost Watering Place."

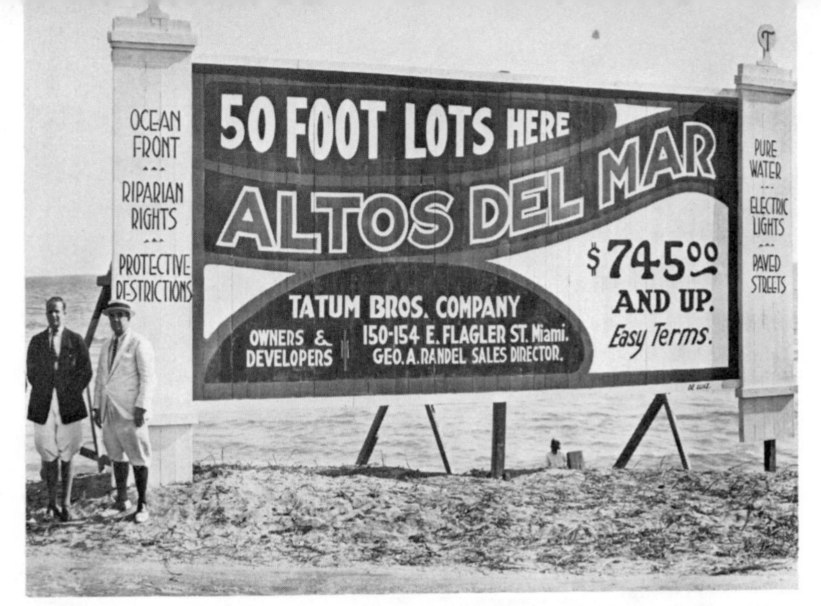

Salesmen, typically attired in knickers, stand by a billboard peddling 50 feet in paradise during the 1920s boom.

Glenn Curtiss planned Opa-locka as "the Baghdad of Dade County," and his architect, Bernhardt Muller, carried out the theme in structures like this administration building.

Entrance gates were the first things to go up in any boomtime subdivision.

Here are two examples, in varying sizes, from the Tampa area.

GONE!!!

•

Florida's good fortune could not go on indefinitely without provoking jealousy elsewhere. Floridians were too euphoric to be diplomatic, and that worsened the outsiders' feelings.

When would the boom end? Everyone was asking, but the answers were flip, calculated to enrage:

"When people stop reading the ads," said one.

"When the sun decides not to shine any more," replied another, "when the Gulf Stream ceases to flow."

"When the Northern businessman becomes a perpetual motion machine and can stand the rush and roar of city life 12 months a year without a let-up or recreation," retorted a third.

Others asked whether all the speculation had a sound base. "One might as well ask whether the Stock Exchange rests upon a sound and stable base," harrumphed the indignant boomers.

But the questions would not go away.

Several Ohio banks, stung by their massive loss of deposits to Florida, teamed up to publicize the fragility of the boom. Floridians responded by boycotting Ohio products.

A New York sportswriter made light of the boom in his

column. "Shut Your Damn Mouth!" was the editorial reply from a Florida paper. The Ku Klux Klan offered to picket.

California, the state's long-time rival in the sun-and-oranges department, anxiously highlighted every shortcoming and downplayed every achievement of the boom.

The fickle public, which had gloried in good news about Florida, was now surfeited on the steady diet of it and demanded the opposite. A vast market opened up for the debunkers, and Florida's response was touchy.

Henry Flagler could have told them that good fortune always provokes jealousy, but they had to learn it themselves, the hard way.

Governor Martin decided a tongue-lashing to the nation's publishers was in order, for the tripe they had been printing about Florida. With the boldness of a man who knows he's right, he went right into their midst to confront them.

He took along some of his big guns: George Merrick, Joseph Young, Paris Singer, Barron Collier, N. B. T. Roney, and other behemoths of the boom. They met the publishers at the Waldorf-Astoria (whose owner, T. Coleman du Pont, was one of the financial backers of Boca Raton) and discussed "The Truth About Florida."

There was nothing muckraking about that truth: rather, it was the plaintive honk of a fattened goose that had laid some golden eggs. Governor Martin considered the meeting a great triumph, noting a diminution in critical coverage afterward.

At the same time, Florida took some practical steps to polish up its tarnished image. Hotel rates, which had been a prominent source of complaints, were regulated. State licenses were required for realtors. The life span of binders was cut back from thirty days to ten, and it was no longer permitted to have additional transactions stuck on them like ticks. The cost of a binder in relation to selling price was upped.

Previously, the binder boys had crowded around the railroad station, hawking their wares to incoming visitors, who had to run the gamut of "sure things" just to set foot in Miami. Binder boys who couldn't crowd into the station assaulted prospects in the streets, where the regular traffic snarls helped provide easy access to a captive audience. This was thought extremely bad for Florida's image, so new regulations required that real estate could only be peddled from offices. Some restaurants found the new law a bonanza; they promptly quit the food business and rented out every one of their tables as "offices."

A committee was set up to screen out-of-state newspapers that ran ads for Florida property and inform them of ventures that were not on the level. A Better Business Bureau was established to handle complaints. Lectures were given on "Truthfulness in Advertising." More concern was given to the appearance of propriety. When Evelyn Nesbit Thaw wanted to open a cabaret across the street from the Halcyon Hotel—designed by her murdered lover, Stanford White—she was denied permission and had to set up in another part of town.

Charles Ponzi—the celebrated swindler whose name entered the language with the "Ponzi Scheme"—was between prison sentences in Massachusetts and needed to raise money for his defense. The quickest place to make it was Florida, so he headed south and set up the Charpon Land Syndicate, which promised handsome—almost stratospheric—profits to its investors. He was promptly nailed for practicing without a license and given a one-year jail sentence: it just would not do to have the highly publicized Ponzi mixed up in Florida's real-estate picture. Getting the message, he fled the state while his case was on appeal.

On the more positive side, a rationale was developed for what was happening in Florida which so satisfied the developers that it came from all their lips in virtually the same words.

Summed up: There was no boom. It was merely the realization of values that had previously been kept unrealistically low by the lack of transportation and by shortcomings in advertising skill. Not only were current prices not too high, they were actually far below value. The bubble was not going to burst, because there was no bubble. Florida was merely growing by leaps and bounds.

That was the boomers' creed, which they recited with all the sincerity of the Lord's Prayer. They preached it from every forum, in public speeches and private sales pitches, in interviews and paid advertisements, on the radio and in subsidized books.

Whether attributed to developers or journalists or public officials or knowledgeable observers, the words came out exactly the same.

• • •

The greatest strain from all the rapid growth was placed on the creaky transportation system. After coping as well as it could, it finally cracked.

In the summer of 1925 more than two thousand freight cars were waiting to be unloaded at Miami. There was no more place to put them, for they were already strung for miles outside the city. The single track that Henry Flagler had laid was simply not adequate to keep up with the booming demand. On August 17 the Florida East Coast Railway declared an embargo on all cargo except fuel, livestock, and perishables. More than seven thousand freight cars stacked up at Jacksonville that fall.

Stocks of building materials soon ran out. One enterprising builder tried to bring in a load of bricks labeled "lettuce," all properly iced down, but he was caught. Others began building flimsier houses. What supplies there were had to be carefully guarded against nighttime raids.

Particularly hurt were those who had large hotels or apartment buildings nearly completed when the embargo went into effect, then could not get what they needed to finish. New projects could not get started. One contractor had to turn down $5 million worth of business in a single month. Addison Mizner opened a new tile factory to supply the needs of his own development.

The Florida East Coast planned to double-track its system, but that would take time. Rival railroads, seeing an opportunity to crack the lucrative Miami market, which had always been an FEC monopoly, promptly announced that they would head their tracks in that direction. The Seaboard Airline borrowed $25 million to undertake the work, getting from George Merrick and Glenn Curtiss the necessary right-of-way to reach the city: the developers wanted no repetition of the deadlock, ever.

A mass rush to other forms of transportation followed, with predictable results. On September 12 the steamship lines were forced to embargo incoming building materials and furniture. City employees and prisoners were pressed into service to unload the boats that were forming the bottleneck. Then warehouse space ran out. The city started to build a new one, but that too would take time.

Perhaps three hundred million people could be stuffed into Florida, as the baseball statistician insisted, but clearly they would not be able to bring their beds and chairs and windows and roofing tiles with them.

Private fleets were the next solution. Never had such an armada descended on Miami. Schooners that properly belonged in maritime museums were commissioned to make one last profitable run. They had to anchor offshore and wait their turn to be guided through the narrow ship channel into the Miami harbor. When one of the boats threw its anchor over the Western Union cable to South America, it cut off communications for several days.

Since buildings could not be completed, there was still a housing shortage on shore, so a group of entrepreneurs decided to bring in a floating hotel. A decommissioned four-masted Danish naval bark, the *Prins Valdemar*, parked on the bay front, would provide a hundred rooms. At 241 feet, it was the largest boat in the invading fleet. Pilots waited for absolute calm before guiding it through the channel. It drew too much to pass easily, so all ballast was jettisoned. A bungling tug ran it aground. When the tide went out, a stiff wind caught the top-heavy masts and rigging and blew the ship right over. It turned as it went down, neatly stoppering the channel completely.

Dredges tried to cut a new opening around it, but ran into a rock ledge. Bringing in the required dynamite took longer. In the end, the channel was closed for twenty-five days. Meanwhile, 45 million board feet of lumber were floating outside on boats waiting to get in. With the tremendous holding costs involved, builders started to go bankrupt.

• • •

Other Florida developments still sold, even as Miami languished. Buyers snapped up lots in Ringling Isles and Davis Shores and a host of future Venices. But a new factor entered into the equation. It was called "silly slump talk." The sound was not music to the boomers' ears.

Sales were slowing, there was no doubt, and lot prices were not running up as fast as they had. Binder boys were taking off for greener pastures on Wall Street. Skepticism was in the air and endless recital of the boomers' creed could not stop it. The smart money was poised to flee.

There were a variety of responses.

George Merrick forged ahead, heaping more fuel on the fire. Coral Gables had sold about $150 million worth of property since that first lot back in 1921. Now he announced even grander plans. The "South Sea Isles of Coral Gables" would turn a chain of islands into a 6.5-mile Riviera along the bay. He imported genuine Polynesians to split open coconuts at his Tahiti Beach for the opening ceremonies, but that was a minor expense. The price tag for this grandiose scheme was $250 million. Let the smart-money Nervous Nellies stick that in their pipes and smoke it!

Carl Fisher, on the other hand, went in for diversification. He had done so well in the boom that his wealth, estimated at $50 million, was ten times what he had come to Florida with. But he knew enough about ballyhoo to be skeptical of other people's, and he was particularly leery of the binder boys and what they represented. So he tightened up his sales terms, upped the required down payment, and even took some of his beach property off the market. Then he headed north for the summer of 1925, leaving the frenzy behind. He had other plans.

He paid $2.5 million for 10,000 acres of Long Island's Montauk Point, announcing that he would create the "Miami Beach of the North." It would gratify his need "to see steam shovels throwing dirt and buildings going up!" There would be three hotels, four golf courses, glass-covered tennis courts, and 15 miles of waterfront.

Florida newspapers, which had treated Fisher like an oracle once the boom got under way, were not at all enthusiastic about his defection. "Imagine a 'Miami of the North,'" snorted one, "with its snow and ice of winter instead of the glowing sunshine and balmy breezes. Probably Mr. Fisher is planning to offer a brand of synthetic sunshine, or something of the kind in lieu of the real health-giving Florida kind."

Although Fisher did not go public with his criticism, he told a friend privately that "The city is literally flooded with 'sharpers' who are pulling all sorts of schemes." He predicted, "We are bound to have a big flare-back and Miami and Miami Beach are bound to suffer as a result."

Less discreet was General T. Coleman du Pont, former chemical-company president, sometime senator from Delaware, and founding member of Boca Raton's financial glitterati.

A devotee of card tricks and sleight of hand, du Pont did not approve of the financial legerdemain of Wilson Mizner. Wilson, in turn, thought him a fool, an old fart wired up with handshake buzzers and squirting flowers, but for once he was underestimating his mark. Du Pont used those gimmicks as a front for his own con games—the biggest of which was taking over the multimillion-dollar family business with a cash outlay of only $700. The old fart clearly outclassed the Abe Lincoln of the underworld.

Du Pont told Addison (as the "day" version of the Mizners) that "I have always, in business, believed in being very, very careful not to make a statement that could not be backed up by facts in every way." He was obviously out of place.

He protested when a nonexistent "hundred million dollar development program" was ballyhooed. When an advertising genius added a line to Boca Raton's publicity inviting buyers to "Attach This Advertisement to Your Contract for Deed. It Becomes a Part Thereof," du Pont looked at the accompanying lies and assumption of responsibility for making them real, and blanched. He was the financial figurehead of the project, the most famous millionaire connected with it—and the first one who would be sued by disgruntled customers. He jumped ship. Publicly.

"I've never been connected with a failure in my life," he said, "and this thing is sure to fail with these people in charge." His departure guaranteed that it would. In the period when bad news about Florida filled a public demand, his statement to the press was widely reprinted. The development's other monied men followed his lead and decamped. "Our efforts to regularize the affairs and the management of the corporation," they complained, "and to eliminate exaggerated publicity have met with criticism rather than cooperation." Sales ground to a halt. The flood of buyers at Boca Raton offices changed almost immediately to a flood of process servers.

"I never open my door," wrote Wilson, "but a Writ blows in." He greeted the servers by showing his collection and asking, "Would you like this on top or in the middle of the deck?"

Addison never got his dream castle off the drawing boards.

• • •

Perhaps the most important convention held in Florida during the winter of 1925–26 was that of the Investment Bankers Association of America, a thousand of whose members gathered in St. Petersburg in December. There had been a lot of hard feelings in banking circles around the country about all the funds that had made their way to Florida, and much alarming publicity about the "inevitable collapse of the boom." The bankers came with critical eyes and hard questions, such as how many of the properties purchased could guarantee a 6 percent return on investment. Florida was anxious to impress.

The weather, however, would not cooperate. St. Petersburg —where the newspaper was given away free when the sun didn't shine—had a record string of free newspapers, and the bankers were not impressed. They wanted to fish and swim and golf in the idyllic tropical paradise they had seen in the ads. Instead, they saw Florida at its worst and most depressing: chilly, wet, and gloomy, the kind of climate nobody would walk across the street to frolic in. They went home singing no praises and recommending no investments.

There was a big freeze on New Year's Eve as the unfortunate winter wore on. Still, there was precedent for hoping that before leaving in February, some people would pick up a last-minute lot on the way out of town. But balancing that was a fear of the Ides of March. Income taxes were due then, and the Internal Revenue Service had descended on Miami as quickly as the con men when the previous year's tales of fabulous wealth were being publicized. They too planned to get their share.

Even the greediest of boom-time operators usually had to settle for 20 percent cash and 80 percent promises to pay over the next four years. That was the financial house of cards on which the boom was built. Uncle Sam, however, wanted all of his money in cash and right away—no four-year delay. Now, with reckoning time at hand, many people did not have the cash to pay. To get it, they would have to put their property up for sale. There was a fear of wholesale dumping, an action that would be disastrous for the already sluggish market.

Which would it be? The last minute pickup or the last minute drop?

The drop, of course. The frenzied lot sales gave way to a mass of land auctions in which people took what they could get. This might have encouraged bargain hunters, but at the same time the stock market registered its biggest dip since 1920, so there were not a lot of adventurous investors around. The pages and pages of real-estate ads gave way to pages and pages of legal announcements dealing with the reclamation or forced sale of the same properties.

There was no summer season in 1926, just a little tropical turbulence in July that gave Miami some high winds and probably would have given the city some more bad publicity if anyone had been around to see it. The boomers were down, but not out. After studying the situation, the silver-lining crowd called it a "lull" and pronounced it a good thing. The fast operators had departed and now Florida could get down to its real destiny. In place of last year's insistence that there was no boom came a new line: the theory of two booms.

Florida, promoters said, had seen not one but two booms. The first, a boom in lot sales and speculation, was now—thank God!—over. The second, a development boom, was just beginning—and the smart money had better get aboard. Much of the construction that had been contracted for during the peak months of 1925 was still under way, or awaiting supplies to begin. This was a strong economic indicator in anyone's book. Add to that the ballyhoo for Florida's new industrial future. The artists went back to their drawing boards to fill in the skylines with smokestacks rather than skyscrapers, while the publicity men cranked out new articles about the rising silk industry or the packing prospects for St. Augustine's hot-as-hell datil peppers. The ad men advised their readers to invest in La Belle, "Henry Ford's choice. The city destined to be the center of the great RUBBER INDUSTRY OF THE UNITED STATES." Baseball-star-turned-realtor Joe Tinker (of the famous Tinker-Evers-Chance double-play combination) boasted, "No Venetian Lagoons for Longwood"—which he projected as a great manufacturing center. Joseph Young added industries to his Hollywood greenbelt, and so did Glenn Curtiss at Opa-locka.

Hold the gondolas! Bring on the steel mills! How about Pittsburgh for a name? How about New Detroit? The lull was just a time for tooling up, like the auto industry's model change. Buy now, before prices go up!

• • •

Monday-morning coffee drinkers and commuters had something to shock them out of their weekend stupor on September 20, 1926. Banner headlines screaming across the front page of *The New York Times* informed them: "1,000 DEAD IN FLORIDA STORM, 3,000 HURT; MIAMI WORST HIT; 60-MILE SWATH OF DESTRUCTION LEAVES 38,000 HOMELESS; SCORE OF TOWNS ARE RAZED OR FLOODED; SHIPPING WRECKED." That was followed by such reassuring subheads as "HEAVY SEAS FLOOD CITIES" and "SPECTRE OF FAMINE RISING."

Other papers reported the death of Glenn Curtiss in the raging storm.

Carl Fisher, in New York to oversee his Montauk development, received a telegram: "MIAMI BEACH TOTAL LOSS. SWEPT AWAY BY HURRICANE."

The reports were exaggerated: a thousand were not dead, Curtiss had survived, and there was still a Miami Beach, though its streets lay buried under 2 to 4 feet of sand. But it had been the worst disaster in the country since the San Francisco earthquake and fire of 1906.

It had caught people unprepared. None of the newcomers had ever seen a hurricane. As soon as the winds stopped roaring, they rushed outside to assess the damage, and many were killed when the fury started up again. They had unwittingly stepped into the eye of the storm.

The barometric readings were the lowest that had ever been recorded in the United States. Winds were measured at 120 miles an hour before the anemometer blew away. Shoddily constructed buildings from the embargo period of the boom were first flattened, then turned into deadly weapons hurled against other targets. The storm surge deposited boats well up on dry land. The *Nohab*, yacht of former Kaiser Wilhelm, was broken in two and sunk. Giant dredges went to the bottom of the bay. Every boat in the harbor was either damaged or sunk, save one: the miscreant *Prins Valdemar* came through unscathed, to be turned into a bay-front aquarium that was a popular Miami tourist attraction for years.

Paradise had turned into a windy, watery, seaweed-drenched hell on earth. The tropical plants were stripped of their foliage. The golf courses had no more greens, just sand traps—acres and acres of them.

Typhoid appeared in the aftermath. Confiscated liquor supplies were broken out in the Miami jail for medicinal purposes—though one diehard prohibitionist threatened to shoot a doctor if "he dared give my wife a drop of liquor."

William Randolph Hearst sent a trainload of doctors and nurses to help. President Machado of Cuba sent a gunboat full of them.

When the Red Cross moved into action, however, raising relief money, they were told pointedly that they might "do more damage permanently to Florida than would be offset by the funds received." Even in the direst straits, Floridians had the booster mentality. Admit nothing! Everything was exaggerated! A booming season was expected!

Believe it or not.

Doc Dammers took out a newspaper ad to answer the question, "When will Florida come back?" His reply was simple: "FLORIDA NEVER WENT AND IT DOESN'T HAVE TO COME BACK."

The silver-lining crowd evolved a whole new set of points to show the bright side of things in the wake of what they euphemistically but unvaryingly called "the gale." It would lead to better construction in the future, they pointed out, with tighter building standards. Wreckage was easy to clear away, and besides, the climate was Florida's main attraction—the storm hadn't blown that away. And, say, did you see how rapidly San Francisco grew back from the ashes of its fire and earthquake. . . .

One of the best things, they said, was that the flood of anti-Florida propaganda had diminished. They were right. The Sunshine State and its boom were being given the dispensation of *nihil nisi bonum de mortuis*.

Only in the hands of a few angry gods were the sinners still being flayed. New York's Reverend John Roach Straton, celebrated guardian of public morality, sermonized his flock: "And yonder is beautiful Florida. How beautiful. But how she did depart from God's way! She turned after the worship of Mammon. Racetrack gamblers were welcomed. The Sunday sermons were forgotten in the mad rush for gold. But God did not forget them. It is to be hoped that Florida will return to God, and it seems now that she will."

Shut your damn mouth, Reverend Straton!

A month later another storm threatened Miami. People quickly boarded up for that one. When it passed by, skirting the area, they went dancing in the streets. Three men were jailed for spreading false rumors about the seriousness of the storm. The boom was gone, but the boom mentality lived on. You had to watch what you said.

• • •

Doc Davis was not doing too well, though it would have been against his religion to tell you so. Like all boom-time developers, he dealt in faith and paper. Buyers trusted Doc Davis and he trusted them. He said the underwater lot they bought would not only become high ground but would be tropically landscaped and bordering a golf course to boot. They believed him and gave him a little cash as down payment. He believed them when they said they would pay the rest in one, two, three, and four years, at the end of which time they would all be fair and square. Their water would have become paradise and their notes would have become cash in his bank.

All those fancy figures he threw around were, therefore, projections. Cash on hand was somewhat less—not enough, for instance, to make all the improvements he promised without continued transfusions from notes as they came due. That was the rub. As skepticism grew about Florida, some people decided to cut their losses at the down payment and forget about the rest. Maybe they could do without the gondola for another few years after all.

Doc Davis was expecting $4 million in second payments to come in on Davis Islands, so he could continue his series of apartment houses based on famous Italian palaces, and other improvements. Instead, he got $30,000 and an instant crisis. If the same thing happened to his St. Augustine project, he would be facing complete disaster. He had a little breathing space there, but not much. A Boston syndicate put up $2.5 million to keep the Islands project going, acquiring 51 percent of Davis's interest in them. That was in August 1926. The timing was good.

The next month came the hurricane. Joseph Young was in New York, trying to stir up the same kind of support. His deal was almost clinched when word of the disaster came in. Hollywood, whose slogan had been "Building for Centuries of Endurance," had a thousand homes destroyed and two thousand damaged. Initial reports, of course, were even worse. The deal was off. Young lost his development to creditors.

Doc Davis knew when a place had exhausted its money-making potential. He had seen it happen in Miami, and now he saw the curse on the whole state of Florida. Time to pack up and take his act elsewhere. He decided on Europe.

He had heard of an island off Holland that might be pumped up to greater size. Riviera real estate was said to be languishing, and might respond to the magic touch of his genius.

He set sail from New York on October 9. Four days later a wireless message from the S.S. *Majestic* reached A. Y. Milam, vice president of Davis Properties (and speaker of the Florida House of Representatives): "DAVE LOST OVERBOARD EARLY THIS MORNING. SHIP CIRCLED OVER HOUR. EVERYTHING POSSIBLE DONE. NO HOPE."

There was a suitable irony. One of his friends wrote that Davis "took great fortunes up from out of the sea. In the sea he died on October 13th, and in the sea he rests."

The mystery surrounding his death has never been dispelled. Although the Davis organization rushed to assure the public that his affairs were in good order and that Davis Shores would carry on, this was patently untrue. By 1927 "America's Foremost Watering Place" boasted only a dozen families in residence and an appraisal noted that "the property is treeless and devoid of top soil; and the white sand tends to drift badly in a high wind. This is a serious drawback to the comfort and beauty of the property for home purposes."

Davis Shores went into receivership, and a few years later the development that was to cost in the high millions was auctioned off on the courthouse steps in the low thousands. All was not well.

When the captain of the *Majestic* flatly called it a suicide, the Davis organization threw up a number of smokescreens. They suggested he had been robbed by "society crooks" and dumped overboard; he was famous for refusing to deposit his valuables in the ship's safe. An alternate theory they advanced was that he had fallen overboard accidentally. This was viewed with skepticism since he had gone out a porthole, but they pointed out it was a very large porthole and he was a very small man.

The insurance company bought that and paid off a huge claim. Davis was known for his rashness in performing athletic feats, and his friends insisted he had foolishly been balancing himself in the porthole when a wave hit the ship and out he went.

Although that was good enough for the claims adjuster, the general public wouldn't buy it. Further revelations titillated them with the *cherchez-la-femme* aspects of the case. The picture that emerged of Doc Davis was not of a modest genius but of a pint-sized braggart who, with growing wealth, sought all the perks, particularly women.

After the death of his wife, he had played for a long time with one of movie maker Mack Sennett's bathing beauties, but she would not marry him. In 1925 he shocked one of his friends by announcing that he would marry the next queen of the Gasparilla Festival, Tampa's mini–Mardi Gras. Since the queen had not yet been chosen, there was a good deal of bravado in his boast, but he went ahead and did it. A whirlwind courtship, elopement, marriage—and then almost immediate divorce. He turned right around and wooed and won her again, and they remarried. Then she left for Europe—without him. It was certainly a stormy relationship.

The fact that he was accompanied on his final journey by a lawyer, a private detective, and his bathing-beauty girlfriend inevitably gave rise to speculation that he was planning to divorce his long-absent wife. After much hemming and hawing, it turned out that the girlfriend was the only witness to Doc Davis's fall. A steward in the hallway outside heard them arguing, heard Davis say, "I can go on living or end it. I can make money or spend it. It all depends on you." Then the final splash.

His death was a shock to the investors who had placed their faith in him. From dreams of vast riches and big quick profits, they were reduced to suing over his pocket change.

The circumstances surrounding his final hours would continue to be a source of speculation. Inevitably, there would be stories that he had turned up in other countries, but few would believe them. Most accepted the fact that Doc Davis was dead.

As dead as the Florida boom.

• • •

Things began to snowball.

The banks watched their vast deposits melt away, for people felt safer having their money elsewhere. All the real-estate loans turned soft. The skyscraper bank buildings, a symbol of boom-time confidence, started to lose their occupants: the vastly diminished number of realtors couldn't begin to fill all the office space that had gone up in anticipation of further frenzied years.

The banks started to fold.

The newspapers, which had waxed fat with real-estate advertising, had also gone in for larger quarters and new printing presses. When they found they couldn't collect for all that ad space from realtors who had either left or gone broke, some of the newspapers were forced to follow suit.

The cities that had expanded their borders to accommodate subdivision developers now rushed to contract. For the hundreds of millions of dollars in bonded indebtedness there was not much more left to show than streets and curbs way out in the sticks, in areas that would not be further developed for a generation. Lot owners stopped paying their taxes and municipalities started defaulting on their bonds.

When the Mediterranean fruit fly made an unwelcome appearance, Florida citrus was quarantined. Many banks that had survived bad real-estate loans could not survive the added burden of bad agricultural loans, and went under.

A 1928 hurricane, coming almost on the anniversary of the 1926 blow, caused an even greater loss of life. Doc Dammers's comforting assurance that hurricanes happen only once in a lifetime was torn to shreds. What didn't blow away froze. The unpredictabilities of every season were visited upon Florida with a vengeance.

While all this happened, the rest of the nation was enjoying booming prosperity. Then in 1929 the stock market crashed, and everything went to hell. Three-fourths of Florida's banks closed their doors. Seven-eighths of the municipalities defaulted on their bonds. The railroads that had rushed to borrow and expand during the boom now went into receivership.

And what of the boomers?

Some went the way of Doc Davis. Particularly poignant was the saga of textile magnate Harry Eagle, who had plunged into the boom in 1925, developing Eagle Crest at St. Petersburg —just in time for the bust. Disillusioned, he went back to his more profitable investments in New York. He managed to corner the silk market—just as rayon became available. A double loser, he committed suicide in 1928.

The bust soured things for many people, though not necessarily to that extent.

John J. McGraw was riding high with his Pennant Park subdivision for a while, but when things turned around he wound up with lawsuits up to his neck. Sarasota didn't look so good to him any more, so in 1927 he decided to take his spring training elsewhere.

The Brotherhood of Locomotive Engineers, which had rushed in where Mrs. Palmer feared to tread, found itself stuck with a first-class white elephant in the town of Venice. When the tides of boom went out, the union discovered it had invested far too much in the property. The additional burden of the national depression nearly made the Brotherhood—like other practitioners of business unionism—go under. Venice itself became a virtual ghost town.

The kings of the boom went their separate ways.

George Merrick lost everything—or everything except the satisfaction of seeing Coral Gables develop according to his plan and become an outstanding suburb. He and his wife ran a fish camp in the keys, on land she had inherited, but the Labor Day hurricane of 1935 swept it away. Merrick went back into real estate in Miami, and again rose rapidly to the top of a much-chastened heap. He chaired Dade County's Planning Council and Zoning Board, two posts for which his background eminently qualified him. He was a founder and the first president of the Historical Association of Southern Florida. During the last two years before his death in 1942, he served as postmaster of Miami.

Carl Fisher, having sensed impending disaster, managed to survive the bust, not unscathed but sufficiently intact to continue his Montauk Point project. That, plus the depression (and drinking), did him in. His $50-million fortune had dwindled to $50,000 by the time of his death in 1939, and the last decade of his life was hard. For his last three years he subsisted mainly on alcohol, an embarrassing relic of Miami Beach's finer days, lamenting to his friends that he was not the Carl Fisher of yore.

Glenn Curtiss fared better than most, because his investments were not limited to Florida. He had to cut back on his real-estate projects—there was no market for them after the bust. But he tried to bolster the economy with some small industrial projects, based on his inventions, which provided jobs for hard-pressed Floridians. He developed a shallow-draft boat pushed by an airplane propeller that was useful for travel in the Everglades, and a streamlined trailer he marketed as the Aero-Car. Convinced that prosperity would return and he could go on developing the Egyptian, Chinese, and English villages he had in mind, he held on to his Florida property. But death intervened in 1930, and his plans died with him.

Addison Mizner spent his last years doing what he was so proficient at: borrowing from friends. Although he designed some more buildings, the taste for Mizner architecture had died with the boom and would not be revived for some years. In order to do some work in California in 1930, he finally had to get a license to practice architecture and was terrified of taking the test. After regaling the examiners with racy tales of how he got his $50 million worth of business, he was given a special dispensation for his shortcomings in spelling and arithmetic. He also wrote his memoirs, which unfortunately end before the Palm Beach years. He died with process servers knocking at the door. Except for Mizner Industries, which was sold and survived another two decades, his estate was insolvent.

Brother Wilson headed off to California's Hollywood, which he compared to "a trip through a sewer in a glass-bottomed boat." Urged to write his memoirs, he declined on the grounds that "It would be blowing a police whistle."

In fact, he wouldn't write anything. So Darryl Zanuck sent a secretary to trail him and copy down his conversations. One of his ad-libbed plots won an Oscar, and some of his wisecracks were uttered by Jimmy Cagney and Humphrey Bogart on the screen. He opened the Brown Derby restaurant, which grew into a chain and left him somewhat better fixed than brother Addison. They both died in 1933. Three years later Wilson appeared on screen, played by Clark Gable: Screenwriter Anita Loos had based her character Blackie Norton in *San Francisco* on her dear, departed friend.

Wilson's post-mortem on the boom had been that "various acts of God and man placed a cosmic pin into one of the most perfectly gassed realty balloons of all time."

For once the quotable aphorist was outdone, at least in terms of pithiness. Walter Fuller, a second-generation St. Petersburg developer (who boasted that his father had made eight fortunes and lost seven and a half of them), boiled it down to a single essential factor. The boom collapsed, he said, because it ran out of suckers.

Looking at the wind-whipped palm trees and waist-deep water, it is easy to understand that initial reports claimed Miami Beach had been swept away by the 1926 hurricane.

Boats in Miami waters were deposited well up on dry land when the storm surge subsided.

Epping Forest, Du Pont's estate in Jacksonville, included among other features a boathouse with a roof garden.

(OPPOSITE, TOP): D. P. Davis was hailed as a genius while the boom went on.

(OPPOSITE, BOTTOM): Alfred I. Du Pont, the family rebel who sat out the boom and picked up the pieces afterward. (*Library of Congress*)

Al Capone's winter home on Palm Island. His presence made the neighbors nervous.

Crowds line up to withdraw their money from a St. Petersburg bank in 1931. Bank runs were frequent—and usually fatal to the institutions—during the Depression.

THE LONG RECOVERY

•

It was an unlikely crew of saviors who came to Florida after the bust. Their patronage was, for the most part, doubly appreciated given the hard times. And for their prescience they profited, by buying when prices were low.

Melvil Dewey, developer of the famous library decimal system, took advantage of the slump to acquire a southern home for his New York resort, the Lake Placid Club. His acreage included the skeleton of a boom-time hotel, which he had completed for use as a "Loj" (a fervent orthographic reformer, Dewey simplified the unwieldy "Lodge" just as he had removed the final "le" from his first name). The state legislature, more eager to please than ever, obligingly renamed the property Lake Placid, Florida, in 1927.

Another colorful character who put down roots at that time was Dr. John Harvey Kellogg, head of Battle Creek Sanitarium in Michigan. Kellogg was a minor language reformer, having coined the word "sanitarium" in place of the then-standard "sanatorium." He is best remembered for his development of breakfast cereal and peanut butter, which he promoted as health foods. An advocate of holistic medicine, he was widely beloved in Florida for his remarks on the beneficial effects of sunshine, which the Chamber of Commerce never tired of publicizing.

For many years he had thought of opening a Florida sanitarium. With the bust, conditions were just right to go ahead. Glenn Curtiss, himself a food faddist (and sometime patient at Battle Creek), had a huge white elephant in the Pueblo Hotel, which was obviously destined to be nothing but a drain on his finances. Dr. Kellogg, after taking a tour of the property, asked him, "How would you like to have this place taken off your hands and used as a sanitarium?" Curtiss slept on it, then appeared at the doctor's door with a contract: a dollar a year, and title free and clear if the sanitarium was a going concern in six years.

"I told him the price was too cheap," Kellogg recalled, "and offered him ten times that amount." Battle Creek had found a Miami home.

More controversial was a new resident on one of Carl Fisher's man-made islands: Al Capone. Feeling unappreciated in Chicago, he threatened to leave the city high and dry (so to speak) for New Year's Eve 1928, and headed for Miami. He became a leading customer of one mayor's clothing store, palled around with the son of another, and bought a Palm Island estate built for brewer Clarence Busch through the real-estate firm of a third. Priests, ministers, and civic leaders approached him for contributions. He praised Miami as "the Garden of America" and noted, "if I am invited, I will join the Rotary Club."

But there were some who did not react with delight to his settling in, or to his prediction that "I believe many of my friends will also join me."

Though Capone listed his occupation as "antique dealer," the *Miami News* openly damned him as "the notorious beer and brothel baron of Chicago." The governor of Florida called on citizens to "cooperate by all legitimate means towards ejecting a public menace and impostor and to exterminate the growth of organized crime."

Carl Fisher testified in court that Capone's presence was detrimental to land sales—something a lesser (or soberer) man would not have dared. The press reported that the onlooking gangster "glared at the witness with all the ferocity of an infuriated beast."

All these efforts were insufficient to dislodge Capone. An income-tax conviction took him away for a while, but he returned to spend his last years at Palm Island, and tour-boat operators regularly pointed out his home as one of the area's attractions. The prediction that his friends would join him proved all too accurate: organized crime became a big factor in Miami's life and economy.

Uncouth on a different order was the man who bought the Mizners' dream of Boca Raton and, at a cost of $14 million, brought it a step closer to reality. The pieces of Addison's and Wilson's mythic realm had first been picked up by the vice president of the United States, Charles Gates Dawes, and his brother, a Chicago financier. After a couple of years the Dawes brothers despaired of putting that particular Humpty Dumpty together again, and passed it on to a one-time associate, Clarence Geist, who was enormously wealthy, but hardly well bred. "Crude" and "coarse" were the adjectives his Palm Beach neighbors applied to him, though he could afford to buy and sell many of them.

Geist had come up the hard way, starting as a farmer, then becoming a horse trader, railroad brakeman, developer of low-income real estate, and finally a public-utilities magnate who controlled so many water companies that he was popularly known as "The Water Boy."

Having been snubbed socially at Palm Beach, Geist was delighted to acquire the barony just south, and proceeded to turn it into a millionaire's club where he (shades of Paris Singer) would pass on the members.

The Cloister Inn, which Addison Mizner considered his architectural epitaph, was quadrupled in size at a cost of $8 million—impressive by boom-time standards, and a knockout in the bust years. Geist lorded it over his manor, holding up entertainments until he made his fashionably late entrance, and having his limousine tear up the turf on his golf course when he didn't feel like walking.

Plagued by a deathly fear of kidnapping, he kept $1 million in cash handy for ransom payment, if need be, and took the precaution of never allowing his photograph to be published. He kept a police dog and bodyguards, and his club was patrolled and protected by men with sawed-off shotguns.

Geist managed to ward off kidnapping, but not the death which must come to all men, and which overtook him in 1938. So attached was he to the social world where he had been king that he left an annual subsidy of $100,000 for five years to underwrite the deficits of his Boca Raton Club.

The boom-time palaces that lacked a sugar daddy like Clarence Geist met with less luxurious fates. Some of them were snapped up by Bible colleges (including Billy Graham's alma mater) and military academies (including one named for Union Admiral David Farragut). Some were taken over for government offices. They were the lucky ones. One became a giant hen house, its basement used for mushroom growing. Others, like Ringling's Ritz-Carlton and Paris Singer's Blue Heron, were never completed. Their hulks remained to haunt the shoreline until the inevitable appointment with the bulldozer.

• • •

John Ringling was sufficiently diversified to avoid destruction in the bust. He was even in a position to help mitigate some of its effects on the Sarasota economy—by making the city winter headquarters for his circus.

This was not strictly a charitable act on Ringling's part. It made a lot of sense, saving the heavy heating bills required by the previous winter headquarters in Bridgeport, Connecticut.

Then too, the Sarasota land was acquired at distressed prices. And there was always the possibility of tourist income from those who wanted to watch rehearsals.

But, despite the hard times, many Sarasotans were inclined to oppose Ringling's plan: circus people, after all, had a fairly shady reputation. It took a convincing chiropractor to talk them into welcoming the boon—which was not the only one that Ringling gave the city.

There was the oil boomlet as well.

A geologist named B. F. Alley insisted rich wells could be drilled in the area. "You people down here haven't seen anything yet," he told the hundreds who flocked to hear his presentation. "Why, the real estate boom was a mere shower compared with the cloudburst that will come with oil."

That was just the kind of talk people wanted to hear. They ate it up when Alley told them, "I can see it now—oil wells up and down the whole coast. It'll be the biggest thing that ever hit this state. It'll make Florida the richest state in the world!"

Thousands gathered to watch baseball superslugger Rogers Hornsby smash a bottle of champagne over the first drilling rig that went in on Ringling's land south of town, as the circus's Czechoslovakian Band played rousing background music.

But the drill never brought up anything but salt water. It was a scene repeated in other Florida communities desperate for solace from the bust. Oil was not to provide salvation.

More productive as a morale booster was the announcement that Ringling planned to build the finest art museum in the south, next door to his Ca'd'Zan. "I intend to put in a college, too," he said, "to teach art and things like that." One of the architects of New York's Metropolitan Museum was brought in to design an appropriate setting for the assorted old masters and Baroque beauties, and work got under way.

Then came 1929.

His wife, Mable, died of Addison's disease in June. "The party is over," grieved John. "I never want to be gay again." He put his nose to the grindstone and in September acquired a near-monopoly in his field by purchasing the rival American Circus Corporation for $2 million.

Six weeks later the stock market crashed. From then on it was all downhill. He made an unhappy second marriage that dragged him through the divorce courts and cost over $200,000 in legal fees. He suffered a stroke and a heart attack, as well as recurrent bouts of gout. His finances were in utter disarray. Defaulting on his notes to buy the American Circus Corporation, he wound up encumbering all his other assets to stave off bankruptcy. Creditors took control of the circus, reducing him to a figurehead president not even able to tap the ticket booth for pocket change. His Bank of Sarasota went under, resulting in a flood of lawsuits.

He could do nothing right. After he gave the John and Mable Ringling School of Art to a nearby college, people started talking about the nude models posing there, and the college—which was church-related—gave it back. He quarreled bitterly with old friends and cut relatives out of his will; he saw "thieving rascals" everywhere.

The Internal Revenue Service got into the act, assigning to his case the same investigator who had sent Al Capone to prison. After the circus was presented with a huge bill for back taxes and penalties, John was personally socked for $300,000—at a time when his assets were frozen, his credit nonexistent, and his telephone cut off for nonpayment.

In November 1936 the Sarasota paper carried a legal notice that the Ringling house and its furnishings would be auctioned off on December 7 to satisfy judgments. John missed the occasion. He died in New York of pneumonia on December 2.

He left about $300 in cash, over a hundred pending lawsuits, and a circus that, according to his nephew, "was losing money like a broken hydrant gushing water." A business associate said, "If John Ringling had spent his entire life trying to mess up his affairs and had hired two lawyers to help him, he couldn't have done a better job."

He also left frozen assets conservatively appraised at over $20 million—adequate to settle all the claims against him and then some. But it took a decade to untangle the estate, the most complicated Florida had ever dealt with. From the web of bitterness and confusion, the state wound up with an impressive art museum and a mansion that reflected the life and tastes of the circus king—before he lost control of the show.

• • •

"They'll all go broke," predicted the man on the porch of Miami's Royal Palm Hotel as he watched the boom-frenzied people scurrying around him. "These people are on the brink of the precipice right now," he said, "and they talk about the good times only getting started."

Alfred I. du Pont knew better. He had been visiting Florida on and off for half a century and had seen the changes. He knew something about shoestring financing, having gone in with his cousins Coleman and Pierre to acquire the family business in 1902 for practically nothing down, at a time when the elders were planning to sell to outsiders.

He knew something of the cycle of boom and bust. During World War I he was making $500,000 a month; in its aftermath he nearly went broke. Understanding the machinations, motivations, and likely results, he decided to sit out the boom and pick up the pieces afterward. In the fall of 1926, as others were fleeing Florida, he moved in. He built one of the last great boom-time homes on the banks of the St. Johns River in Jacksonville, and named it Epping Forest, after the home of Mary Ball, mother of George Washington and ancestor of Mrs. du Pont. The third Mrs. du Pont. Like Flagler before him, he had a stormy marital career, which served to isolate him from his family and break the alliance of cousins that ran the corporation. In one sense, changing his legal residence to Florida was a final thumbing of the nose at his Delaware relatives.

It was not the first thing he had done to spite them: A. I. du Pont was the family rebel. His Wilmington estate (designed by Carrère and Hastings) was surrounded by a 9-foot wall—to keep other du Ponts out. The first time most of them saw inside was when the house was opened, on a paying basis, for a charity benefit.

He was a bundle of contradictions: generous and spiteful; a friend of the poor who lived like a king; a music lover who lost his hearing; a war hero who never wore a uniform; a supporter of prohibition who maintained his own hundred-thousand-dollar liquor supply.

"I am a very poor mixer," he wrote, "do not make friends readily and when I do I am exceedingly disagreeable."

Yet, when Florida was flat on its back, this prickly character decided to devote the rest of his life to getting it on its feet again. "It's a challenge we can't pass up," he told his friends, adding, "In my last years I'd much rather have the people of Florida say that I had helped them and their state than to double the money I now have."

Newspapers in search of glad tidings screamed: "DUPONT MILLIONS TO FLORIDA!" He brought with him assets of $34 million, which the press quickly inflated to $100 million or $200 million. No matter. He was a major stockholder in both Du Pont and General Motors. As their stock boomed in the late twenties, his wealth grew to match any hyperbole.

Five million dollars were to be invested for openers. He put them into the two least sought-after things in Florida at that point, land and banks (the bust had soured land investment, and banks were collapsing right and left). Du Pont bought up hundreds of thousands of acres in the northwest Florida Panhandle, and quietly acquired control of the Florida National Bank in Jacksonville.

He also took a dip into politics. Al Smith was the Democratic presidential candidate in 1928. Although many Florida Protestants looked askance at his Catholicism, that didn't bother du Pont—but Smith's intimacy with the other faction of his family did. So du Pont decided to back Herbert Hoover, who became the first Republican to carry Florida since Reconstruction.

It was one of those textbook campaigns that will long be cited as an example of dirty politics. Prohibitionists, fundamentalists, anti-Catholics, and Ku Klux Klanners all did their part in a meticulously orchestrated effort that was highly successful and left a very bad taste. Du Pont was in Europe while the fireworks took place: having made the decision, he left the implementation in capable hands, with his brother-in-law, Ed Ball, as maestro of the campaign. It set a pattern. When money was needed, du Pont supplied it. When something had to be done, Ed Ball arranged it. It was a financial and political one-two punch that knocked out many an opponent.

Just as he had predicted the bust, du Pont also saw the stock-market crash in the offing, and he got prepared. When it hit, he owed no money and had a cash reserve in the millions. He was in a position to aid others who had not been so prescient —or so rich to begin with.

When the depression caused widespread unemployment and hardship, du Pont was there to help alleviate conditions. In Delaware he financed an old-age pension program out of his own pocket—until the state was embarrassed into taking it over. In Jacksonville he launched a public-works project that paid the unemployed to clean up streets and parks.

He expanded his bank holdings, feeling that a sound system was a prerequisite for recovery. From Jacksonville he spread out to Lakeland, Bartow, Orlando, Daytona, St. Petersburg, and Miami. This was at a time when public confidence was at a minimum. Mattresses bulged with life savings, and many agreed with the man who swore, "I wouldn't put my money in another bank if God Almighty was the president and Jesus Christ the cashier."

But du Pont's banks were solid—"as liquid as the lakes," one admirer put it. His millions protected them from collapse during runs. "Pull our banks through" was his instruction to his brother-in-law. Ball scurried across the state by plane and car to deliver cash where it was needed, guarding it himself with a shotgun (in whose use he had become proficient as a boy, serving as night watchman of the family oyster beds).

Du Pont bought up Florida bonds for his banks at rock-bottom prices. There was not a great market for the defaulted municipals, but du Pont believed they would come back, and he could afford to wait. He was a Rock of Gibraltar in a sea of intranquillity, but there was one complaint, heard so frequently it became a litany: "Damn that man du Pont; comes here with all that money and won't loan a nickel."

The soundness of his banks was not based on any kind of venturesome lending policy. "Banks are public trusteeships" was his philosophy; "their primary object should be the safe custodianship of the money entrusted to them, not the making of money for their shareholders. If all Florida banks had had this in mind, there would have been no failures."

While other banks vanished, his grew: deposits of $27.5 million at the end of 1930 had increased to over $40 million by 1935.

One reason du Pont could buy his land so cheaply was that it was almost inaccessible. The political experience he had gained in the Hoover campaign proved invaluable when it came time to lobby for roads to be built—one of the most political questions in any state. Du Pont was titular president of the Gulf Coast Highway Association, and Ed Ball did the work. Roads began to join together the isolated Panhandle settlements. Links were forged between the du Pont interests and the "Pork Chop Gang" that controlled the state legislature. It was a powerful combination.

Du Pont sold some of his land to the government for Apalachicola National Forest, in a profitable deal arranged by Ball, and pondered the possibilities for the rest of it. There was a lot of waterfrontage with resort possibilities, but the times were not right: Florida's resort possibilities had been overdeveloped in the boom. A lot of the acreage could be farmland, but crops were being plowed under just then, with the blessings of the government. That left the trees, millions and millions of them. Du Pont decided to set up a paper mill, and to build a town to go with it, a model town, where the workers would be able to buy model homes, their families could be educated out of backwoods primitivism, and their lot in life would improve. His utopian strain came into bloom again, though it was kept within reasonable limits by Ed Ball's constant focus on the bottom line.

Du Pont lived long enough to plan, but died in 1935, before the St. Joe Paper Company became a reality. He left $58 million to finance its creation, along with instructions that somewhere down the line all the money must go to benefit the elderly sick and the crippled children of Delaware. This was in line with his belief that "it is the duty of every one in this world to do what is in his power to alleviate human suffering." In the meantime, Ed Ball was in charge.

This arrangement embraced all the contradictions of du Pont's personality and—some would say—left the fox securely guarding the chicken coop.

• • •

Herbert Hoover was not half as popular in Florida in 1932 as he had been in 1928, and he didn't get half as many votes when he ran against Franklin D. Roosevelt. Ready to jettison the laissez-faire approach to solving the problems wrought by the depression, the public was calling for a New Deal, and Florida chimed in with its electoral votes.

Then Roosevelt did what Harding and Hoover and others before had done: he headed for Florida. It nearly proved fatal. The New Deal might have died aborning if left to the tender mercies of Vice President John Nance Garner.

Roosevelt was no stranger to the Sunshine State. His father had been one of Henry Plant's investors in building up the railroads, and while recuperating from polio in the 1920s, FDR often sailed his houseboat in Florida waters, stopping off at Miami to mend political fences with William Jennings Bryan.

James M. Cox, who headed the 1920 Democratic ticket with Roosevelt as vice-presidential nominee, had also located in Miami. At the urging of his friend Carl Fisher, he bought a newspaper and built for it one of the great boom-time skyscrapers, topped by the ubiquitous Giralda Tower.

Roosevelt's houseboat, the *Larooco*, was a casualty of the 1926 hurricane. It had been moored in Fort Lauderdale, awaiting his next trip, when the wind and rising waters carried it 4 miles inland. After the tides receded, the boat was deposited in a pine forest a mile from the nearest water. Nearly impossible to move, it was offered for sale as a hunting lodge, but it found no buyers, and was sold for junk in 1927.

That put an end to Roosevelt's Florida cruising until 1933, when, awaiting inauguration, he went on a fishing trip aboard Vincent Astor's palatial yacht *Nourmahal.*

Coming ashore on February 15, 1933, he told an enthusiastic crowd at Miami's Bayfront Park: "I am not a stranger here. It is true that I have not been here in seven years, but I often have visited here. I am firmly resolved that this shall not be the last time I shall come here to Miami."

Then the shooting began.

The crippled president-elect miraculously escaped, though his bodyguard and his companion, Mayor Anton Cermak of Chicago, were among those wounded. Police and spectators pounced on the gunman, a thirty-three-year-old unemployed bricklayer named Giuseppe Zangara, who had once tried to assassinate the king of Italy.

He had been lured from his home in Hackensack, New Jersey, two months before by reports of Miami's healthful climate. "I thought it would do my stomach good to come here," he said, "but it seemed to get worse instead of better. The pain seemed to make my extreme hatred for the rich and for everybody in authority all the more." So he bought an eight-dollar pistol at a North Miami pawnshop and went after Roosevelt.

Mayor Cermak lingered with his wounds, then died on March 6. On his deathbed, he expressed the belief that Al Capone was behind the shooting. Three days later Zangara pled guilty to Cermak's murder and, with swift justice, was electrocuted at Raiford State Prison on March 20, 1933.

But Roosevelt survived and launched the New Deal. Soon its alphabet-soup agencies were funding a variety of projects: paving roads, building bridges, civic centers, airports, bathing pavilions, fishing piers, and all the other things necessary to resuscitate the tourist industry—including post offices from which the visitors could mail home their postcards of Sunny Florida.

They were not booming times. However, people placed a high priority on vacations as soon as these became possible. As the hard times eased off, ever so slightly, there was a perceptible increase in the number of tourists. They were welcomed warmly when they came to visit, though those who had other things in mind were bluntly discouraged. A billboard at the St. Petersburg city line proclaimed: "WARNING. DO NOT COME HERE SEEKING WORK. A CITY'S FIRST DUTY IS TO EMPLOY ITS OWN CITIZENS."

By the late 1930s some of Florida's cities were again able to pay interest on their share of the half billion dollars in bonded indebtedness incurred during the boom. But it was not until Dr. New Deal turned into Dr. Win the War that the economy really recovered.

At first, however, it portended yet another disaster for Florida.

There are certain preconditions for successful tourism, and the war played havoc with all of them. Rationing of tires and gasoline and limitations on train space made it hard to get to Florida in the first place, while an attitude of "work, don't play" acted in advance to discourage vacationing. Those who arrived found conditions less than idyllic. Coastal areas were blacked out (even automobile headlights were painted over), and access was limited by checkpoints at bridges and barbed wire stretched along beaches.

The concern was real: German U-boats were patrolling Florida waters, landed saboteurs at Ponte Vedra Beach, and shot down a blimp near Miami. Many large ships—the exact number was concealed by military censorship—were torpedoed. The incoming slicks from sunken oil tankers did awful things to the vaunted sandy beaches.

Florida's fragile economy could not survive under these conditions, so the only thing to do was enlist. Five hundred resort hotels were placed at government disposal, and where sun-and-funners had once frolicked, soldiers were trained instead. This saved the government from building barracks, and gave the hotels an enviable occupancy rate. The flying season was wonderfully long, and the state blossomed with forty military airfields.

Clark Gable, mourning the death of his wife, actress Carole Lombard, enlisted in the service and was sent to officer-candidate school in Miami Beach. A picture of him shaving his famous mustache was sent around the world. The training was no cinch. "The courses are getting as stiff as a groom on his wedding night," reported America's heart throb. Like the rest of the cadets, he was permitted no outside contacts during training—much to the regret of area hostesses.

Ballyhoo turned patriotic for the duration. Bathing beauties painted their fingernails red, white, and blue. Betty Grable and Veronica Lake, Sabu and Sonja Henie all sold war bonds. One of the causeways to Miami Beach was renamed to honor Douglas MacArthur.

Bars did a booming business, but the military decreed that professional houses of prostitution—some of them venerable Florida institutions—be put out of business. The pros were then replaced by amateurs known as Victory Girls, who plied their trade so assiduously at Miami's Bayfront Park that all the shrubbery was trimmed back to avoid providing cover for their activities.

What was not done for pay was done for fun. One reporter noted that the "bacchanals of ancient Rome were re-enacted on the sands by naked WACs and GIs." Florida had seen merry-making before, but never on this order. These were the people, after all, who could say, "Tomorrow we die."

The war pumped money into the economy. Massive unemployment was replaced by a labor shortage, to the extent that prisoners of war were put to work harvesting agricultural crops. All the slack was taken out of the housing market glutted after the boom. No vacancies were reported on all fronts, living-room couches again became rentable, and people even kept a running check on funeral homes to see what houses or apartments might be coming available.

Many of the soldiers who passed through for training decided they liked Florida and would return there, so that a whole new generation was introduced to the charms of the Sunshine State. Two decades had diminished the memory of past problems. Now the stage was set for a new boom, which began as soon as the war ended. The flood of tourists was so great that many had to sleep in their cars, while the demand for homesites was sufficient to quadruple the price of building lots. VA- and FHA-guaranteed mortgages fueled the flames.

Florida was off again!

• • •

The war changed the world and the war changed Florida.

Not only the resulting prosperity, but also many of the technical advances gave the state economy a shot in the arm. Experimental work carried on in Orlando with DDT found immediate peacetime application on Florida's tremendous bug population and the agricultural crops on which they munched.

The development of orange-juice concentrate was a patriotic achievement, saving valuable transport space during the war by eliminating bulk that people were just going to throw away anyhow. In peacetime it became the sensation of the food industry and the breakfast table.

Minute Maid opened its first plant in 1946. Half a million gallons were produced that season. Then Bing Crosby crooned its praises and the housewives of the nation embraced it as a labor-saving invention. Demand soared. Sales zoomed. Fifty million, 75 million gallons a year.

Effects on the citrus industry were dramatic. In the fresh-fruit days, oranges were sold for their looks, which meant that a third or more of the crop might be discarded for cosmetic reasons. With concentrate, appearance became irrelevant—no one beyond the production line ever got a peek. The result was a more stable citrus industry, moving inexorably in the direction of larger growers and larger-scale production. Even the by-products became a big business: Florida cows get their vitamin C by devouring great quantities of dried citrus pulp.

Aviation had undergone tremendous improvements, which, in the form of better, larger airports and bigger, faster planes, were turned from military to civilian use. New York–to–Miami became the breadbasket route for Eastern Airlines. Flying became less rare and risky in the public mind: certainly the GI who had bailed out at several thousand feet would not be intimidated by the prospect of a smooth flight in a relatively plush, pressurized cabin where the talking was done by reassuring stewardesses rather than barking sergeants.

It was not the same old paradise these planes brought their passengers to, but a new, improved version. Things were once more on the move, as boom-time building levels were being surpassed, Miami Beach leading the way.

It was the age of Lapidus. What Carrère and Hastings had done for Flagler's St. Augustine, and Addison Mizner had done for Palm Beach, Morris Lapidus did for Carl Fisher's resort in the postwar period. Like its predecessors, it was a period piece. It was the height of style or the pits of taste, according to your point of view. But it was there, and growing—out, up, and all around—in the era of "this year's hotel"—buildings that occupied center stage for a single season before being ruthlessly upstaged by the next Lapidus creation.

Given all this staginess, it was appropriate that the architect had served his apprenticeship as a stage designer and storefront-façade remodeler. The tricks he had learned he put to use in Miami Beach's hotels, from the Sans Souci in 1949 through the Fontainebleau, Eden Roc, and others in the fifties. One comedian attributed the architecture to Frank Lloyd Wrong.

"My hotels are to tickle," Lapidus said, "to amuse." Giving the Beach an international reputation for garish glitter, they were the well-paying home-away-from-Vegas for the nightclub entertaining set, from Frank Sinatra on down.

Not all visitors were delighted. Senator Estes Kefauver, bringing his highly publicized investigations to Miami in 1950, damned the place as the winter capital of "upper-bracket hoodlumdom." He called for a crackdown in the area, which had become "the plunderground as well as the playground for America's most vicious criminals." That got headlines and it got action, but it didn't win the senator a warm spot in the hearts of Floridians. He lost the state's presidential primary when he went off hunting the White House in 1952.

Walter Winchell nattered about the scene, but his day was passing. The new stars were in television, and the Beach had them. Arthur Godfrey brought his show there in 1952, a move so important in the local scheme of things that Julia Tuttle Causeway now runs right into Arthur Godfrey Road. When his star faded, Jackie Gleason was brought in as the celebrity-in-residence. His presence is celebrated with Jackie Gleason Drive —and a similar honor was paid to Ed Sullivan, dean of the first generation of television hosts.

Elsewhere, motels rather than hotels lined the roads. The convertible was the car of the hour, and Florida's beaches were where the boys were.

• • •

A short season is the curse of any resort. Florida's season has expanded considerably since the changing of flags in 1821. In the early days the coastal areas were off-limits in the summer months (abandoned even by all the locals who could afford it) because of the threat of yellow fever. When that came under control, Henry Flagler experimented with a summer hotel, The Continental, on the beach near Jacksonville, but it was a consistent money-loser.

On a much more modest scale, the Methodist church promoted St. Augustine Beach for summer bungalows just before World War I. The pattern developed that inland Floridians spent their summers at the beach, but northerners were scared off by linear incremental estimates of what the August temperatures must be if it was 80 in January. That made the beaches restful for the natives, but the secret of their habitability could not be kept forever while airlines and hotels were losing potential revenue. Throughout the fifties a concerted effort was made to turn Florida into a year-round resort.

The development of air conditioning ranked right alongside the conquest of yellow fever in making this possible. It also made it feasible to recruit year-round residents. Florida did not have the industrial base to offer jobs, or it would long before have depopulated large parts of the country. But with the growth of Social Security and company pensions, there arose big groups of retirees who had portable incomes, and who formed the base for the most conspicuous aspect of the postwar boom: the retirement community. "The ceiling on our operation," boasted one builder, "is the number of retired people in the United States."

First the old subdivisions were filled. Davis Shores became, if not "America's Foremost Watering Place," at least St. Augustine's most popular suburb. Miles of roads and curbs that had earlier led to nothing but bonding defaults now led to settlements dotted with new homes. The demand was so brisk that some took shortcuts. Jim Walter launched his fortune putting up shell houses. Others took trailers. Bradenton became the mobile-home capital of the world. It had taken a generation, and it had discarded the spirit of elegance by the wayside, but the old tracts from the twenties were finally filling up. Even Venice boomed, a quarter century after it nearly sank the Brotherhood of Locomotive Engineers. Land prices headed back up.

Then the developers went farther afield, out to where the land was cheap. Levittowns-in-the-sun sprouted from cow pastures all over the state.

The transformation of raw land into a self-contained city is no small job, and the companies that took it on were giants. King of them was the General Development Corporation, weighing in at $125 million and claiming to be the largest city-builders in the world. They were not afraid to think big. Matching future projections with land areas, they pointed out that their Port Charlotte development was larger than Detroit or Miami. Port Malabar was nearly the same size as Cleveland or Cincinnati, and Port St. Lucie outranked Pittsburgh.

The "Port" in the titles highlighted an important requirement: land bought for such developments had to have some kind of water. Not necessarily the world's greatest beach or finest natural harbor. Given just a little to work with—a creek and some lowlands, even—developers could whip it into shape. It was the heyday of dredges and draglines, bulldozers, steam shovels, and sea walls that picked up where the Lord rested on the seventh day. It was the age of finger-islanding, a real-estate revolution that altered the face—and upped the value—of many a low-lying area.

The father of finger-islanding was Charles G. Rodes of Fort Lauderdale. Back in the twenties he had learned that the cheapest way to create waterfront property was to dig ditches in lowlands, use the spoil to create high ground, and sell it all at a fancy price. This process made him a millionaire. Then came the bust. During the thirties he was reduced to hefting a shovel on a WPA project, but he kept his land, and in the postwar boom he made back all he had lost and much, much more.

If imitation is the sincerest form of flattery, then Rodes was the most flattered man in Florida during the 1950s. Waterfront property was mass-produced as never before. Doc Davis would have been green with envy.

General Development was a flatterer when it came to finger-islanding but a pacesetter when it came to ballyhoo. They raised the cry of "$10 down, $10 a month" and spread it around the world. The easy terms made it well-nigh irresistible, an offer people couldn't refuse. They sold a hundred thousand lots for openers, largely by mail order. Attractive ads in national magazines (GDC's chairman was Gardner Cowles, Jr., publisher of *Look*), booths in railroad and subway stations and airports, gave them broad outreach. You could sign up for a lot on your way to work in the morning and have it paid for by the time you retired. The complete model home built in New York's Grand Central Station let you see just what you were getting.

Once GDC set the standards, others took off from there. Some offered more frills. For $20 down and $20 a month, for instance, you could buy a lot at Cape Coral, which boasted 76 miles of dredged waterways—three times the length of canals in Venice, Italy. Those who could afford $90 down and $90 a month could get into Jamaica Island, the sea-walled, choicest section of an ex–tomato field that had been rechristened Apollo Beach. The geographically mixed metaphors were further complicated by billboards proclaiming that Royal Canadian "Guy Lombardo Wants You as a Neighbor."

Other developments were promoted with even more hoopla. Coral Ridge Properties, weighing in at $50 million, was headed by an ex–car dealer who definitely believed in the hard sell. He brought in color guards and majorettes and brass bands playing

"Happy Days Are Here Again" for his land sales—one of which chalked up a respectable $4-million sellout in just twenty-one minutes.

As things took off, everyone wanted to get in on the action. One new town catered to retired cops and featured a Policemen's Hall of Fame among its attractions. The Upholsterers Union launched Salhaven, and the National Association of Letter Carriers founded Nalcrest for their superannuated members.

The baseball contingent was prominent. Connie Mack, Jr., son of the game's grand old man, was executive director of Cape Coral. New York Yankees co-owner Del Webb developed Sun City (open only to those "lucky enough to be over 50"), where street signs warned, "DRIVE SLOWLY. GRANDPARENTS PLAYING."

Palm Beach Lakes was the project of Lou Perini, who owned the Milwaukee Braves. It was located west of West Palm Beach —"the city Flagler built for his help"—but the point was not belabored in the choice of its name.

Top-of-the-line as well as garden-variety millionaires got involved. The Texas-oil-rich Murchisons planned to duplicate Carl Fisher's success on the keys off St. Petersburg, figuring their Tierra Verde could become a city of fifty thousand. Ninety percent of the lots were waterfront.

Shipping magnate Daniel K. Ludwig bought 18,000 acres of mangrove swamp on Biscayne Bay, on which he was reported to be planning a luxury resort that would rival Miami Beach.

These were the types of place whose ads began, "ATTENTION ALL MILLIONAIRES." They aimed their pitch at "well-bred people of discriminating taste," or "the few who want the utmost in exclusive luxury."

But at the heart of the boom were those several rungs down the economic ladder. As *Fortune* magazine pointed out in 1960, "This, if not a poor man's boom, is one made by people who count the pennies." Such were the vast bulk of the three thousand homeseekers coming in each week, giving Florida five times the national growth rate. Developers loved these modest-income people because God made so many of them, and offered them mass-produced homes, rather than Miznersque uniqueness. This did for the house what Henry Ford had done for the car. You could have any model you wanted as long as it was A, B, or C (in Florida those prosaic letters were usually given the names of exotic trees or shrubs).

These new city builders boasted of their creative financing —"money engineering," one called it. Not only were easy terms extended to buyers, but the developers themselves were given long credit by the cattlemen and farmers who sold them tracts. Low down payments, followed by gradual reimbursement as things started moving, then a nice fat plum at the end, in gratitude for waiting.

Even so, development was an expensive business: so much money had to be poured into streets and drainage and the like before anything came back. But when it came back . . . Wow! Sixteen dollars' worth of pasturage formed your basic thousand-dollar lot, and lot prices were going up to meet the demand.

The giants of development went public—those that had not already done so. In the winter of 1958–59, about forty Florida land stocks went on the market, and they were hot. They doubled, tripled, and quadrupled in price. Generous dividends were declared.

They were the sensation of the season.

Many strange outfits have been seen on Miami Beach over the years, but these soldiers exercising with their gas masks during World War II probably take the cake.

Finger-islanding created extra miles of waterfront for enterprising developers to sell. Land in the foreground here at Port Canaveral is being raised up and shaped in 1966; houses have already been constructed on the rest of the property.

The high-rise development of Miami Beach during the postwar boom set the pattern for the rest of the state's waterfront property.

SHOOT THE MOON

•

To every thing there is a season.

The fall of 1959 was the rainy season. For sixty days running the heavens shed their beneficence on the Florida land boom. Streets, subdivisions, and houses flooded, canals silted, and cesspools backed up.

Weather influences outlook, as dreary skies give rise to dreary minds. People who thought they were buying paradise felt, instead, like refugees from Noah's Ark, and they did what people will do: they complained.

They were not the only ones. Most of those who bought into the boom didn't live on their land; a good percentage of them had never even seen it, having bought from artists' renditions in the pages of their favorite magazines. They held it either for speculation or future building, and they were scattered far and wide—one development had customers in forty-four states and fourteen countries.

1959 was a pinching year, as far as the economy was concerned. Because of the recession, those masses who always watched their pennies were watching them even more closely. Some, deciding their Florida investments were not so wise after all, stopped making their payments of $10 or $20 or $90 a month. The state developed one of the highest foreclosure rates in the nation.

That caused problems for the developers. Most of them—even the biggest—were undercapitalized. The cow pastures had an amazing ability to absorb money—even as their ability to absorb rainwater was proving somewhat less than desired.

Tremendous sales had been chalked up, impressive figures given to the press, but there was a touch of funny money in it all. A million dollars in sales might represent as little as $10,000 in cash, and that wouldn't build many roads or lay many sewers or dredge many canals—all of which the developers were pledged and obligated in advance to do.

While pioneer residents of the new cities worried about pumping out their dining rooms, those they had bought from got ulcers over the cash crunch. Florida land stocks tumbled—25, 50, 75 percent. The media ground their gears into reverse to cover the new phenomenon.

On the defensive, its good image at stake, Florida issued new regulations for real-estate advertising. No longer could the euphemistic and expandable "nearby" or "minutes away" be used; Paradise Beach would have to come right out and say it was 51.7 miles from the ocean. That took a lot of the romance out of advertising copywriting—but, then, regulators are always killjoys.

Another killjoy compared the population growth rate with the available subdivisions and announced that Florida had enough building lots to meet its needs for the next twenty years. The price of pastureland dropped abruptly. Tomato crops were put in once again on what the farmer had previously thought might make a nice Garden of Eden Mobile Home Estates.

In 1960 a hurricane hit, and the freeze of the century, in 1962, killed six million bearing trees. Concentrate plants had to import their oranges from Haiti, Mexico, South America, and Africa.

Then there was trouble in Cuba. Fidel Castro had taken

over, and many Cubans were heading for Miami. In 1962 it looked as if there might even be war. Pleasure seekers seldom choose to vacation in war zones.

Things were hard all over.

One project, slated to be a city of fifty thousand with a billion-dollar investment, got only as far as the first two hundred homes—and only five of these were occupied, all by employees of the developer.

Port Charlotte, largest of the new cities, was supposed to have a population of seventy thousand by 1965 (and half a million eventually). Thrown off stride, it was credited in the 1970 census with just 10,769.

All that remained was to wrap it up and give it a sufficiently colorful label. That honor fell to the president of the Better Business Bureau. "Swamp merchants in Florida have accumulated many hard-earned dollars from the elderly," he complained to a congressional committee in 1963. Not only had the property not yet been drained, he pointed out, but "some of the area is in a water conservation zone where it is government policy to maintain water."

That did it. The Florida swampland scandal was the funeral dirge for the postwar boom.

• • •

The senior citizen who lost the most from that boom was one who could easily afford it. His name was Arthur Vining Davis, and he was very old and very wealthy.

Once, overhearing some people at a party discuss whether he was the second- or third-richest man in America, he came up behind them and snapped, "Fifth." Then he walked briskly away.

But that was atypical, and he later regretted it. Usually he took the position that it was nobody's damn business how much he was worth. On occasion he even stretched credulity by saying, "I'm not rich."

No one believed that.

A product of the Horatio Alger era, he was yet another son of a poor but honest minister. After graduating, Phi Beta Kappa, from Amherst in 1888, he went on to Pittsburgh and a job that paid $60 a month "when I could get it." There he helped produce the first commercial aluminum in the world, found uses for it, sold it to the public—and got Andrew Mellon to invest in it. In 1907 he was a founder of the Aluminum Company of America. In 1910 he became president and in 1928 chairman of the board.

In 1948, past 80, he left Pittsburgh and settled in Miami. But he did not give up the reins. "I operate the Aluminum Company of America lock, stock and barrel," he told an inquiring reporter.

Pint-sized, gruff-voiced, and secretive, he set as his goal in Florida not to retire, but "to make money." He had a few hundred million stored up, but saw no reason to stop. His constant lament was "Nobody wants to work any more"—excluding himself. He was one of the nation's senior workaholics. Why not just take it easy for the last few years? "I don't plan to die," was the reply.

He bet on the Florida boom and sank his money into it at a rapid pace—$1.5 million a week during one extended period. Despite his distaste for publicity, this inevitably drew attention. Articles in national magazines called him the "World's Fastest Spender" and "The Man Who Is Buying Up Florida."

A glimpse of his private plane or helicopter in an area was enough to heat up the real-estate market, resulting in what were popularly called "Davis Prices."

In 1956 he purchased Mizner's Boca Raton Hotel and Club for $22.5 million. This landmark transaction was the costliest Florida had ever seen, four and a half times as much as it had taken to acquire the whole state from Spain. Another relic of the twenties' boom—Sarasota's Ringling Isles—he picked up for $13.5 million.

Usually big spenders are welcomed in Florida, but Davis riled an inordinate number of smaller operators. The increased prices, once he got involved, destroyed the margin for a lot of speculators. Those who bought land surrounding his holdings found to their regret that he was prepared to leave it in its raw state practically forever. There were not many fringe benefits to be gathered from his investments. Worst of all, given his advanced age and vast holdings (he owned about 10 percent of Dade County, among others), were the fears that he might die suddenly and that all his property would be dumped on the market to pay estate taxes, which would spell disaster. When he fainted, it was front-page news.

People said unkind things about him, pointing to the incredibly wide range of his investments as a sure sign that the multimillionaire had entered senility and was throwing his money away. Airlines, steamship companies, shopping centers, orchid nurseries, banks, tomato farms, ice-cream factories, pineapple plantations, hotels, golf courses, gas stations, islands, and swamps all formed part of his Florida empire.

His detractors underestimated the old fox, however. His holdings were a harbinger of the conglomerates that would shake and roil the economy in coming years. If the pieces were put together, he could have done everything from mortgaging to clearing the land to building to landscaping to bringing in the furniture and occupants, providing them places to shop, stocking the shelves of the stores, and even pumping the gas that went into the cars. If it had all worked out.

But he lost on airlines, steamships, pineapples, tomatoes, and other ventures, enough to make another man—or several—quite wealthy. The biggest loss came off shore. In 1956 Davis paid $14 million for half of the Isle of Pines in Cuba, intending to develop it as the *ne plus ultra* of island resorts. But Fidel Castro, who had once been imprisoned there, came to power. He had different plans for it and confiscated the whole thing.

The most profitable thing Davis did was to incorporate. His Arvida Corporation (the name, which he had earlier used for a Canadian mining town, was made by taking the first two letters of Arthur, Vining and Davis) was one of the hot stock issues of 1958–59. Almost overnight the value of his holdings doubled. Then the boom hit the skids, and by the time he died in 1962 at the age of 95, the debacle was almost complete.

It is ironic that he lost. The Arvida Corporation was (and is) an upscale developer. It didn't peddle cow pastures, engage in hard sell, do mail-order installment sales, or push mass-produced housing. It was innocent of the most widespread abuses of the boom, yet it suffered along with the rest.

Still, in Davis's tax bracket a few good losses are helpful in equalizing the bite taken by Uncle Sam. He was in no danger of going under. Time was on his side. He could afford to indulge during his last years.

He spent $250,000 moving a road away from his Coral Gables estate because the headlights bothered him. After virtually rebuilding his house from the ground up, he tore it down and built another. When he died, he left the place to his secretary.

Arthur Vining Davis was well padded against the hardship of loss. But when it came to making money, Florida land proved far less profitable for him than aluminum.

• • •

Florida might have faced some awfully hard times after the swampland scandal if there hadn't been something to fall back on. Fortunately, there was.

Something new had been added to the heavens in 1957. Sputnik. Then a dog named Laika. Then Yuri Gagarin. The fallout on earth was distinctly unpleasant for America's image makers: the country was not used to being second-best. So on May 25, 1961, President John F. Kennedy told a joint session of Congress: "I believe this nation should commit itself to achieving the goal, before the decade is out, of landing a man on the moon and returning him safely to earth. No single space project in this period will be more impressive to mankind, or more important for the long-range exploration of space; and none will be so difficult or expensive to accomplish."

Floridians applauded. They were particularly intrigued with the last part, about the expense. Taking it for granted that Cape Canaveral would be the launching pad, they wanted to know just what this would do to the local economy.

A year later they got a better idea, when Kennedy told a Miami Beach fund-raising dinner that the space program would soon "have five times as many persons working in the Canaveral area as we do today."

Senator Spessard Holland probed a little deeper at budget hearings, trying to get "a clear picture of just what exactly you intend to do in Florida next year." It needed to be pinned down: a new boom was under way, and people's livelihoods were at stake, not to mention their speculations.

The space race was a great consolation to the Sunshine State in the aftermath of the swampland scandal. The real-estate developers had dealt in the millions, but the moon shot would run into billions.

The area adapted accordingly. A neon strip sprouted rocket-shaped signs. Places like the Missile and Galaxy lounges served astronaut cocktails, moonshots, and lift-off martinis. Nightclubs advertised "Girls in Orbit" and combos played "Fly Me to the Moon."

And the space program adapted. Once its earlier secrecy was dispensed with, reporters no longer had to sneak up at marsh-side with binoculars or rely on tipsters in local bars and barbershops to figure out when launches were scheduled. Instead, press releases were rained on them.

Tourists were catered to. Stores were crammed with space toys for them to buy, and even the paper placemats in restaurants were take-home souvenirs. Professional bus tours started running through the space center in 1966. Visitors could take their pick of the Sea Missile or Vanguard motels, or the Cape Colony Inn, a joint investment the astronauts made with money they received for telling their stories to *Life* magazine.

The space center was a wildlife refuge as well. Workers fed spare bits of their lunch to alligators, and rattlesnakes occasionally warmed themselves in the sun on the concrete launch pads. Part of the government acreage was leased back to citrus growers.

A single building cost more than Henry Flagler's entire investment in Florida. At the time of its construction, the Vehicle Assembly Building was the largest in the world: 525 feet high and covering 8 acres, using enough structural steel to build thirty thousand automobiles. A special ventilating system was required to prevent clouds from forming in the spacious interior. To give it solid support in the shifting sands, 135 miles of steel piping were driven into the bedrock 160 feet below. The doors of the structure were large enough for the Statue of Liberty to walk through.

In the fifties, when missiles were being launched from Canaveral, surrounding Brevard County was the fastest-growing in the country—zooming up at five times the Florida rate and twenty times the national. The moon program did nothing at all to slow that down.

The area had been passed over by Henry Flagler and largely untouched by the twenties' boom. Now, making up for those earlier slights, it was fat and happy. People started to call it the Platinum Coast, in one-upmanship to the hitherto more prosperous Gold Coast on the south. The beautifully expressive name, however, never caught on like the inevitable Space Coast.

Booms bring their own set of problems, of course. All of Uncle Sam's computers and all the wise and well-paid Ph.D.'s could never seem to penetrate the growth-rate problem and match it up with housing. The situation was chaos from the beginning.

In the early days, when the base was first being established, some of the workmen were reduced to sleeping in sections of sewer pipe. Then came the mobile homes—in such huge quantities that when the concrete-block tract developers finally caught up with demand, there seemed to be no place to dispose of the trailers, short of shipping them to Latin America.

Building turned to overbuilding, and by 1965, two thousand homes went begging for buyers, and 22 percent of the apartments in the Cape area were unoccupied. Still—and this was the madness of it all—more were under construction.

The careful synchronizing necessary to put a man in space was never applied to the local housing situation. From one year to the next it was either feast or famine.

Other growth pains were not inconsiderable: water, schools, sewers, hospitals, and roads were constantly pressed to keep up with enlargement.

Then there was the human element. The matrix of the community was as loose as sand on a windy beach. Churches and civic groups—the glue that binds other places of similar size together—were relatively weak. An us-and-them mentality grew up between those employed in and out of the space industry.

Nothing is without its cost. If a little anomie and a higher-than-average divorce rate were the price of all this progress, most people were willing to pay—particularly if the problems didn't affect them personally.

• • •

The boom was not only at the Cape, but extended out in all directions. Government contractors sought nearby sites for development and brought their payrolls with them. Martin Marietta's Orlando plant rapidly became the state's largest, with over ten thousand employees.

A group of investors bought land between Orlando and the Cape to build Rocket City, under the direction of retired missile General John B. Medaris. But Rocket City never took off. It was later taken over by the International Evangelistic Association, whose members evidently thought it a good launching place to be Nearer My God to Thee.

Since people kept a close watch on large real-estate transactions, the area was abuzz with rumors in the mid-sixties when a huge tract was being put together south of Orlando. So secretive were the methods, with buyers using dummy corporations and negotiators using false names, that speculation centered on the elusive, reclusive billionaire Howard Hughes as the likely purchaser. Reporters pestered distinguished visitors for hints. When cartoonist Walt Disney was in the area to visit the space center he was asked if he knew anything about it, or would ever consider launching something like his Disneyland in Florida.

No, he replied, he had a heavy investment in his California operation and was all booked up.

He lied.

He was the mysterious purchaser. Word slipped out before the final acquisitions were made, and just what Disney feared happened: the last acres shot up in price from $183 to $1,000 each.

Even so, the tariff was not excessive. A 27,000-acre area—about twice the size of Manhattan—was bought for less than $6 million. The California attraction he opened in 1955 covered only 230 acres, but Disney had been distressed at the "second-rate Las Vegas" that quickly surrounded it—for commercial as well as aesthetic reasons, since the fringe operations were making four times as much as he was.

In Florida he would control the land for miles around, and reap the benefits thereof. When the inevitable related businesses tried to cluster up, they found they couldn't get very close. And where space was available, they had to pay through the nose. One gas station paid $155,000 for its acre of land; another put up twice that. Disney had given an average of less than $200 an acre for his tract.

It was big news. The governor of Florida himself insisted on announcing it, introducing the cartoon magnate as "the man of the decade, who will bring a new world of entertainment, pleasure and economic development to the State of Florida." When the Orlando paper saw the plans, it hailed them in bold headlines as "Supercalifragilisticexpialidocious." Central Florida had never been much of a tourist area, but now it was going to start, with the biggest name in the business.

For Disney, the public announcement culminated years of planning. He claimed a certain sentimental attachment to Florida since his parents had been married there. But his father, after failing as both a hotelier and an orange grower, had packed up and moved to the Midwest, which was where the future cartoonist was born in 1901.

In 1958, three years after opening his California park, Disney commissioned the first of several studies to pick an eastern location. Florida was the overwhelming choice. His friend John D. MacArthur, the insurance billionaire, tried to lure him to the Palm Beach area, but Disney didn't want to be near the ocean.

"I want to be inland," he said. "We'll create our own water." He didn't want the deteriorating action of the salt air to affect his equipment, and sought a land buffer against the inevitable hurricanes.

Most of his investigations were made through surrogates, because he didn't want prices to skyrocket, as they surely would if his involvement were known. The one time he let down his guard and went to look at land himself, he was recognized at the airport.

"Are you Walt Disney?" a man asked.

"Hell no," he replied. "I get mistaken for him all the time, and if I ever run into that s.o.b., I'm going to tell him what I think of him."

The pressure of that kind of secrecy ended when Disney World went public. But there were still to be five years of planning and construction between the initial announcement and the grand opening.

• • •

In the meantime eyes focused back on Cape Kennedy—as Canaveral had been renamed for the martyred president who gave it its biggest boost. The greatest show on earth was opening: the manned shot to the moon.

In July 1969 the Cape area was packed with a million visitors for the event, including Lyndon Johnson, Jack Benny, Spiro Agnew, Ralph Abernathy, and three hundred Poor People's Campaigners. With motels all sold out within a 50-mile radius, people slept in cars, campers, trailers, tents, and cots around motel pools. Public parks were used as campgrounds, as were beaches. Hundreds came by boat. Homeowners rented out spare beds at good prices, while youngsters rented out their front lawns for viewing space.

Never before—not even for John Glenn's flight—had there been such crowds gathered, and they brought with them the potential for trouble. The civil-defense director expected "the equivalent of 1,000 miles of automobiles parked bumper to bumper," and pointed out that "we only have 1,000 miles of highways here, so physically, cars could cover every road in the county." Tourist gridlock. Restaurant owners stocked up in advance, afraid that food trucks wouldn't be able to get through.

But all the hardships were forgotten as the ecstatic crowds watched the launch. "Go, baby, go!" was the roar from the VIP stands. Lyndon Johnson called for peace on earth. Spiro Agnew called for a man on Mars. Ralph Abernathy sang "We Shall Overcome." A good time was had by all.

A few days later an estimated half billion people saw Neil Armstrong climb out on to the lunar surface and proclaim it "one small step for man, one giant leap for mankind."

For two thousand space workers back in Florida, the next step was to the unemployment line. The moon program had shot its load and was in the process of contracting. Although there would be a few more launches, the Florida space boom was decelerating with a thud.

Defense contractors packed up and left. NASA trimmed

back its rolls. Employment fell by two-thirds. Specialists in esoteric space skills wound up peddling fishbait, rubber alligators, and plastic ray guns to tourists. Foreclosures rose. Builders and bankers found themselves stuck with two thousand unwanted homes.

• • •

Central Florida was saved by a mouse. Mickey.

By the fall of 1971, the watery domains of Hamilton Disston were transformed into the wonderful world of Walt Disney.

The boom didn't wait for the grand opening. Land speculators got to work as soon as the initial announcement was made, and over $100 million worth of property changed hands.

The buyers were nothing if not persistent. "People were knocking on my door almost every day," recalled one cattle rancher, "from Chicago, California, Palm Beach, Miami." He found it was not so simple to say no. "I didn't want to sell, but my taxes got so high I couldn't hold out any longer. In one year the assessment on some of my property went from $6 an acre to $16,000." He sold—and became a multimillionaire.

Disney had a track record that speculators found irresistible. The California park had prospered mightily, and Florida's was to be a much bigger operation. So people shamelessly gobbled up everything they could get. "We don't mind being the world's greatest parasite to Walt Disney World," said one major realtor assembling nearby acreage.

Disney Productions itself did not await the first tourists to start cashing in on its investment. Lucrative, tightly drawn contracts were signed with major corporations, leading *Business Week* to dub the place "Promotionland." Disney's negotiators, far from being starry-eyed or pixieish, drove hard bargains and brought home the bacon.

"You pay Cadillac prices with them," said one executive

who went through the process, "but you get what you pay for. They represent the state of the art. Nobody does a better job at what they do."

Eastern Airlines paid $1 million a year to become "The Official Airline of Walt Disney World" and was delighted to see Orlando's air traffic take off.

Others did it more for the public-relations value than the potential cash returns. "A company will pay us to sponsor an attraction like the Mickey Mouse Musical Revue," said a Disney official, "because people feel happy when they are here, and they are in the right mood to accept a corporate message. If we can show them that AT&T, for example, plays a part in an image of America like Mickey Mouse, they might be able to forget the busy signals."

The grand opening was quite an event. Arthur Fiedler conducted a symphony orchestra with musicians from sixty-six countries. Mrs. Walt Disney and Mickey Mouse appeared while the carillon played "When You Wish upon a Star." But Walt himself couldn't make it. He had died just a year after the initial announcement, though not before presiding over the first seven master plans for the attraction.

Disney World immediately shot to first place among tourist destinations, drawing over eleven million visitors the first year. In a state that had heard so much hype, it was pleasant to note that Disney's estimates were invariably conservative. The initial projection of a hundred-million-dollar venture was quadrupled by opening day. Although four thousand employees had been spoken of, by late 1973 that number had more than tripled.

That was a great boon to the local economy, but not just anyone need apply for those positions. "We do not think of 'hiring for a job,'" explained the personnel director, "but rather of 'casting for a role.'" Long-haired men and braless women did not fit the role.

There was a significant ripple effect. Not just motels and gas stations clustered in the nearby acreage, but every other kind of tourist attraction as well. "We're all trying to milk whatever we can by riding on the coattails of Disney," said one of the promoters.

Farther afield, at Cape Canaveral—as it was renamed after a decade as Kennedy—the ripples were felt and welcomed. The number of visitors at the space center increased dramatically, and the area billed itself as "the closest beach to Disney World." The Vanguard Motel changed its name to the Beach Park. Things started to look up again.

Disney Productions bought some beach property near the Cape for future development. One enthusiastic booster even suggested that "had we had a Walt Disney, the space program would never have been cut back," pointing out that it "hasn't been sold so that your average folk, Little America, can identify with it." Now, if Mickey Mouse had been on the nosecone, who would have had the heart to cut the funding? Who would have complained about the costs or priorities if it meant knocking Donald Duck?

Financial giddiness was widespread in the wake of Disney's success, but not universal. Even Chamber of Commerce officials denigrated the belief that "Tinker Bell will wave her magic wand and Orlando will become a wonderland," and warned, "If those who buy land for speculation don't use more common sense, they are going to get stung."

"I can tell you that we are not making loans on unimproved real estate," said one local banker. "Prices have gone out the window and someone is going to be burned badly."

Against this wariness was the obvious evidence of the present. A Howard Johnson's executive noted, "some of our motor inns in the Orlando area are running at 100% capacity for days on end, and our restaurant sales have increased 100%. All of us should learn to sing 'M-I-C-K-E-Y M-O-U-S-E' much more loudly."

So they ate, drank, and made merry, building, building all the time, until the fateful day in January 1974 when Disney World announced it was letting two thousand employees go. The nation was suffering from inflation, recession, and gas shortages, all of which took their toll on the tourist trade. With the mouse boom hitting the skids for a while, some of the motels that went up in the wave of overbuilding were foreclosed and auctioned off, and Orlando earned a reputation as the worst apartment market in the country.

But it was temporary. The urge to vacation was deep in the American blood, and the lure of the Magic Kingdom was, statistically, like nothing else Florida or the country had ever seen. Disney Productions primed the pump by moving up a year the construction date for their next extravaganza: EPCOT, an acronym for Experimental Prototype Community of Tomorrow and a project that might best be described as Walt Disney's Folly.

In addition to being a cartoonist, filmmaker, advertising genius, and entrepreneur of history, Disney was also a frustrated city planner. No less than Franklin Smith, he felt an urge to move things from the drawing board to a semblance of reality.

The mere idea of transporting his Magic Kingdom across the country did not excite him: that represented no new challenge. So he relegated the routine tasks to his subordinates and spent his last year going over and over what would be unique to Florida: a model community for twenty thousand people. It was, his associates teased him, to be "an experimental, absolute monarchy." He readily agreed: "I'm the last of the benevolent monarchs."

The governmental form may have been archaic, but in all other ways the community was to be modern, up-to-date, state-of-the-art. He sent forth his representatives to see what industry had in mind for the future so it could be incorporated into EPCOT.

"It will be a planned, controlled community," Disney said, "a show case for American industry and research, schools, cultural and educational opportunities. In EPCOT there will be no slum areas because we won't let them develop. There will be no landowners and therefore no voting control. People will rent houses instead of buying them, and at modest rentals. There will be no retirees. Everyone must be employed."

It would, in short, be a smiling Brave New World, a cartoonist's 1984, representing the absence of everything Disney disliked in society. Its residents, in their climate-controlled, technologically advanced tomorrowland, would be the ideal guinea pigs for market-testing every new product.

Walt Disney died before it got beyond the planning stage, but his successors vowed to carry on. Having poured eight hundred million highly publicized dollars into what was the largest private construction project in the world, they opened it with great fanfare in 1982—as an amusement park.

Walt Disney's Folly got derailed along the way and turned into the selfsame thing the Disney organization had been peddling for a quarter of a century—in a new, improved, up-to-date version, complete with computer glitches. The public loved it. Attendance nearly doubled, from twelve and a half to twenty-three million people. As other tourist attractions rushed to keep up, Orlando entered its second generation of the pleasures and pains of booming.

• • •

After the swampland scandal and the collapse of the lot-sales boom in the sixties, developers turned their attention from the cow pasture with the low down payment to the urban land whose higher cost led naturally to high-rise construction. The single-family home was replaced by the apartment, the "site city" by the "vertical subdivision."

Apartments are expensive investments, but there were ways to share the burden. One widely used traditional method was to organize as a cooperative. This had advantages for tenants, but a serious pitfall in that one person's investment depended on the fidelity of others in making their payments. The role of "brother's keeper" was not an attractive one to the sun-hunters flooding into Florida.

Fortunately there was another form of ownership which avoided that problem. It was called "condominium."

Other places had used it, as far back as ancient Rome, but it was a novelty in the United States. It consisted of combined joint and private ownership. In an apartment situation it meant that people held title both to their unit and to an undivided share of such common amenities as outside walls, roof, and lawn. An individual's share could be bought and sold and even used for speculation. Property taxes and mortgage interest were credited by the IRS even as they were for owners of single-family homes.

Special laws were needed to recognize this form of property and enable mortgage lenders to participate in its financing. They swept through state legislatures like a wave of the future in the 1960s. The federal government gave its imprimatur by permitting Federal Housing Administration loans for "individually owned units in multi-family structures" in the 1961 Housing Act. Even more portentously, it sanctioned the creation of Real Estate Investment Trusts (REIT) with gooey tax benefits like the most fattening of French pastries.

Condominium is a form of ownership that has been applied to things as diverse as parking lots, campgrounds, office buildings, boat slips, grain silos, airplane hangars, ocean liners, and horse stables. But in Florida it came early on to mean high-rise waterfront buildings, which gave the beaches all the charm and tropicality of a big-city skyline. From within, some of them had majestic views—though a good proportion overlooked nothing more scenic than blacktopped parking lots and nearby traffic jams. As they lined the coast, one right after another, they so dominated the vista that the casual passer-by might be unaware there was a beach anywhere in the vicinity.

They had a name for it.

Condomania.

Beach prices shot up. The little cottages that had dotted the area behind the dunes since beachgoing first became popular were bought up in clusters and bulldozed along with their surrounding vegetation. Sometimes the dunes were leveled as well, their natural protective function ignored as they were seen merely to clutter up the ocean view and consequently act as a drag on prices. Condos were put up. Where four families had frolicked before, 680 units now rose like a beacon on the coast, complete with swimming pool, sauna, parking lot, and a sprig of pampas grass to show it was not New Jersey.

Then the bulldozers moved over a few feet and the whole process started again.

Things were booming.

It was the Levittown concept applied vertically to the most heavily hyped land in the country. They were selling not just a unit but a way of life—Jacuzzis, tennis courts, cool drinks, skimpy bikinis, gorgeous sunsets, summer weather in wintertime—the complete, maintenance-free existence of your dreams.

"Come with me to my condo" was as fetching a come-on as "Have you seen my etchings?" It was the best of all possible worlds the advertisers could imagine.

Anyone with a winning smile and a firm handshake could cash in by becoming a developer. Money was no problem. REITs were springing up all over the country, gathering billions and funneling a fair share of it into construction loans for Florida condos.

"Money was choking them to death," recalled one builder. "All you had to do to get some was pick up the phone—and I mean to *answer* it."

It was the age of leveraging—five will get you ten. A developer with savvy could leverage himself right out. No risk. If it went over big, he got rich. If it collapsed, he didn't lose a dime: he didn't have a dime in it.

That's just what happened. The condos were built and built and overbuilt and everybody leveraged to the hilt and counted on quick sales as salvation from the day of reckoning.

Then the economy ground to a halt, particularly the housing

sector. As interest rates went up, making holding costs unbearably high, the developers started to take their leave, with a last smile and handshake. The REITs were left holding the bag and promptly collapsed. Florida's big ones registered losses of 64 to 95 percent—no mean drop—and their collapse triggered national disaster, for nearly one-fifth of all REIT money had been invested here.

"It's a cross between Hiroshima and the St. Valentine's Day Massacre," said one surveyor of the wreckage. The go-go approach had gone-gone.

To complicate matters, some landlords—tired of tenant complaints and ready to unload depreciated property—converted their apartments to condos just at that time, adding to the glut and, ironically, causing some shortages in the rental market. It was frosting on the cake of disaster.

Meanwhile, sufficient time had elapsed for complaints to start surfacing from the first generation of condo dwellers—and surface they did. People talked in harsh tones of swindles and gimmicks and loopholes and gravy trains. They had read the fine print and found it a fertile field for the next best thing to fraud. Clauses tied them to long-term recreation and management leases that siphoned off a continuing income for the original developers. The quality of service might be abominable, but it still had to be paid for (one condo paid the developer off *not* to manage it). The stink grew so that one man in the business said, "the ability to say you don't have one of those clauses is a positive selling point these days."

Some developers had retained ownership of the condo's water- and sewage-treatment facilities and regularly raised the rates, providing themselves with a lifetime income. Others hadn't even sold the land, but had merely leased the property for ninety-nine years. For them it was something to pass on to their grandchildren.

Those who bought condos based on artists' renditions or salesmen's promises found that some of the amenities so vividly pictured or described never made their appearance. Some who believed only what they saw with their own eyes were shocked to learn that everything was "extra"—even the parking place!

Novelist John D. MacDonald catalogued all these things and more in his 1977 chiller *Condominium*, which, if it did not slay the dragon, certainly did nothing to resuscitate it.

Florida Trend, the state's leading business magazine, described condos as a good idea "ambushed by a pack of quick-profit artists." It damned the industry as "thoroughly prostituted" and predicted, "when the smoke clears it's likely some developers will be behind bars."

The investigators jumped in. Not only the Florida attorney general, but the Federal Trade Commission, Interstate Commerce Commission, Securities and Exchange Commission, and—most feared of all—CBS's *60 Minutes*. Laws were rewritten, new regulations laid down. For instance, builders were now to be held liable for their product for three years, as an incentive to less shoddy workmanship. The offending fine-print items were henceforth to be disclosed in boldface type. Certain kinds of financial hanky-panky were expressly forbidden.

Given this, the most odoriferous situation Florida had been confronted with since the swampland scandal, the market was in a blue funk; most real-estate activity was in the foreclosure field.

With all those empty condos out there, there was nothing to do but ballyhoo. Free boat rides, turkeys, watches, gift certificates, televisions, even cash, were offered to people to come look. Advertising campaigns featured Red Buttons and Milton Berle, Jackie Gleason and Bobby Riggs, Chris Evert Lloyd and Nancy Lopez Melton. Still, people were wary. "You've got to buy a condominium," cautioned one architect, "like two porcupines courting. Very, very carefully."

Some of the unsold complexes descended a rung down the ladder and went in for time-sharing or interval ownership—one fifty-second of a unit at a not exactly prorated price. Although this opened up a new market in a lower income bracket, it was not enough to turn the situation around, so the hard sell was brought in. Telephone callers harassed the general public. Sales reps buttonholed people on the streets. And the reaction was negative.

They hit rock bottom. Nothing to do but recast them as "luxury condominiums." Shag carpets, glass coffee tables, butcher-block counters, a coat of paint, a new advertising pitch, and a higher price.

"Luxury" is a word so cheapened through overuse that it will inevitably go into the lexicon, along with "Heights" and "By-the-Sea," as a buzz word for the wise buyer.

Author Theodore Dreiser, who traveled through Florida during the 1920s boom, noted the stress on "*luxury*—always luxury—luxury to the point of nausea!" If he had returned half a century later, he might have made the same comment.

Then came a blessed lull, during which efforts were focused on peddling an overstocked inventory. But with the next outbreak of prosperity, "For Sale" signs sprouted like mushrooms overnight on the last pieces of greenery. They rapidly became the dominant element in coastal stretches, each designed to be more eyecatching than the last, with sock-it-to-em Day-Glo garishness. The bulldozers returned, uprooting the native foliage and preparing the way for Phase II, which could be had at preconstruction bargain rates while no more than a blueprint, a billboard rendering, and a gleam in the developer's bank account. Paradise had never looked so good. The vacation was over; it was time to get back to work.

On March 27, 1981, the construction crews went to work at Harbour Cay condominium in Cocoa Beach. The building collapsed on them. With eleven killed and twenty-three injured, it was the worst construction disaster in Florida history. It led to fines, investigations, suspension of licenses, and new legislation. Two years later the developer spawned a new subsidiary to build a "sturdier luxury condominium" on the site.

Thus far, financial collapses have been more frequent than structural ones, but the condos have not yet faced a great hurricane. It is only a matter of time. The results will be closely watched—particularly for those complexes where the protective dunes were removed.

Condominiums spark many sentiments in Florida, few of them neutral. Some see them as the greatest thing since white bread, the finest investment since Boca Raton, a way for people to enjoy collectively the amenities of the good life that they could not afford singly. Others see them as the great rip-off of the age, the worst despoiler of beaches Florida has ever seen; John D. MacDonald predicts that in the long run they are "doomed to become seaside slums."

Whatever the future holds for them, they remain one of the most controversial and discordant elements in Florida's present.

Signmakers in the Cape Canaveral area were quick to adapt to the Space Age.

Mandarin, once the peaceful winter home of Harriet Beecher Stowe, has been confronted with the pressures of development, as have other desirable Florida areas. (*Cartoon by Ed Gamble © 1983 the* Florida Times-Union)

Walt Disney (*left*) and his brother and business partner, Roy (*right*), flank Florida Governor Haydon Burns at the grand announcement in 1965 of Disney's plans for the state.

Crusty Ed Ball, a Florida institution for more than half a century.

BRINGING IT ALL BACK

•

Ed Ball watched these varied booms and busts—from swampland to space shots to condomania—with the bemused grin of a superannuated pixie. He had been there before they came and was there after they left to pick up the pieces, profiting from all of them.

He was old as the hills, and behind his back everyone speculated about when he would "cross the creek." But there were those who insisted the question was "not *when* Mr. Ball dies, it's *if* Mr. Ball dies."

The old man himself once told a critical congressional committee, "You will be happy to know that I am not going to live forever"—but he didn't get any more specific than that. Four heart attacks slowed him down slightly, but in 1973, at eighty-five, he still made two round-the-world trips and over twenty transatlantic flights, searching out business opportunities on four continents.

In the era of the Man in the Gray Flannel Suit, Ed Ball was one of the last of the old-time operators.

Years before a member of the rival du Pont faction had

dismissed Ball as the rebel Alfred's "head ass-licker." He didn't get it quite right.

Alfred found Ball "as tenacious as a bulldog on a tramp's pants" and even admitted he found it "necessary to bat Ed over the head with a club once in a while."

Together they achieved symbiotic completeness. Du Pont had a lot of money and a great talent for losing it. Ball, a product of the decayed southern gentility that was rich in background but poor in cash, was a wizard at making money. Du Pont was visionary, Ball eminently practical.

Du Pont lived like a king, with yachts and grand estates and all the trappings, but Ball was the quintessential simple liver. A multimillionaire many times over, he still wore dime-store glasses, ate at lunch counters, and lived in a commercial-hotel suite. Although he owned a castle in Ireland, he built himself, typically, a more modest home on the grounds and rented out the grand place to paying guests. He could afford to indulge but usually declined, feeling it would make him "vulnerable and susceptible to decay."

When du Pont had suggested Ball as a director of the chemical corporation, relatives dismissed him as "a common little drummer." Wrong again.

Ball had served his apprenticeship on the road, but there was nothing common about him. He had been an ace salesman of lawbooks, office furniture, cash registers, and automobiles before his sister married du Pont and he hired on as business manager. A native canniness was his greatest asset. He liked to call himself "just an old farmer," but he had all the slyness of a country boy preparing to skin the city slicker. There is no telling what the Du Pont company might have done with Ball in its leadership.

He took the Alfred I. du Pont Estate in Florida and turned it into the state's largest landowner, largest banker, and largest taxpayer. He ran the $58-million estate up to an estimated $2 billion. He built the Florida National group up to thirty-one banks, with over $1 billion in assets. He made the St. Joe Paper

Company an incredible land bank with over 1 million acres in holdings. Ball's personal investments extended to England, Ireland, Morocco, Iran, and Japan. Not bad for a country boy.

His philosophy was simple: avoid debt, keep down expenses, and don't let anything go.

"If you hold that sand and earth long enough," he was fond of saying, "sooner or later it will be worth something."

In a state plagued by hot-shot developers, he stood out as the great underdeveloper. They said he preferred trees to people, since trees couldn't vote. That made for some hard feelings. The Panhandle, where he loomed so large, was Florida's poorest region. One local editor complained, "that part of Florida where I live cannot free itself and prosper behind Mr. Ball's pine curtain."

As a banker he was criticized for wanting to keep all the money in the vault, rather than lend it out to foster growth. As a businessman he was faulted for never delegating authority. A consummate detail man, he made sure that everything from the biggest bond issues to the smallest postage and paper-clip costs crossed his desk. He was notorious for paying low wages and making all the decisions himself.

Ed Ball was not a lovable character, unless you were within his charmed circle. Outsiders called him willful, arrogant, autocratic, cantankerous, and arbitrary, as well as the full run of noble titles, from duke and baron to emperor and czar.

He gave back as good as he got. Those who stood in his way were chumps, Wall Street wolves, blackmailers, and buzzards. When George McGovern, running for president, criticized Ball's labor policies, the old man shot back a telegram informing the candidate that "THE GREATEST TRAGEDY IMAGINABLE TO THE UNITED STATES OF AMERICA WOULD BE YOUR ELECTION TO THE POSITION YOU NOW SEEK." The idea of a McGovern victory was enough to make Ball threaten to leave the country.

His battles were many and epic. "I'll fight till hell freezes over," he vowed. Litigation was his pleasure. A measure of his determination can be seen in his protracted struggle to take over Henry Flagler's Florida East Coast Railway. The line had fallen on hard times after the bust and depression and gone into receivership in 1931. A decade later, Ball started buying up FEC bonds at a few cents on the dollar. When he put together enough of them, he made his bid to take over management of the railroad. The rival Atlantic Coast Line had the same idea—and an influential advocate in Senator Claude Pepper, a New Dealer who believed the du Pont Estate controlled quite enough of Florida without gobbling up the FEC as well.

In 1944 and 1950 Ball raised war chests in an effort to defeat Pepper, and in the latter year he was successful. It was an even more memorable campaign than the one he had waged against Al Smith in 1928. Still, another decade of argument and litigation was to follow before the FEC finally fell into Ball's lap.

He proceeded to modernize it, convinced it could show a profit. There was nothing old-fashioned in his approach: automation and other technological advances were used to cut back on the payroll. The unions asked for a raise, in line with national railway policy, but Ball flatly refused. FEC was not an interstate carrier and would not be bound by interstate agreements. Take it or leave it. The unions struck. It was bitter. Ball ran the line with supervisory personnel and strikebreakers. There was sabotage. Trains were derailed and dynamited.

When Ball cut out passenger service, he cited the danger—but the move provided a healthy boost to the balance sheet, getting rid of that unprofitable aspect of the business. Even though two presidents and a congressional committee tried to intervene, Ball defied them all, willing to wait for hell to freeze over. Years went by. It was the longest strike in railroad history. He ground them down. Some said Ed Ball was tough as nails. No, said others, at least nails bend sometimes. He broke the union, set up his railroad the way he wanted, eliminated featherbedding, and turned a profit—just as larger carriers were declaring bankruptcy. It made him a folk hero to the far right.

But there was a price.

The octopus of the du Pont Estate had many tentacles.

Labor decided to cut one off. Due to their lobbying, a law was passed that offered Ball the unpalatable choice of giving up his railroad or giving up his banks.

He hated it. Having nursed them from sickliness to health, he wanted them both. Selling assets was anathema to him. So he stalled, stretching it out in subterfuge and keeping them guessing. Year after year, as the 1960s gave way to the 1970s, people wondered what part of the du Pont empire would be sold off. Ball, as always, played it very close. That part of it he liked. "Confusion to the enemy!" was his invariable toast when he gathered his cronies together for after-hours drinks (this was a ritual; he said he found four or five highballs "*very* relaxing").

What was the world coming to? Socialistic drift in all directions. Unpleasant things were happening in politics too. When the Florida legislature was reapportioned to represent people instead of pine trees, the Pork Chop Gang lost its control to the lamb-choppers. Ed Ball liked pork, hated lamb—at least in Tallahassee. His influence diminished accordingly.

Eventually, he gave up his banks—perhaps because the union was hoping he would give up the railway to someone who might bend a little. He wouldn't give them the satisfaction. They could complain as much as they wanted about low pay. Nobody made less than he did: as head of the railroad he earned $12 a year, while the du Pont Estate, which he had run up into the billions, never paid him but $16,000 a year, and even that had stopped in 1951. Although he had become one of the richest men in the country, it wasn't on wages. He was one of that breed of entrepreneurs who "seen their opportunities and took them."

"I always answer my own phone," he said, "because you never know when Santa Claus might be calling and I don't want to miss him."

Santa called him many, many times.

Back in the 1930s he got an option on a large piece of Panhandle property, together with five businesses. Just as it came due, he was able to sell 190,000 acres of it to the federal government for Apalachicola National Forest. That was only a part of the land, but the price he received paid the entire bill, with $70,000 to spare. The five companies and an additional 240,000 acres fell into his lap, free and clear. Things like that can make a man rich.

About the same time, he bid for and got the food and souvenir concession at Mount Vernon, which was fitting, since George Washington was an ancestor of his, in a lateral sort of way. He ran it—at a profit—for forty-three years, then traded the remainder of his lease to a company that gave him stock in return. The stock went up. He sold it for nearly $2 million. Not bad for a small sideline.

Ed Ball had come to love hotels in his days as a traveling salesman. "I have lived in hotels 70 to 80 percent of my life, and I am perfectly at home," he said. "I can walk into a hotel no matter where it is, and after I throw my hat on a piece of furniture, I feel just as much at home as I possibly could in any private house."

It was only natural he would invest in a few of them, and—since he was Ed Ball—only natural that they would turn out to be bonanzas even though their previous owners had pegged them as white elephants. He paid $46,000 for Key West's La Concha Hotel. During just two years of World War II it paid $240,000 in dividends.

He had an enviable record when it came to things like that. Enviable, but not perfect.

Raymond Mason, a business associate and protégé of Ball's, wrote in 1976 that "he has been greatly moved by the accomplishments of Iran, in the stability of their government and the methods they are employing to bring their country solidly into the twentieth century." Any money he invested on that basis certainly came a cropper. Ball outlived his friend the shah.

Then there was the marriage contract.

Ball remained a bachelor till he was forty-five. When he took a wife, he decided to apply some of his financial acumen and experience toward guaranteeing marital harmony. Accordingly, he drew up a lengthy instrument, signed by both parties, that pledged them to avoid company the other found objectionable, forgo close friends of the opposite sex, bar in-laws from lengthy visits, spend four nights a week at home, take pride in their personal appearance, forgo nagging and fault-finding and the like. Infractions were punishable by forfeiture of "one percent (1%) of such party's portion of the monthly community earnings or income for each such violation." The most serious offense, infidelity, was punishable by dissolution of the marriage.

This free-enterprise approach to wedded bliss didn't work, unfortunately. After a decade Mrs. Ball filed suit for divorce, claiming her husband was "dogmatic, domineering, self-opinionated and moody." He returned the compliment.

After dragging through the courts for six years, the case was finally settled when a lawyer demanded a free hand and bluntly told Ball, "You go run your banks and paper mills."

"Well," protested Ball, "I usually participate in my litigation more than that."

The lawyer, knowing this was precisely the problem, stuck to his demand and got results.

Ball didn't write any more marriage contracts, but he had other battles to occupy his final years. As long as his sister lived, she was the beneficiary of the du Pont Estate. Ball's philosophy was to let the assets appreciate rather than squeeze out all possible income, and she went along with that. Her tastes were simple enough so she could make do with the $13 million or so he produced for her annually.

(Once, when a senator suggested that income was excessive—especially in light of Ball's penny-pinching toward railroad employees—Ball shot back: "Mrs. du Pont has been criticized for the income she gets, but most of those years she was in the 91 percent bracket and when you take 91 cents out of each dollar, it doesn't leave too much to give to charitable and education institutions which she has done. At times I have wondered how she was able to eat." That tear-jerking peroration qualified him for the chutzpah award, southern division.)

After Mrs. du Pont's death in 1970, the income from the estate was to go to crippled children and the elderly poor of Delaware, who obviously had a vested interest in high return, rather than asset appreciation. Two of the trustees (including du Pont grandson Alfred Dent) felt that there should be a restructuring of investments with that in mind. Dent figured a return of only 0.13 of one percent on the du Pont billions was going for the purpose his grandfather had intended. The state of Delaware agreed. But not Ed Ball. He would fight to the finish to prevent the dismantling of the empire he had built.

Every place needs its curmudgeon, and Ed Ball was Florida's. Business success alone is always limited in the amount of public interest it engenders. A crusty, colorful character like Ball is required to give it a little sex appeal, to keep it from being dry as a balance sheet. He was aware of that, and not beyond fostering his own legend. An editor who had published an exposé of the du Pont holdings was surprised to have Ball order ten thousand copies of it. The old man knew the value of publicity in creating and maintaining an image.

One reporter noted, "Mr. Ball loved to tell stories about how tough a son of a bitch he was, particularly to journalists." A good number of these stories worked their way into print, adding to his public persona. Some of them at first provoked outrage, then aged gracefully into regular thigh-slappers.

There was the time a policeman stopped him for going 60 in a 15-mile-an-hour zone (Ball habitually drove like a bat out of hell). Getting ready to issue a ticket, he found he had nothing to write with.

"Mr. Ball, do you have a pencil?" he asked.

"Yes, chief, I have a pencil," Ball replied.

"Would you mind lending it to me?"

"Chief," asked Ball, "do I look like a damn fool?"

He got away without a ticket.

Ball was no great respecter of authority other than his own.

Once President Kennedy called the principals in the railroad strike to come to the White House for a little jawboning.

The FEC served Cape Canaveral, and the strike was having a deleterious effect on the space program. When reporters beat a path to Ball to find out what he planned to say, he told them he wasn't going to be able to make it, because he had a dentist's appointment that day.

Another time Ball suggested that a recalcitrant governor who disagreed with him was on an LSD trip.

Scratch an old-time Floridian and you'll find a favorite Ed Ball story. He was a man you hated to tangle with—he could "lean real hard" on people—but he will not soon be forgotten.

In 1981 he entered New Orleans's Ochsner Clinic, hung on for ten weeks, and finally died at the age of ninety-three. Even Claude Pepper, who had managed a stunning comeback after being one of the main victims of Ball's "leaning," managed a brief eulogy. Like the death of Flagler, it was a watershed mark in Florida history. More passed away with Ed Ball than one mean old man.

It is not hard to picture him, from the other side of the creek, whispering back to his successors, "this old Florida sand will look after you if you let it," and hoisting a last toast of "Confusion to the enemy!"

• • •

What of the other titans that strode across Florida history? If they were to come back, what would they see? What would they think? What would they recognize? What would they miss?

So many of them suffered short-range disappointments, and were gone by the time their dreams reached long-term fulfillment.

What if Peter Sken Smith, the general with no eyebrows who cut such a wide swath in St. Augustine in the 1830s, were to return for a glimpse of the Ancient City today?

He would be gratified to learn that his pioneer suburb, North City, was added in 1983 to the National Register of

Historic Places—but sorry to learn it was attributed to a subsequent developer, Miss Lucy Abbott. The street running through it to which he gave his middle name has been changed by the sign painters over the years from Skenandoah to Shenandoah—effectively concealing the interesting history behind it.

His grand mansion on the Plaza went through many transmogrifications. During the Civil War it provided sanctuary to the occupying Union soldiers. Later, an entrepreneur took Smith's advice and turned it into a hotel—just in time for the Flagler boom. It was expanded over the years, but the mansion remained at the heart of it, even though dwarfed by the massive additions. Rudolph Valentino stayed there while making one of his early movies in St. Augustine.

At the beginning of World War II, just after the mansion passed the century mark, there was a small fire in its upper reaches. The firemen put it out with dispatch, but it worried members of the church next door: they were afraid it would blaze up again and sweep away their house of worship. They bought the hotel and had it torn down as a fire trap, resisting the suggestion of the historical society that the ancient coquina foundations be preserved. It vanished without a trace. The church complex later expanded to cover the site. It was, ironically, the church that the owners of the *Herald*, Smith's goading nemesis, had joined after the general had them excommunicated by the Presbyterians. They must have had a last heavenly (or hellish) laugh over that.

The other fascinating Smith—Franklin—would both recognize and miss parts of his legacy to the Ancient City.

Villa Zorayda still stands, a tourist attraction garishly billed as Zorayda Castle, hemmed in by blacktop and featuring an "exotic gift shop." Beyond the hype, however, the extraordinary building survives. The Alhambra traceries still cover the walls, and many of Smith's internationally purchased furnishings remain. But the visitor can only learn that the builder was a Boston millionaire; no more of his colorful career is told.

At least he is now given credit for his creation: for many years it was attributed to the better-known Stanford White, which drove Smith's dutiful daughter up the wall. She solicited letters from White's son, as well as Henry Flagler's, citing her father as the real architect. She also threatened to take legal action against the falsification that had robbed him of his place in history.

Smith's adjoining shopping arcade and its hotel addition are no more. They burned in the 1950s.

Across the street, the magnificent Casa Monica Hotel prospered no more for Flagler after he bought and renamed it the Cordova than it had for Smith. In the 1890s it was remodeled for apartments, then, early in the twentieth century, linked by an over-the-street walkway to the Alcazar to become an annex of that hotel. The depression did them in. Their doors were closed after 1932.

During the civil-rights demonstrations in the 1960s, police dogs were billeted in the abandoned Cordova lobby.

It was not seemly to have such a major part of the downtown idle and vacant, so the Cordova was remodeled for the county courthouse, and the neighboring Alcazar was redone as a city hall (with its casino portion housing Otto Lightner's museum of hobbies). That put the grand old buildings back to use but, unfortunately, the interior of Smith's hotel was gutted, its scenic sun parlor and Moorish decorations replaced with nothing more exotic than standard 1960s design—the architectural counterpart of Muzak. The Alcazar lost its ornate wooden windows to modern metal frames, and plywood paneling was liberally applied to the interior. Such is the price of progress.

Smith might look around and see other examples of his Moorish Revival style—of which St. Augustine has an unparalleled collection—surviving, though not yet fully appreciated for their uniqueness. As the father of Florida's fantasy architecture, he could look around at the many exotic relics of subsequent booms and see that he had indeed wrought a plentiful revolution. If he went to Disney World, he could see that some of his wild-eyed proposals have been put into effect, profitably. Replicas of famous buildings rise, far from their native soil, so that tourists can rush by the millions to see them. They are the greatest success in Florida history. So much for those who dismissed him as a dreamer! His dreams have come true.

Henry Flagler—the student who surpassed his teacher—would find he is far from forgotten in Florida. Flagler Beach, Flagler County, Flagler Boulevard, Flagler College, and countless other memorials perpetuate his name. His finest hotel—the Ponce de Leon—has been recycled into a school. The skyline of St. Augustine still owes its enchantment to the towers and domes of his grand buildings.

But he would not be able to find his own home. Kirkside, with its sterling-silver faucets, was torn down in 1950, when his third wife's heirs considered the $20,000 required to fix it up an unwarranted expenditure. The spacious grounds were subdivided for a modern housing development.

If he looked carefully enough, he could see the fluted colums and leaded-glass windows incorporated into the Kirkside Apartments on a corner of the property. Various houses in town boast their relics from the great old mansion: the black-and-white tile floors, the marble mantel, other last remains cherished as the whole was not.

Flagler could follow his rail line south, but not as a passenger, since Ed Ball did away with that service. He could see the massive Ormond Hotel, which he bought and enlarged, now sadly asbestos-clad and with a checkered past as an old-folks' home. But he would be pleased to learn it was slated for the monumental task of restoration, to mark its hundredth birthday.

At Palm Beach he could see his old private railroad car, lemon-painted in Florida East Coast yellow. It is on display at Whitehall, the marble palace he built for his Cinderella wife. That home has fared better than Kirkside. A luxury hotel for many years, with a huge tower addition, Whitehall was finally bought by a granddaughter the oilman never met and restored as a monument to him, returned to scale by the removal of the overbearing hotel wing. It is one of the few things a tourist can visit in the still-exclusive resort.

Flagler's Folly—the Key West Extension—was the biggest loser among his Florida ventures, wiped out by the Labor Day hurricane in 1935. The remaining roadbeds were sold—for 3 percent of what they cost—and formed the base for the later Overseas Highway to the island city.

If he followed the crowds to Tampa—assuming he ever did—he could see that Henry Plant's Folly, the Tampa Bay Hotel, has survived. Though missing some of its gingerbread and without the flower gardens that spelled its name, it still rises like a mirage to amaze visitors. No longer a hotel, it has been home to the University of Tampa since the depression.

Addison Mizner, were he to return, would search in vain for some of the finest examples of his architecture. He may not have known mathematics, but that wasn't why his buildings collapsed. They put up a valiant, though losing, fight against the wrecking ball that claimed so many of them as tastes and styles changed.

The seventy-room Playa Riente, which had been hailed in the twenties as "certainly one of the most perfect great houses in America," bit the dust in 1957. Its ballroom murals were donated to an art museum, its furnishings auctioned off, the public given a last look to benefit charity, and Playa Riente was no more. Mrs. Stotesbury's El Mirasol and countless other Mizner villas suffered the same fate.

The architect would be surprised to learn that his best-known Palm Beach mansion is a comparatively minor one he designed for department-store heir Rodman Wanamaker, which derives its fame from having been purchased in 1933 by Joseph P. Kennedy.

Going south to Boca Raton, Mizner would be pleased—if not amazed—to see that it had lived up to the advance billing as an exclusive community. Ads for the area have stated that one out of every forty-three residents is a millionaire. Although that

(BELOW AND OPPOSITE BOTTOM): This modern 26-story tower overshadows the original Mizner wing and later Geist addition to the Boca Raton Hotel and Club.

The Kennedy home in Palm Beach. John F. Kennedy worked on *Profiles in Courage* here.

may not be quite the ratio Wilson was promising in his heyday, it is far from unimpressive.

Addison's architectural epitaph, the Cloister Inn, still stands as part of the much larger Boca Raton Hotel and Club. It is doubtful whether Mizner would approve of the additions—what architect likes to be second-guessed?—or of the changes made to his own section. His favorite part is dwarfed by the rest, particularly an utterly out-of-scale twenty-six-story tower added under the Arvida regime.

Mizner, who was fond of creating stories to go with his buildings, would have a field day with this complex. Let us imagine his portly figure reclining in an imitation-antique Spanish chair (Mizner Industries produced them in oversized versions for the likes of the maestro), regaling the members of his court, a pet monkey on his shoulder and a malicious twinkle in his eye.

"This building started as a work of genius," he would intone, "a flowering of the ages. I did it myself. People came from far and wide to marvel at it. Even John L. Sullivan signed the guest register. But, with the unpredictability of history, it fell almost immediately on hard times and was snapped up at bargain prices by a big boor with more money than taste who tried to overwhelm it with his own grandiose addition."

Here Addison would sniff with displeasure, gather his dignity together, and continue:

"People offended his ego by insisting on the original, so in revenge he chopped up some of its grandest rooms and painted over some of its finest features." He wipes away a tear from his eye. "But still it survived. Then another rich man came along, as wealthy as he was aged, and as tasteless as the tin foil he peddled. What can such people know of beauty? They have ice-water running through their aesthetic arteries. He feared invasion by bearded armies from Cuba, where they had recently confiscated his property. Since he had paid the most fabulous price in history for my hotel, he didn't want them to capture that as well. He upgraded the security system. Before it had been thought sufficient to have police dogs and sawed-off shotguns. Now nothing less than a missile silo would do. It was so massive that it scared off every miscreant with thoughts of robbing the guests, raping the maids, or pillaging the hotel rooms. It was accounted a great success by the paranoid. Its style was copied on surrounding buildings. Still, people of taste came—not to see the silo, but the architectural gem at its base. It is not easy, but there is a way. They whisper the secret to their friends in the tasteful minority.

"'Go immediately into one of the monstrosities,' they say. 'Wear dark glasses or eye patches, if necessary. Then gaze outward—carefully blocking out all peripheral vision—upon the original section, the unequaled architectural gem. And marvel at the genius of the man who designed it.'"

King Addison's court would chuckle appreciatively, the philistines having been once more put in their place.

On his visit to Boca Raton, Mizner would look in vain for the island where he planned to build his dream castle: Arvida had it dredged out of existence. So much for the permanence of the land. But the lowest blow of all would be the taking of his name in vain. Boca Raton's rising condominium is named The Addison. Its advertising splashes his name about liberally, suggesting that somehow it represents the fulfillment of his dreams. But wait. . . .

A distinctive feature of the condo age is the curvilinear design, which provides the maximum number of units with ocean exposure. The shape is thus financially motivated, for a slice of ocean view shoots the price way up. In other ways it is a disaster. As the bend increases to almost horseshoe proportions, the condo begins to rival La Scala for fine acoustics. Every mealtime's clinking of forks and plates reverberates throughout the complex. The squeals of joy from the swimming pool serve to remind people that their paradise is not an unshared blessing. There are no Robinson Crusoes in Florida condos.

The Addison is an exemplar of the curvilinear style. It would never be mistaken for any of the architect's own work. The only thing Miznerian about it is the price. Two- and three-bedroom units go from $332,000 to $1.1 million each.

They include such amenities as "decorator designed elevators," and an in-house "color coordinator." Those who pay top-of-the-line prices for the penthouse can enjoy "towel warming bars" in the master bathroom. All of the units have individual safes, to foil those burglars who get past the security-controlled gatehouse, by the TV-monitored lobby, around the security assistance desk, and through the secured elevator access to each apartment lobby.

Mizner would like the hype and appreciate the flattery. It would stroke his ego to think his name could still sell real estate. That has not always been the case.

But to be associated with what look for all the world like a pair of slightly warped and squashed United Nations buildings would surely rile his architectural soul.

AUTHOR'S NOTE

A book like this owes an inestimable debt of gratitude to libraries. Extensive use was made of the University of Florida Library and its P. K. Yonge Library of Florida History, the St. Augustine Historical Society Library, and the St. Augustine Public Library. The Florida Photographic Collection in the Florida State Archives was invaluable in illustrating the book. Pictures are still worth thousands of words.

Of particular interest to any writer is that part of history not already neatly packaged and recorded: the raw material that walks and talks in the form of vivid memories of people who lived through some of the situations described. No other single source is quite so good for giving a feel of the past, a flavor to history more enticing than blandness.

I have been extremely fortunate over the years in encountering many kind souls who have shared their memories with me and have not bridled unduly at my sometimes probing and impertinent questions. To them should accrue no blame for the opinions expressed herein, but a share of whatever credit is to be had.

Let me thank, alphabetically: Roy Barnes, Norton Baskin, Alfons Bernhard, Marie Bradfisch, Hubert Carcaba, Eugene Carter, Manuel Castrillon, Dora Center Chauvin, Charles Coomes, Wilma Davis, W. I. Drysdale, Marguerite Lopez Dunne, Carle Elkins, A. E. Ferrell, June Moore Ferrell, William Forrester, Mary Lee Gannon, B. M. Hall, George Hamilton, J. Carver Harris, Eloise Herndon, John Ingle, James Knott, Sister Mary Albert Lussier, Dolly Fletcher Maestre, Albert Manucy, George Maust, William McGuire, Rubye Lee Moeller, William Moeller, Mena Oliveros, Thomas Pacetti, X. L. Pellicer, Slade Pinkham, Lucius Rees, J. W. Richbourg, Clement Slade, Caca Smith, John Spengler, Roland Spicer, H. H. Stackhouse, Helen Hindry Stephens, Leslie Stephens, Les Thomas, Pierre Thompson, Charles Walker, Jean Parker Waterbury, and Larry Westbrook.

SELECT BIBLIOGRAPHY

(An * denotes an unpublished manuscript, master's thesis, or doctoral dissertation.)

Adams, Charles Francis, ed. *The Works of John Adams.* 1856.
Akin, Edward N. "Southern Reflection of the Gilded Age: Henry M. Flagler's System, 1885–1913." 1975.*
Allen, Frederick Lewis. *Only Yesterday.* 1931.
Amory, Cleveland. *The Last Resorts.* 1952.
Amundson, Richard J. "The American Life of Henry Shelton Sanford." 1963.*
Babson, Roger W. *Actions and Reactions.* 1935.
Bacon, Eve. *Orlando: A Centennial History.* 1977.
Ballinger, Kenneth. *Miami Millions.* 1936.
Barbour, John. *Footprints on the Moon.* 1969.
Baumann, Franklin A. "Disney World: A Modern Feudal Kingdom?" 1973.*
Beach, Rex. *The Miracle of Coral Gables.* 1926.
Blackman, E. V. *Miami and Dade County, Florida.* 1921.
Blake, Nelson M. *Land Into Water—Water Into Land.* 1980.
Branch, William S. *The Eppes-Shine Families of Orange County, Florida.* 1949.
Brown, Warren J. *Florida's Aviation History.* 1980.
Butcher, Lee. *The Condominium Book.* 1980.
Cantacuzène, Princess Julia. *My Life Here and There.* 1922.
Carrère, John M. *City Improvement from the Artistic Standpoint.* 1908.
Carter, Clarence E., ed. *The Territorial Papers of the United States,* vols. XXII–XXVI. 1956–62.
Cash, W. T. *History of the Democratic Party in Florida.* 1936.
Cash, W. T. *The Story of Florida.* 1938.
Cash, W. T., and Dodd, Dorothy. *Florida Becomes a State.* 1945.
Castleden, Louise D. *The Early Years of the Ponce de Leon.* 1957.

Clark, Morita Mason. "The Development of the Citrus Industry in Florida Before 1895." 1947.*

Cohen, Isidor. *Historical Sketches and Sidelights of Miami, Florida.* 1905.

Cole, Arthur H. "Agricultural Crazes." *American Economic Review.* (1926).

Collins, Leroy. *Forerunners Courageous.* 1971.

Cowles, Frank Jr. *What to Look For in Florida.* 1964.

Cox, James M. *Journey Through My Years.* 1946.

Dahl, Curtis. "Mr. Smith's American Acropolis." *American Heritage.* (June 1956).

Dahl, Curtis. "Quartet of Pompeian Pastiches." *Journal of the Society of Architectural Historians.* (October 1955).

Dain, Phyllis. *The New York Public Library.* 1972.

Dau, Frederick W. *Florida Old and New.* 1934.

Davidson, James Wood. *The Florida of To-day: A Guide for Tourists and Settlers.* 1889.

Davis, Richard Harding. *The Cuban and Puerto Rican Campaigns.* 1898.

Davis, T. Frederick. "Digest of the Florida Material in Niles' Register 1811–1849." 1939.*

Davis, T. Frederick. *History of Jacksonville, Florida.* 1925.

Dawe, Grosvenor. *Melvil Dewey.* 1932.

Dewhurst, W. W. *The History of St. Augustine, Florida.* 1881.

Diamond, Edwin. *The Rise and Fall of the Space Age.* 1964.

Dinkins, J. Lester. *Dunnellon: Boomtown of the 1890's.* 1969.

Doherty, Herbert J. "The Florida Whigs." 1949.*

Doherty, Herbert J. *Richard Keith Call.* 1961.

Douglas, Marjory Stoneman. *The Everglades: River of Grass.* 1947.

Douglas, Marjory Stoneman. *Florida: The Long Frontier.* 1967.

Douglas, Marjory Stoneman. *Hurricane.* 1958.

Dovell, J. E. *History of Banking in Florida.* 1955.

Dozier, Howard D. *A History of the Atlantic Coast Line Railroad.* 1920.

Dunn, Donald H. *Ponzi! The Boston Swindler.* 1975.

Dunn, Hampton. *Florida Sketches.* 1974.

Dunn, Hampton. *Re-Discover Florida.* 1969.

Dunn, Hampton. *Yesterday's St. Petersburg.* 1973.

Edwards, Virginia. *Stories of Old St. Augustine.* 1973.

Engelbrecht, Curt E. *Neighbor John.* 1936.

English, John W., and Cardiff, Gray E. *The Coming Real Estate Crash.* 1980.

Fitzgerald-Bush, Frank S. *A Dream of Araby: Glenn H. Curtiss and the Founding of Opa-Locka.* 1976.

Flynn, John T. *God's Gold.* 1932.

Flynn, Stephen J. *Florida: Land of Fortune*. 1962.
Forbes, James Grant. *Sketches Historical and Topographical of the Floridas*. 1821.
Fox, Charles D. *The Truth About Florida*. 1925.
Frisbie, Louise K. *Florida's Fabled Inns*. 1980.
Frisbie, Louis K. *Yesterday's Polk County*. 1976.
Frothingham, Octavius B. *Gerrit Smith*. 1878.
Fuller, Walter P. *St. Petersburg and Its People*. 1972.
Gannon, Michael V. *The Cross in the Sand*. 1965.
Goode, James M. *Capital Losses*. 1979.
Gore, Eldon H. *From Florida Sand to "The City Beautiful."* 1950.
Graff, Mary B. *Mandarin on the St. Johns*. 1953.
Graham, Philip, ed. *Sidney Lanier: Florida and Miscellaneous Prose*. 1945.
Graham, Thomas. *The Awakening of St. Augustine*. 1978.
Graham, Thomas. *Flagler's Magnificent Hotel Ponce de Leon*. 1975.
Gray, David. *Thomas Hastings: Architect*. 1933.
Gray, Lewis Cecil. *History of Agriculture in the Southern United States to 1860*. 1933.
Griffith, Leon Odell. *Ed Ball: Confusion to the Enemy*. 1975.
Grismer, Karl. *The Story of Fort Myers*. 1949.
Grismer, Karl. *The Story of St. Petersburg*. 1948.
Grismer, Karl. *The Story of Sarasota*. 1946.
Groene, Bertram H. *Ante-Bellum Tallahassee*. 1971.
Haden-Guest, Anthony. *The Paradise Program*. 1973.
Hanna, Alfred J. *A Prince in Their Midst*. 1946.
Hanna, Alfred J., and Kathryn Abbey. *Florida's Golden Sands*. 1950.
Hanna, Alfred J., and Kathryn Abbey. *Lake Okeechobee*. 1948.
Harcourt, Helen. *Home Life in Florida*. 1889.
Harlow, Ralph Volney. *Gerrit Smith*. 1939.
Harner, Charles E. *Florida's Promoters*. 1973.
Hartsfield, Annie M.; Griffin, Mary; and Grigg, Charles, eds. *NASA Impact on Brevard County*. 1966.
Hecht, Ben. *A Child of the Century*. 1954.
Hill, Dorothy E. "Joseph M. White." 1950.*
In Memoriam: Henry Morrison Flagler. 1914.
Jacques, David H. *Florida as a Permanent Home*. 1877.
Jahoda, Gloria. *Florida: A Bicentennial History*. 1976.
Jahoda, Gloria. *River of the Golden Ibis*. 1973.
James, Marquis. *Alfred I. du Pont*. 1941.
James, Marquis. *The Life of Andrew Jackson*. 1938.
Johnson, Malcolm B. *Red, White, and Bluebloods in Frontier Florida*. 1976.
Johnson, Stanley. *Once upon a Time: The Story of Boca Raton*. 1979.

Johnston, Alva. *The Legendary Mizners.* 1953.
Jones, Howard Mumford. *America and French Culture.* 1927.
Kefauver, Estes. *Crime in America.* 1951.
Keller, William F. *The Nation's Advocate.* 1956.
Kenan, William R. Jr. *Incidents by the Way.* 1955.
Kendrick, Baynard. *Florida Trails to Turnpikes.* 1964.
Kendrick, Baynard. *Orlando: A Century Plus.* 1976.
Kinney, Henry. *Once upon a Time: The Legend of the Boca Raton Hotel & Club.* 1966.
Klamkin, Marian. *The Return of Lafayette.* 1975.
Knauss, James O. *Territorial Florida Journalism.* 1926.
Kobler, John. *Capone.* 1971.
Kofoed, Jack. *Moon over Miami.* 1955.
Lazarus, William C. *Wings in the Sun.* 1951.
Leonard, Irving A. *The Florida Adventures of Kirk Munroe.* 1975.
Levasseur, A. *Lafayette in America in 1824 and 1825.* 1829.
Levine, Lawrence W. *Defender of the Faith: William Jennings Bryan.* 1965.
Long, Ellen Call. *Florida Breezes.* 1883.
Loos, Anita. *Kiss Hollywood Good-by.* 1974.
Lynes, Russell. *The Tastemakers.* 1954.
Macartney, Clarence E., and Dorrance, Gordon. *The Bonapartes in America.* 1939.
MacDonald, John A. *Plain Talk About Florida.* 1883.
MacDonald, John D. *Condominium.* 1977.
Marth, Del. *Yesterday's Sarasota.* 1973.
Martin, Sidney Walter. *Florida's Flagler.* 1949.
Mason, Raymond K., and Harrison, Virginia. *Confusion to the Enemy: A Biography of Edward Ball.* 1976.
Mayer, Martin. *All You Know Is Facts.* 1968.
McGrane, Reginald C. *Foreign Bondholders and American State Debts.* 1935.
McKenzie, Howard G. "William Jennings Bryan in Miami, 1915–1925." 1956.*
McLendon, James. *Pioneer in the Florida Keys.* 1976.
McMakin, Dorothy P. "General Henry Shelton Sanford and His Influence on Florida." 1938.*
McPhee, John. *Oranges.* 1967.
Mehling, Harold. *The Most of Everything.* 1960.
Mencken, H. L. *Prejudices: Fifth Series.* 1926.
Mizner, Addison. *The Many Mizners.* 1932.
Morris, Allen. *Florida Place Names.* 1974.

Mosley, Leonard. *Blood Relations*. 1980.
Muir, Helen. *Miami, U.S.A.* 1953.
Mullen, Harris H. *Florida Close-Up*. 1972.
Mullen, Harris H. *A History of the Tampa Bay Hotel*. 1966.
Munroe, Ralph Middleton, and Gilpin, Vincent. *The Commodore's Story*. 1930.
Murat, Achille. *America and the Americans*. 1849.
Nelson, Wallace M. "The Economic Development of Florida 1870–1930." 1962.*
Nevins, Allan. *John D. Rockefeller*. 1941.
Ney, John. *Palm Beach*. 1966.
North, Henry Ringling, and Hatch, Alden. *The Circus Kings: Our Ringling Family Story*. 1960.
Orr, Christina. *Addison Mizner: Architect of Dreams and Realities*. 1977.
Packard, Vance. *A Nation of Strangers*. 1972.
Paige, Emeline K., ed. *History of Martin County*. 1975.
Parks, Arva Moore. *The Forgotten Frontier*. 1977.
Pearce, Billee Peeler. "Resorts in a Pioneer Land: The Development of Florida Resorts 1821–1880." 1969.*
Pettengill, George W. Jr. *The Story of the Florida Railroads 1834–1903*. 1952.
Plowden, Gene. *Those Amazing Ringlings and Their Circus*. 1967.
Post, Charles Johnson. *The Little War of Private Post*. 1960.
Pratt, Theodore. *The Story of Boca Raton*. 1963.
Proctor, Samuel. *Napoleon Bonaparte Broward*. 1950.
Redford, Polly. *Billion-Dollar Sandbar*. 1970.
Reid, Whitelaw. *After the War*. 1866.
Rerick, Rowland H. *Memoirs of Florida*. 1902.
Rezneck, Samuel. *Business Depressions and Financial Panics*. 1968.
Roberts, Kenneth. *Florida*. 1926.
Roberts, Kenneth. *Sun Hunting*. 1922.
Rockefeller, John D. *Random Reminiscences of Men and Events*. 1909.
Roof, Katherine M. *Colonel William Smith and Lady*. 1929.
Roseberry, C. R. *Glenn Curtiss: Pioneer of Flight*. 1972.
Ross, Ishbel. *Silhouette in Diamonds: The Life of Mrs. Potter Palmer*. 1975.
Sedgwick, Henry Dwight. *La Fayette*. 1928.
Serling, Robert J. *From the Captain to the Colonel: An Informal History of Eastern Airlines*. 1980.
Sewell, John. *John Sewell's Memoirs and History of Miami, Florida*. 1933.
Shofner, Jerrell H. *History of Jefferson County*. 1976.
Shoumatoff, Alex. *Florida Ramble*. 1974.

Simmons, William. *Notices of East Florida.* 1822.
Smiley, Nixon. *Florida: Land of Images.* 1972.
Smiley, Nixon. *Yesterday's Florida.* 1974.
Smiley, Nixon. *Yesterday's Miami.* 1973.
Smith, Franklin W. *Design & Prospectus For the National Gallery of History & Art.* 1891.
Smith, Franklin W. *Designs, Plans, and Suggestions for the Aggrandizement of Washington.* 1900.
Smith, Julia Floyd. *Slavery and Plantation Growth in Antebellum Florida 1821–1860.* 1973.
Smyth, G. Hutchinson. *The Life of Henry Bradley Plant.* 1898.
Stockbridge, Frank Parker, and Perry, John Holliday. *Florida in the Making.* 1926.
Stockbridge, Frank Parker, and Perry, John Holliday. *So This Is Florida.* 1938.
Stover, John F. *The Railroads of the South.* 1955.
Stowe, Harriet Beecher. *Palmetto Leaves.* 1873.
Swanson, Allan A. "Pilo-Taikita: A History of Palatka, Florida." 1967.*
Tarbell, Ida M. *All in the Day's Work.* 1939.
Tarbell, Ida M. Introduction to *Florida Architecture of Addison Mizner.* 1928.
Tebeau, Charlton W. *A History of Florida.* 1971.
Thane, Elswyth. *Mount Vernon Is Ours.* 1966.
Thomas, Bob. *Walt Disney: An American Original.* 1976.
Thomas, David Yancey. "A History of Banking in Florida." 1907.*
Thomas, Richard. *John Ringling.* 1960.
Tornabene, Lyn. *Long Live the King: A Biography of Clark Gable.* 1976.
Travers, J. Wadsworth. *History of Beautiful Palm Beach.* 1929.
True, Alfred C. *A History of Agricultural Experimentation and Research in the United States 1607–1925.* 1929.
Upham, Samuel C. *Notes from Sunland.* 1881.
Vignoles, Charles. *Observations upon the Floridas.* 1823.
Webb, Wanton S. *Webb's Historical, Industrial and Biographical Florida.* 1885.
Weeks, Jerry Woods. "Florida Gold: The Emergence of the Florida Citrus Industry, 1865–1895." 1977.*
Weidling, Philip J., and Burghard, August. *Checkered Sunshine.* 1966.
Weigall, T. H. *Boom in Paradise.* 1932.
Whitney, John F. *St. Augustine, Florida.* 1873.
Wilford, John Noble. *We Reach the Moon.* 1969.
Williams, John Lee. *The Territory of Florida.* 1837.

Williams, John Lee. *A View of West Florida.* 1827.
Wolfe, Tom. *The Right Stuff.* 1979.
"The Work of Messrs. Carrère & Hastings." *The Architectural Record.* (January 1910).
Wright, Albert Hazen. *The Atlantic-Gulf or Florida Ship Canal.* 1941.
Zehnder, Leonard E. *Florida's Disney World.* 1975.

In addition, use was made of the following newspapers, newsletters, and magazines:

Business Week, Christian Science Monitor, East Florida Gazette, East Florida Herald, El Escribano, Florida Business and Opportunity, Florida Grower, Florida Historical Quarterly, Florida Times-Union, Florida Trend, Fortune, Kiplinger Florida Letter, Miami Herald, Nation's Business, The New York Times, Orlando Sentinel-Star, St. Augustine News, St. Augustine Record, Suniland, Sunrise, Sunshine, The Tatler, Tequesta, Update.

ACKNOWLEDGMENTS

The writer accumulates debts of gratitude with a speed matched only by the running up of bills.

My publisher, William Jovanovich, suggested the topic and signed the contract. Without him there would have been no book.

My editor and friendly nemesis, Marie Arana-Ward, maintained reasonable good humor in the face of late deadlines. Her assistant, Nancy Schauffler, helped to shoot down some high-flying allusions in the text. Copyeditor Anne Zaroff worked wonders with my eccentric grammar, not to mention my lapses of logic.

Two fine women, Sudie Hicks and Mozelle Brown, read the manuscript in progress, squirreled away a copy of it for safekeeping, and came up with an unending stream of nice things to say about it. Every author needs one such fan: I was blessed with two.

The cares of the workaday world do not cease merely because the writer chooses to ignore them and concentrate on the task at hand. My wife, Becky, can testify how an unequal share of the load falls on others in the vicinity. Those foolish enough to befriend an author will be called on to run errands, loan money, and go out of their way on a regular basis.

They also serve who babysit, fix typewriters, clip, proofread, dig out dusty tomes and brittle photos, or just manage to look interested when really bored to tears. For these and other beneficences, let me thank: Jackie Bearden, Bob Dewart, Tom Gardner, Cam Gates, Tom Graham, Margaret Hamilton, Roger Hickey, Ken and Jill John, Jan Lowell, Bill McGrath, Bea Miner, Joan Morris (St. Joan of the Archives to writers in need), Donna Nobrega, Becky Hamilton Nolan, Joseph and Virginia Nolan, Dorothy Puma, Charlyn Rainville, Corinne Richardson, Carol Rigolot, Bill and Helen Stewart, Craig Thomson, Nell Webb, and last, but certainly not least, Cyndi Westbrook.

INDEX